Incarnation Anyway

AAR
AMERICAN ACADEMY OF RELIGION

Academy Series

SERIES EDITOR
Kimberly Rae Connor, University of San Francisco

A Publication Series of

The American Academy of Religion
and
Oxford University Press

INCARNATION AND PHYSICS
Natural Science in the Theology of Thomas F. Torrance
Tapio Luoma

OF BORDERS AND MARGINS
Hispanic Disciples in Texas, 1888–1945
Daisy L. Machado

YVES CONGAR'S THEOLOGY OF THE HOLY SPIRIT
Elizabeth Teresa Groppe

HSIEH LIANG-TSO AND THE *ANALECTS* OF CONFUCIUS
Humane Learning as a Religious Quest
Thomas W. Selover

GREGORY OF NYSSA AND THE CONCEPT OF DIVINE PERSONS
Lucian Turcescu

GRAHAM GREENE'S CATHOLIC IMAGINATION
Mark Bosco, SJ

COMING TO THE EDGE OF THE CIRCLE
A Wiccan Initiation Ritual
Nikki Bado-Fralick

THE ETHICS OF ANIMAL EXPERIMENTATION
A Critical Analysis and Constructive Christian Proposal
Donna Yarri

PAUL IN ISRAEL'S STORY
Self and Community at the Cross
John L. Meech

CROSSING THE ETHNIC DIVIDE
The Multiethnic Church on a Mission
Kathleen Garces-Foley

GOD AND THE VICTIM
Traumatic Intrusions on Grace and Freedom
Jennifer Erin Beste

INCARNATION ANYWAY
Arguments for Supralapsarian Christology
Edwin Chr. van Driel

AAR
AMERICAN ACADEMY OF RELIGION

Incarnation Anyway

Arguments for Supralapsarian Christology

EDWIN CHR. VAN DRIEL

OXFORD
UNIVERSITY PRESS

2008

OXFORD
UNIVERSITY PRESS

Oxford University Press, Inc., publishes works that further
Oxford University's objective of excellence
in research, scholarship, and education.

Oxford New York
Auckland Cape Town Dar es Salaam Hong Kong Karachi
Kuala Lumpur Madrid Melbourne Mexico City Nairobi
New Delhi Shanghai Taipei Toronto

With offices in
Argentina Austria Brazil Chile Czech Republic France Greece
Guatemala Hungary Italy Japan Poland Portugal Singapore
South Korea Switzerland Thailand Turkey Ukraine Vietnam

Published by Oxford University Press, Inc.
198 Madison Avenue, New York, New York 10016

www.oup.com

Oxford is a registered trademark of Oxford University Press

Library of Congress Cataloging-in-Publication Data
Driel, Edwin Chr. van (Edwin Christian van), 1969–
Incarnation anyway : arguments for supralapsarian Christology / Edwin Chr. Van Driel.
p. cm.
Includes bibliographical references and index.
ISBN 978-0-19-536916-8
1. Incarnation—History of doctrines. I. Title.
BT220.D68 2008
232'.1—dc22 2007045682

9 8 7 6 5 4 3 2 1

Printed in the United States of America
on acid-free paper

To the memory of my father

Gerrit van Driel (1916–1989)
Dienaar des Woords

Lieve Heer, Gij zegt 'kom' en ik kom,—
want mijn leven is onder de macht gesteld
van de Heer die mijn dagen en nachten telt
en de Heer zegt 'kom' en ik kom.

O mijn God, Gij zegt 'ga' en ik ga,
Gij zegt 'ga' en ik ga, laat mij niet alleen
wees het woord in mijn vlees en de geest om mij heen
wees de adem waaruit ik ontsta.

Want o Heer, ik zeg 'kom' en Gij komt,
ik zeg 'kom' en Gij komt en uw bloed wordt wijn
en uw lichaam brood voor wie hongerig zijn
en uw naam wordt een lied in mijn mond.

Willem Barnard

Preface

It is a pleasure to open this book with a thank you to all who supported me before, during, and after its delivery.

The book started out at Yale University as a dissertation. Therefore, I wish to start by thanking my *Doktorvater*, David Kelsey. He is a master of close reading, and reviewed each chapter and offered wise suggestions to improve and shape my arguments. I am honored by the close attention he gave my work in his first year of retirement.

My professors at Yale shared with me their knowledge, wisdom, advice, and triple chocolate cookies. I thank them all: Marilyn McCord Adams, Robert Adams, Serene Jones, Rowan Greer, Miroslav Volf, and Nicholas Wolterstorff.

I first encountered supralapsarian Christology at the theology department of Utrecht University, in the context of what was then known as the Utrecht School—an exciting program in medieval and Reformed scholastic theology, philosophy of religion, and systematics. I thank Willem van Asselt, Eef Dekker, Antonie Vos, and all other members of the Research Group John Duns Scotus.

At Yale my friends in the Theological Discussion Group, fellow graduate students, provided a forum for discussion and debate when the ideas presented here were in a germinal state. For their incisive questions, their collegiality, and their friendship, I am most grateful.

My parents were the ones who first put me on the path of theology. My father, the late Gerrit van Driel, read me theological books in utero. I can recommend this method to all parents who would rather see their child become a theologian than a business major. Tonnie van Driel-van den Berg has encouraged my theological endeavors for decades in many and various ways; her self-sacrificial support was crucial in my decision to pursue further studies abroad.

From the delight with which she would put herself on an open Barth volume, one would think Miep van Driel liked supralapsarian theology as much as I do.

Finally, the best Yale gave me is my wife, Kimberly Miller van Driel. I thank her for her love, her support, and many, many conversations and discussions, in which she learned more about supralapsarianism than she probably cared to know. She was the first reader of the manuscript, and the readability of what follows owes a great deal to the great care with which she translated my many Dutchisms into proper English.

An abbreviated version of the second chapter of this book was published earlier as "Schleiermacher's Supralapsarian Christology" in *Scottish Journal of Theology* 60 (2007): 251–270. Parts of the fifth chapter go back to "Karl Barth on the Eternal Existence of Jesus Christ," *Scottish Journal of Theology* 60 (2007): 45–61. I thank Cambridge University Press for permission to reprint.

The hymn by Willem Barnard on the dedication page is taken from *Liedboek voor de kerken* ('s Gravenhage: Boekencentrum, 1973), published for the *Interkerkelijke Stichting voor het Kerklied.*

Contents

THE ARGUMENT FROM CREATION

THE ARGUMENT FROM CONSUMMATION

Incarnation Anyway

I

Introduction: Divine Motives for the Incarnation

. . . What was from the beginning,
what we have heard,
what we have seen with our eyes,
what we have looked at and touched with our hands,
concerning the word of life . . . (1 John 1:1)

In 1991, the year I entered divinity school, the church in the Netherlands was involved in a reprise of a perennial theological debate: what should we think of the resurrection? Articles were written, debates organized, and pamphlets published. One of these pamphlets was written by a professor in systematic theology of the school where I studied, and as a dutiful new student I bought and read it. My professor engaged a number of philosophical and scientific arguments against the resurrection, and finally came to speak of its theological meaning. There, at the end of the pamphlet, a short passage caught my attention. In the midst of his argument on the resurrection, the author switched subjects—almost without noticing—and wrote on the incarnation in general:

> Without incarnation God cannot see us with his own eyes. And what would we desire and need more than to be

> seen by him? Without incarnation God cannot listen to us and hear us with his own ears. God could not speak to us with his own voice, and what do we dream of and desire more than to hear the music of God's very own voice? . . . Without incarnation God cannot touch us, and what would we more intensely long for than that God were so close to us that it is hand on hand, skin on skin? If we long to hear the beat of God's heart, to taste his love, there is nothing we desire more than the warmth of his hands, the peace of his embrace. But how could God see us, hear us, and make himself to be heard and touched, than by the *humanity* of his eyes and ears, his voice, his tongue, his hands?[1]

This passage struck me because it set forth the meaning of the incarnation in a different way than that to which I was accustomed. Reared as a son of a Netherlands Reformed minister, I had been taught to think about the incarnation in the context of sin and forgiveness: God becomes human in order to take care of the problem of human sin. Although it is the prevalent view in the Reformed circles in which I grew up, it is certainly not a view unique to Reformed theology. It is in fact the majority report of Western theological accounts of the person and work of Jesus. Different confessional traditions have different ways of construing the way in which the Incarnate takes care of the sin problem, but they all agree that the incarnation is contingent upon sin. We can call such a Christology *infralapsarian*: the divine will to become incarnate logically follows (*infra*, after) the divine will to allow sin (*lapsus*, fall).

By contrast, my professor suggested that God had motives to become incarnate that were not contingent upon sin: a desire to be with human beings, to fulfill their longing for God's presence, to be available to them in a way that is so central to human existence: embodiment. Such a view does not exclude the idea that the incarnation is also motivated by God's desire to take care of the sin problem. It simply suggests that there are other, deeper motives behind the incarnation than only the need for reconciliation. We can call such an understanding of the incarnation *supralapsarian*: the divine will to become

1. Antonie Vos Jaczn., *Het is de Heer! De Opstanding voorstelbaar* (Kampen: Kok, 1990), 157–58 (my translation).

incarnate logically precedes (*supra*, before) the divine will to allow sin.[2] While this view is the minority position in Western theology, supralapsarian Christology experienced something of a resurgence in nineteenth- and twentieth-century theology, when major theological figures like Friedrich Schleiermacher, M. J. Scheeben, Karl Barth, and Karl Rahner embraced this view.[3]

Infralapsarianism and supralapsarianism are both family names. Neither of them stands for a particular theory; they stand for two families of ideas. Infralapsarians agree that God had to become human in order to take care of the sin problem, but they disagree widely on the reasons why. The result of this disagreement is a variety of atonement and reconciliation models. Likewise, supralapsarians agree that the incarnation is not contingent upon human sin, but they differ widely on the reasons why. The result of this disagreement is a variety of supralapsarian approaches to the meaning of the incarnation.

This book is concerned with an analysis and evaluation of the ways in which supralapsarian arguments can be construed. Whereas there are many studies devoted to a comparison of different forms of infralapsarianism, this book is the first scholarly monograph to systematically map and analyze different approaches to supralapsarian Christology. My goal is to draw up the supralapsarian family tree. I will give a thick description of supralapsarian arguments in their particularity, draw out their consequences for other theological loci, and evaluate the theological gains and losses of each approach.

The analytical part of the book is governed by two theses. The first is that each of the three ways in which God is taken to relate to what is not God—in creation, in redemption, and in eschatological consummation—can function as the basis for a supralapsarian argument. In the first four chapters I illustrate this thesis with detailed case studies of the Christologies of Friedrich Schleiermacher (redemption), Isaak Dorner (creation), and Karl Barth (eschatological consummation). I point out in advance that since these case studies

2. The terms *infralapsarian* and *supralapsarian* were originally situated in the doctrine of election. The earliest application of these terms to Christology in German or English literature that I am aware of is by Karl Rahner (e.g., in his article "Grace," in *Sacramentum Mundi* II (New York: Herder and Herder, 1968), 422 [415–24]. However, Rahner's ingenious move is predated by a nineteenth-century Dutch theologian, Daniel Chantepie de la Saussaye, who suggested the application of these terms to Christology in his *Beoordeeling van het werk van Dr. J.H. Scholten over de leer der Hervormde Kerk* (1857–1859), reprinted in D. Chantepie de la Saussaye, *Verzameld Werk*, deel 2 (Zoetermeer: Boekencentrum, 2000), 271.

3. Cf. the bibliographical appendix at the end of this book.

serve to illustrate an overall systematic argument concerning the different ways in which theological loci can be made to relate, I focus on the inner logic, coherence, and inner strength of each author's particular proposal, and ignore the wealth of important scholarship that in recent decades has appeared on the historical, sociopolitical, and economic positions of these figures, especially Schleiermacher and Barth.

In the course of these case studies, I introduce a second analytical thesis that concerns the nature of the receiver of the gift of incarnation. One can hold the incarnation to be a gift to human nature; one can also hold the incarnation to be a gift to human persons. I argue that each of these two approaches leads to a very different understanding of the work that the incarnation does. Taking the incarnation to be a gift to human persons leads to an account of the incarnation in which God, by assuming human nature, makes Godself available for interpersonal interaction, from one human being to the other. Taking the incarnation to be given to human nature leads to an understanding of the incarnation on which God, by assuming human nature, is able to change the ontological status of humanity from the inside out. As I will show, supralapsarian theologians are prone to blur this conceptual distinction, resulting in incoherent Christological accounts.

In the penultimate chapter, I cover the material of my three case studies one more time—this time to determine and evaluate what is not particular to each of these authors but characteristic for the three kinds of supralapsarian strategies I want to distinguish.

In weighing these different approaches, I commend as the theologically most fruitful supralapsarian strategy one that is rooted in a notion of eschatological consummation, and which takes the goal of incarnation to be the interpersonal interaction with God. In the final, constructive chapter I develop three arguments along these lines.

My first supralapsarian argument is premised on the relation between the eschaton, the goal of creation; and the proton, the beginning of creation. I appeal to a deeply rooted intuition of both Western and Eastern theology that the eschaton is not the restoration of the proton. In the eschaton there is an abundance, a richness in intimacy with God and in human transformation, which the proton did not know. However, the argument goes, such gain cannot be contingent upon sin. Sin, by its very nature, never brings us closer to God; it only alienates us from God. If we gained the richness of the eschaton because of sin, this would amount to a notion of *felix culpa*, but, I argue, such a notion needs to be rejected. Therefore, the richness of the eschaton has to be understood in supralapsarian terms: it is not contingent upon sin. And since Christ is the embodiment of the abundance of the eschatological life, neither is the incarnation contingent upon sin.

My second supralapsarian argument looks closer at the way in which Christ embodies the abundance of eschatological life. Again I appeal to a notion deeply embedded in theology: the eschaton brings humanity the enjoyment of full intimacy with God, the *visio Dei*. However, for bodily, sensory beings such enjoyment cannot consist only of an intellectual vision but needs to include sensory contact. And, I argue, eschatological humans will be bodily, sensory beings, as the Gospel depictions of Christ's resurrection attest. Therefore, if the eschatological goal of humanity is to enjoy God in the beatific vision, this vision should not be understood purely in terms of intellectual cognition but also imply sensory perception. However, this can only take place if God makes Godself present in bodily form.

Finally, my third supralapsarian argument is based on the notion of friendship with God. I argue that there is a discernible line in both the Hebrew Bible and the New Testament which suggests that God's ultimate goal is to be a friend of his creatures. The deeper friends are involved, the more available they make themselves to each other. The incarnation can be interpreted as God making Godself ultimately available, by offering the friendship in a mode previously not present—visible, tangible, audible in human form, and with a human face. This friendship is not based on the divine desire to reconcile estranged humanity; it is the other way around: the divine desire to reconcile strayed humanity is based on, and therefore logically follows, divine friendship. Therefore, if the incarnation is the fullest expression of this divine friendship, the incarnation also logically does not follow human estrangement and divine reconciliation, but precedes it—in other words, is supralapsarian.

These three arguments together amount to an eschatological vision: a vision of lively, intimate, abundant enjoyment of the incarnate Lord as the goal of creation. But that which is the goal of life also determines its meaning. Our understanding of that for which we were created shapes our understanding of ourselves, our world, and our God. And if it is Christ for whom we were created, if the incarnate presence of God in Christ is the goal of all things, then Christ is intimately bound up with the meaning of all aspects of our lives. Here, on the level of our daily lives, lies the deepest difference between a supralapsarian and an infralapsarian Christology. In an epilogue to the book I tease out some of these implications of supralapsarianism for our eschatological imagination and daily spirituality. Most of this will, however, have to wait for a sequel to the current book.

2

Schleiermacher's Supralapsarian Christology

Schleiermacher is the first major supralapsarian theologian since the Middle Ages, and his defense of it is one of the most original created. Most supralapsarian theologies turn on a distinction between the incarnation as the primal and essential goal of God's relationship with humankind, and sin and redemption as its accidental companion. Schleiermacher's approach is very different. As a "Hernhuter of a higher order," he did not give up on the central place his Pietist forefathers had given to the notion of redemption. For Schleiermacher, this is still the central concept to describe Christ's relation to us. But redemption is placed in an ontological framework inferred from the notion of absolute dependence. It is this ontological framework that leads Schleiermacher to construe redemption in a supralapsarian rather than an infralapsarian way.[1]

1. Several commentators have pointed at the supralapsarian nature of Schleiermacher's Christology and its medieval predecessors. However, none of them offers a thorough analysis of Schleiermacher's approach. The most extensive discussion to date, by Eugene TeSelle, describes Schleiermacher in terms of the traditional distinction between incarnation as essential completion and accidental redemption. In this, my analysis differs significantly. Cf. Friedrich Beisser, *Schleiermachers Lehre von Gott, dargestellt nach seinen Reden und seiner Glaubenslehre* (Göttingen: Vandenhoeck und Ruprecht, 1970), 241–43; Eugene TeSelle, *Christ in Context: Divine Purpose and Human Possibility* (Philadelphia: Fortress Press [1975]), 69–86; Robert James Sherman, *The Shift to Modernity: Christ and the Doctrine of Creation in the Theologies of Schleiermacher and Barth* (New York: T and T Clark, 2005), 199, 200.

Therefore, first I look at Schleiermacher's notion of absolute dependence and the ontological framework inferred therefrom; only thereafter do I lay out the details of Schleiermacher's Christology. Finally I argue that an inconsistency between Schleiermacher's ontology and Christology fatally undermines his proposal.

I. Schleiermacher's Ontological Framework

Redemption and Absolute Dependence

Schleiermacher's theology is a reflection upon the experience of redemption and absolute dependence. Redemption is an experience in which we relate to Christ. We feel how he brings us under his influence. He assumes us into his community; he shares with us his power and thereby transforms our existence.[2] By contrast, the experience of absolute dependence is one in which we are conscious of God. Schleiermacher explains this experience by contrasting it with relative dependence. In relationship to finite reality, we experience ourselves to be relatively free and relatively dependent, resulting in a relationship of reciprocity. We are both active and passive; we are on both the giving and the receiving end.[3] However, we also experience both ourselves and all of finite reality to exist in a relationship of absolute dependence. In such relationship there is no reciprocity. We exercise no freedom at all toward the Whence of our absolute dependence. In fact, we experience our relative dependence as well as our relative freedom to be included in this absolute dependence.[4] The Whence of this absolute dependence is identified as God.[5]

In the Christian life, the experience of redemption and the experience of absolute dependence always go hand in hand.[6] We cannot have one without the other. There is no general God-consciousness that is not bound up with a

2. Friedrich Schleiermacher, *The Christian Faith*, ed. H. R. Mackintosh and J. S. Stewart (Edinburgh: T and T Clark, 1999), § 100–101, pp. 425–38. References to this translation of *Der Christliche Glaube* (1830–31) use the abbreviation CF followed by section (§) and page numbers.

3. CF § 4.2–3, 13–16. Cf. for the identification of "that which is co-determined by other things" as the finite: CF § 56.1, 231.

4. CF § 4.3, 16.

5. CF § 4.4, 16.

6. CF § 32, thesis, 131.

relation with Christ.[7] Without the redeeming activity of Christ, the feeling of absolute dependence is clouded by sin. It is, says Schleiermacher, in bondage, and only set free by redemption.[8] Therefore, everything that is said about the God-consciousness without reference to the experience of redemption should be seen as an abstraction from the concrete experience of the believer.[9] On the other hand, there is no relationship with the Redeemer that has no bearing on the general God-consciousness. One cannot build a relationship with Christ at the expense of the priority of the experience of God, without leaving the boundaries of religion.[10]

Schleiermacher's formulations not only express a close relationship between these two sides of the believer's experience but also betray a referential order. The experience of Christ serves the experience of God. The activity of the Redeemer is no goal in itself, but serves to bring us to a greater understanding of intimacy with God. To put it differently, the absolute dependence of human beings on God is essential to human existence. It is given with the relationship between creation and creator. By contrast, the need for the redemptive work of Christ is accidental, needed because of the influence of sin on our relationship to God. Sin, however, is not given with creation.

The experience of absolute dependence, modified by the experience of redemption, is for Schleiermacher not only the source but also the limit of theology: "All the divine attributes to be dealt with in Christian Dogmatics must somehow go back to the divine causality, since they are only meant to explain the feeling of absolute dependence."[11] All that we say of God does not denote "something special in God, but only something special in the manner in which the feeling of absolute dependence is to be related to him."[12] Our language about God never goes beyond God's causal working on us. But neither, of course, does our experience of God. This will have important consequences for our experience of the incarnation.

7. CF § 62.3, 261.
8. CF § 63.2, 263.
9. CF § 62.3, 262.
10. Ibid.
11. CF § 50.3, 198.
12. CF § 50, thesis, 194.

Absolute Dependence and Omnipotence

The notion of absolute dependence has a wider range than our own existence. Not only ourselves but all of finite reality is taken to exist in absolute dependence on the divine causality.[13] This wider scope is implied by the absoluteness of the experienced dependence. As noted above, we are relatively independent in relation to finite reality. If finite reality in its turn were relatively independent vis-à-vis the divine causality, this would leave our dependence on God incomplete. Dependence and independence are in this sense transitive. Absolute dependence is also uniform: absoluteness does not allow for variations.

The exact way in which divine causality relates to the web of finite reciprocal relations is of less relevance to our topic.[14] More important is the modal status of this relationship. Schleiermacher spells it out in two theses. Together they contain his doctrine of divine omnipotence. First, "the entire system of Nature, comprehending all times and spaces, is founded upon divine causality, which as eternal and omnipresent is in contrast to all finite causality."[15] This is mainly a repetition of the aforementioned. The second thesis is more distinctive: "the divine causality, as affirmed in our feeling of absolute dependence, is completely presented in the totality of finite being, and consequently everything for which there is a causality in God happens and becomes real."[16] What God actually causes exhausts all possibility. What this means is that there is no alternative for reality as it is. Things cannot be otherwise than the way they are.

Schleiermacher gives four arguments to support this latter thesis. The first refers back to the notion of absolute dependence as the only basis for theological statements. If we say that God could do something other than God does, we go outside the immediate experience of divine causality. We have no ground to do so.[17] When answered that the divine causality extends to all reality, and that reality consists both of the actual and the possible, Schleiermacher tries to undermine the latter part of this thesis. This is his second argument. We come at our notion of the possible by too narrow a focus on the individual and its nature. We call possible that which we ascribe as potential for an

13. CF § 5.1, 19.
14. See especially CF § 46, 170–78, and § 49, 189–93.
15. CF § 54, thesis, 211.
16. Ibid.
17. CF § 54.2, 212–13.

individual based on its nature. But if we took into account the whole web of finite interaction in which the individual had its place, we would say that what was not realized was also not possible.[18] Third, if we held that God does not realize all that is possible for God's omnipotence, we would have to accept the notion of divine self-limitation. This, however, is a notion not given in the experience of absolute dependence.[19] Finally, Schleiermacher's last argument refers to the conceptualization of the possible as Platonic forms or possible words. In many classical conceptions of creation, God's causal activity is conceived as electing and creating one of these eternally existing forms or worlds. But this suggests the existence of entities independent of the divine causality, which is excluded by the first thesis of divine omnipotence.[20]

Each of these two theses has a different ontological profile. I refer to them, economically but somewhat inelegantly, as omnipotence I and II. One of the most characteristic features of the profile of omnipotence I is a qualified notion of creaturely freedom. Schleiermacher does not deny that human beings are free. They are active and not merely passive participants in the system of nature. However, this is a particular kind of freedom. It is, to use some medieval terminology, a freedom of spontaneity, but not a freedom of indifference. Human beings are free to do as they choose, but their spontaneous choosing is founded upon and determined by the divine causality: "The whole of our spontaneous activity comes from a source outside of us."[21] Vis-à-vis the divine causality, human beings do not have the freedom to choose or originate another action than they do.

The ontological profile of omnipotence II is more restrictive. Omnipotence I restricts freedom on the level of creation, but it does not restrict freedom for God. It could, for instance, be combined with a libertarian notion of divine freedom. Such freedom is, however, excluded by the second thesis. In omnipotence II, God cannot do otherwise than what God does. The distinction between divine ability and divine willing collapses. There is nothing that God could do but does not. Conversely, there is nothing that God does, but that God could refrain from.[22] The result is a lack of ontological space for an alternative

18. CF § 54.2, 213.
19. CF § 54.2, 214.
20. CF § 41.1, 153–54, and § 59, postscript, 341.
21. CF § 4.3, 16.
22. CF § 54.3, 214–15.

reality. It is this last point that has earned Schleiermacher the name of determinist.[23]

Omnipotence I and II not only have their own ontological profiles but are also logically independent. We do not have to hold to omnipotence II if we hold to omnipotence I. A reading of the arguments for omnipotence II underscores this. The first and third arguments are based on the experience of absolute dependence. The second argument tries to undermine certain intuitions about the possible. Only the fourth argument is based on omnipotence I. The possible as a Platonic pantheon of eternal ideas, existing independently of God, is inconsistent with the notion that everything is absolutely dependent on the divine causality. The problem with this argument is that one does not have to conceive of the possible in this way. At least two other options are available. Cartesian voluntarism holds that possibilities are caused by divine deliberation and choice. The possible is causally dependent on divine willing. Theistic activism holds that possibilities are caused by divine contemplation. The possible is causally dependent on divine knowing.[24] Cartesian voluntarism is not consistent with Schleiermacher's rejection of divine choosing, but theistic activism is. It holds that God's mind necessarily produces the possible. If Schleiermacher were willing to construe the origin of the possible according to theistic activism, there is no argument that leads from omnipotence I to omnipotence II.

It is important to make this last point. As we will see below, the supralapsarian nature of Schleiermacher's Christology is based on omnipotence I. It is, however, omnipotence II that causes problems for Schleiermacher's

23. Jacqueline Mariña aims to exonerate Schleiermacher from the charge of determinism by reinterpreting the relationship between God and world by appealing to his notion of freedom of spontaneity; "Schleiermacher's Christology Revisited: A Reply to His Critics," *Scottish Journal of Theology* 49 (1996): 177–200, especially 185–88, 195–98. Julia A. Lamm also qualifies the notion of determinism by expounding Schleiermacher's take on individuality and freedom; *The Living God: Schleiermacher's Theological Appropriation of Spinoza* (University Park: Pennsylvania State University Press, 1996), 171–85. However, both discussions are concerned with determinism as implied by omnipotence I. This leaves aside the determinism implied by omnipotence II. We might, in omnipotence I, be free to do spontaneously what we desire; given omnipotence II, our spontaneity has nonetheless only one option open to itself. And not even God could change this option, since God too is limited to only one way of acting.

24. For a recent discussion of Cartesian voluntarism: Gijsbert van den Brink, "Descartes, Modalities, and God," *International Journal for Philosophy of Religion* 33 (1993): 1–15; and Alvin Plantinga, *Does God Have a Nature* (Milwaukee: Marquette University Press, 1980), 95–126. For a recent defense of theistic activism: Thomas V. Morris and Christopher Menzel, "Absolute Creation," *American Philosophical Quarterly* 23 (1986): 353–62, reprinted in Thomas V. Morris, *Anselmian Explorations* (Notre Dame: University of Notre Dame Press, 1987), 161–78.

construal. If omnipotence II is not based on omnipotence I, this leaves open the possibility to try to repair Schleiermacher's proposal by relinquishing omnipotence II.

Redemption and Decree

One single divine willing encompasses all history. History unfolds in time and numerous individuals and events, but God does not govern history by a series of decisions, initiatives, and reactions. History unfolds in time, but it is an unfolding of what is determined in God's single, eternal, and nonreciprocal will. That is the upshot of the experience of absolute dependence, as interpreted by omnipotence I. God's willing needs to be timeless, Schleiermacher argues, because otherwise time would condition God, instead of God being the nonconditioned conditioner of all.[25] What omnipotence II adds to the picture is that God's willing is not a form of deliberation and deciding choice but "simply an absolute approval."[26]

For us the most important aspect of the decree is that it is nonreciprocal. Schleiermacher calls this his "primary and basal presupposition."[27] This is the basis for Schleiermacher's supralapsarianism. If God does not respond to human actions, the incarnation cannot be interpreted as a divine answer to the human problem of sin. The latter is the heart of the infralapsarian approach. An infralapsarian might conceive of this idea of divine response in different ways. She does not have to conceive of it as being temporal. She might conceive of it as eternal. God might from all eternity foresee that human beings will fall and consequently foreordain the coming of Christ. In fact, the majority of infralapsarians have taken it this way. However, central to the infralapsarian position is the logical priority of human sin over divine incarnation. For Schleiermacher, such a position is excluded.

Absolute dependence not only has important consequences for the place of the incarnation in the divine decree but also influences our take on sin. If everything falls within the scope of divine causality, it seems that this must also hold for human sin. Schleiermacher indeed does not shy away from this

25. CF § 52, 203–6.
26. CF § 55.2, 225–26.
27. CF § 147.2, 673.

conclusion. Sin is "grounded in human freedom," he says.[28] But our freedom is not more than a freedom of spontaneity, as we noted. And "the whole of our spontaneous activity comes from a source outside of us."[29] Therefore, "sin's being grounded in our freedom is all the more compatible with its being rooted likewise in the divine causality because, with regard to the feeling of absolute dependence, we recognize no difference between the greater and the less activity of temporal causality."[30] God is "the author of sin."[31]

Schleiermacher qualifies this last statement. He does this by comparing the relationship between divine causality and sin with the relationship between divine causality and redemption.[32] Redemption is the goal of the divine causality. Sin is not; it is only a means. That "the emergence of sin preceded the advent of redemption in no sense implies that sin was ordained and willed purely for itself." On the contrary, Schleiermacher continues—and here is a key text for his supralapsarian stance—"the very statement that the Redeemer appeared when the fullness of time was come makes it quite clear that from the beginning everything had been set in relation to his appearing."[33]

With this last point, we have reached the heart of Schleiermacher's theology: that of divine teleology. To talk about the content of divine teleology, we need a firmer ground than the experience of absolute dependence, though. That experience cannot distinguish between means and ends.[34] All existence is uniformly dependent on the divine causality. The nature of things or the course of history therefore cannot teach us anything about divine purposes.[35] All we can know is that everything is included in the divine decree, not how the divine decree is ordered.[36] For that we need to reflect on that other experience: the redemptive activity of Christ.

28. CF § 81, thesis, 330.
29. CF § 4.3, 16.
30. CF § 81.2, 333–34.
31. CF § 79, thesis, 325.
32. CF § 80, thesis, 326.
33. CF § 80.2, 328.
34. CF § 46, postscript, 177.
35. CF § 166.1, 728.
36. Robert Merrihew Adams questions whether a divine decree governed by omnipotence II can be said to have ends and means. If there are no real possible alternatives, is there anything for purposes to explain? Robert Merrihew Adams, "Schleiermacher on Evil," *Faith and Philosophy* 13 (1996): 571–72 [563–83]. In this chapter, I leave this question aside.

II. Schleiermacher's Supralapsarian Christology

Christ the Redeemer of Creation

While the feeling of absolute dependence is an essential feature of humankind,[37] it is also a universal experience that this consciousness is hampered in its development. Our God-consciousness does not permeate all activities of our self-consciousness. There are lower powers in the soul that are not susceptible to the impulses proceeding from the God-consciousness. They strive to secure for themselves in the finite what can only be given in dependence on God. This obstruction of the free development of the God-consciousness Schleiermacher defines as sin.[38]

Sin is inevitable for us; the strength or weakness of the causal impulses issued from the God-consciousness is not ours to control.[39] Despite its inevitability, sin is, however, not an essential part of human existence.[40] Human nature has the potential to be free from sin and completely permeated by the God-consciousness. Such is the ideal (*Urbild*) of humankind. In Christ this ideal has become history. In him there are no powers that darken his awareness of God; his God-consciousness is "absolutely powerful" and has perfectly integrated all other parts of the soul. His God-consciousness gives "impulse to all life's experiences and determines them."[41] Catherine L. Kelsey gives us a powerful metaphor to understand what such a life is like. She likens the God-consciousness to the experience of a preacher, when "our attention and all our best skill is directed toward the congregation in front of us and toward being open to what God is using us to show or say at that moment. After the fact, we realize that we said more than we knew to say. Somehow God did something better or bigger than our best effort, yet God worked through that effort. Rather than a 'God-and-me' experience, the experience is one of 'God-through-me-toward-others.'" The life of Jesus, the life of the ideal, was entirely like this precious experience of the preacher, Kelsey suggests. Although for the preacher

37. CF § 6.1, 26.
38. CF § 66, 271–73.
39. CF § 66.3, 272–73, 86.2, 356.
40. CF § CF 68, 275–79, 94.1, 385.
41. CF § 93.2, 378.

these experiences are few and far between, for Christ life was an unbroken series of those moments.[42]

Schleiermacher makes two important and related caveats concerning Christ's ideality. First, he does not mean that Christ embodied all talents and possibilities of humankind—"as though Christ must have been ideal for all knowledge or all art and skill which have been developed in human society."[43] Rather, the ideality of Christ concerns only his God-consciousness. In all other areas of human existence "he could only develop in a certain similarity with his surroundings."[44] Second, ideality does not exclude growth and development. Christ's awareness of God and the integration of the powers of his consciousness were ideal for every moment of his existence, but would never be stronger than the possibilities of stages of life—be it childhood or adulthood—permitted. If this were not the case, it would deny Christ the completeness of his humanity. The ideal does not become history by embodying only a certain moment of human development; it is ideal by embodying, throughout its development, a God-consciousness that is free from any impediment.[45]

Christ's perfect God-consciousness cannot be explained as a natural product of human development. Until Christ, humans had universally wrestled with sin; and "in the corporate life of sinfulness sin propagates itself naturally."[46] Christ's presence in the midst of history cannot be explained out of the causal nexus of finite reality. It is none other than a "miraculous fact"; his God-consciousness a new implanting of supernatural origin.[47] "The Kingdom of God and the divine procedure in its harvesting and propagation is represented as a special divine activity by itself, apart from the divine government of the world in general."[48] Nonetheless, this supernatural origin should be carefully qualified. Christ's presence goes back to divine, not finite, causality. This divine causality is not, however, new in relation to the divine decree. It is not an addition to the original plan. The divine decree does not allow for add-ons; it is after all "one, undivided, and eternal," the expression of God's nonreciprocal

42. Catherine L. Kelsey, *Thinking About Christ with Schleiermacher* (Louisville: Westminster John Knox Press, 2003), 9.

43. CF § 93.2, 378.

44. CF § 93.3, 382.

45. CF § 93.3, 381–82.

46. CF § 89.4, 365.

47. CF § 93.3, 381; § 95.3, 389; § 89.4, 365.

48. CF § 120.1, 552.

good pleasure.[49] The appearance of the ideal is not addition, but completion.[50] This is the ground for the notion of divine teleology. Nothing in the general dependence of all finitude on God betrays a purpose in the divine causality, except for this new implanting.

According to Schleiermacher, "to ascribe to Christ an absolutely powerful God-consciousness, and to attribute to him an existence of God in him, are exactly the same thing."[51] Schleiermacher wants to hold to the confessional theorem that in Christ we meet one person in two natures. He believes, however, that subsequent ontological explanation of the formula is marred with difficulties and ripe for revision. The majority of his arguments target the supposed incoherence of the ontological approach. In passing he mentions another argument which, on his own criteria, should be just as convincing.[52] An ontological explanation suggests, in one way or the other, something about the being of God. But how God is in Godself does not lie open to our immediate impression; only God's causal activity does. Theology should therefore be confined to a reflection on God's causal working. It is in those terms that Schleiermacher's alternative formulation is cast. He wants to uphold the unique divinity of Christ, by saying that Christ differs from any other human being in that in him "always and everywhere all that is human in him springs out of that divine."[53] Note that in this formula the difference between Christ and other human beings is merely quantitative. The reason that our God-consciousness "cannot fittingly be called an existence of God in us" is that it is "always dominated by the sensual self-consciousness." And if it is "able neither to portray God purely and with real adequacy in thought, nor yet to exhibit itself as pure activity, it cannot be represented as an existence of God in us."[54] But this, of course, is not an insurmountable difficulty. It is overcome in the redemption.

"The Redeemer assumes believers into the power of his God-consciousness, and this is his redemptive activity," reads Schleiermacher's famous formulation.[55] Based on the foregoing, we can understand what this means. There is a power going forth from the Redeemer, a "pervasive influence," an impulse that

49. CF § 95.3, 389.
50. Ibid.
51. CF § 94.2, 387.
52. CF § 96.2, 396.
53. CF § 96.3, 397.
54. CF § 94.2, 387.
55. CF § 100, thesis, 425.

is issued from him and now also starts to work in us.[56] But we just noted that the uniqueness of Christ is that in him all powers of the soul are issued from his God-consciousness, which is the existence of God in him. This must then also hold about the causal influence of him on us. "And thus the total effective influence of Christ is only the continuation of the creative divine activity out of which the Person of Christ arose."[57] In the redeeming activity of Christ, what had happened to him now happens to us. As the special divine activity began in Christ, it now continues through him in us. The divine causality, which integrates all Christ's life's experiences in his perfect God-consciousness, now, through his, empowers ours. It is "the essence of redemption that the God-consciousness already present in human nature, though feeble and repressed, becomes stimulated and made dominant by the entrance of the living influence of Christ."[58] And the being of God in Christ is paralleled by and continued in the being of Christ in humanity as a whole.[59] The special divine activity creates thus a pyramid, a corporate life of divine causal indwelling, with Christ as its head and mediator. In the life of the church, the causal influence of its founder is thus still palpable and "in its deepest inwardness, or as an impulse, [it] corresponds to its origin, and consequently, in spite of all reactions, [it] will also increasingly work itself out."[60] The ideal's epiphany in history has influenced history's direction decisively.

Christ the Completion of Creation

By influencing history's direction decisively, Christ completes the creation of human nature. Schleiermacher believes that God ordained the creation of humankind in two stages. The first stage is a preparation for the second; the second the completion of the first. The first, inaugurated by the appearance of the first human, constituted the physical life of the human race. It is a phase in which "the impartation of the Spirit to human nature . . . was insufficient, in that the spirit remained sunk in sensuousness and barely glanced forth clearly

56. "[P]ervasive influence," CF § 100.2, 427; "impulse active in us," CF § 104.3, 455.

57. CF § 100.2, 427. Cf. CF § 100.1, 425: "But his act in us can never be anything but the act of his sinlessness and perfection as conditioned by the being of God in him. And so these too in addition must become ours."

58. CF § 106.1, 476.

59. CF § 106.1, 477; § 100.1, 427; § 94.2, 387–88.

60. CF § 88.3, 365.

at moments as a presentiment of something better."[61] The second phase, inaugurated by the appearance of the second Adam, Christ, constituted a new spiritual life.[62] It is the time of the special causal influence of divine presence. Schleiermacher therefore does not shy away from calling Christ's inauguration of the second phase a work of creation, even while creating is a divine act. After all, all God's activity proceeds from the being of God in him.[63]

Redemption and completion are closely interconnected. In the next section we will see that, for Schleiermacher, redemption serves completion. However, completion is also necessary for redemption. To see this, I call attention to Schleiermacher's argument about the necessity of Christ's perfect God-consciousness.[64] Schleiermacher asks whether it would not have been enough if Christ had a heightened but not ideal God-consciousness. He refutes this idea on two grounds. If Christ's God-consciousness were not ideal, we would always carry the hope that one day humankind might surpass Christ and reach the fullness of consciousness of God. It is good to have a consciousness that is strongly directed at God. It is far more desirable never to be deluded by sin at all. However, such a hope would mark the end of the Christian faith. A Christian hope is only directed at an ever-deepening understanding of Christ. Second, if the God-consciousness could continually progress, the creation of humankind would not have been completed. This would, deplorably, place human creatures below other creatures. The unspoken premise here seems to be that humankind is thereby ranked below creatures it should surpass. That is, of course, a rather anthropocentric argument. Schleiermacher might have fared better by connecting his thesis with his notion of redemption. He is correct in saying that if Christ's God-consciousness were not completely perfected, the creation of humankind would not have been completed. The problem with this is not that our ranking in creation's order would be undermined. The problem is that we would not be redeemed. After all, the incompleteness of human nature is precisely the underdevelopment of its God-consciousness. This in turn leads to sin. Redemption comes when Christ, through the perfection of his God-consciousness, takes us up in this perfection and thereby brings our human nature to completion. Without his consciousness of God being perfect, he might have been

61. CF § 89, 365–69.
62. CF § 95.3, 389.
63. CF § 100.1, 426.
64. CF § 93.2, 378–79.

able to bring us to a higher level. He would not, however, have been able to secure our blessedness. Therefore, for Christ to be the Redeemer, he has to have perfection; because only given his perfection could he bring completion, and only by bringing completion could he bring redemption.[65]

The Supralapsarian Christ

We now have all the material needed to make an analysis of the conceptual structures of Schleiermacher's supralapsarian Christology. Its profile is determined, both negatively and positively, by the notion of absolute dependence and the consequent inferred forms of divine omnipotence. Omnipotence II prevents us from analyzing Schleiermacher's supralapsarianism in terms of counterfactuals. Much older supralapsarian Christologies are formulated as a positive answer to the question: would God have become incarnate even if humans had not sinned? But if there are no alternatives for reality as it is, as omnipotence II says, this question is meaningless. Schleiermacher's Christology can therefore only be analyzed in terms of the order of the divine decree.

The order is determined by omnipotence I, and this in a twofold way. First, as we noticed above, a decisive point is the nonreciprocity of humans' relationship with God. If we are absolutely dependent on God, God never responds to human actions. And if God does not respond to human actions, the incarnation cannot be interpreted as a divine answer to the human problem of sin. It has to be supralapsarian. "The Christian faith that all things were created for the Redeemer implies . . . that by creation all things (whether as prepared for or as overruled) were disposed with a view to the revelation of God in the flesh, and so as to secure the completest possible impartation thereof to the whole of human nature, and thus to form the Kingdom of God."[66]

I gave this last quotation in full because it calls our attention to an ambiguity in Schleiermacher's thought. To say that "all things were created for the Redeemer" suggests that the incarnation in Christ is God's prime intention. Other formulations used by Schleiermacher suggest the same.[67] However, the last part of the passage implies something different. The revelation of God in the flesh is given with an eye to the most complete impartation thereof, not to just

65. Contra TeSelle, *Christ in Context*, 84.
66. CF § 164.1, 723.
67. For instance: "from the beginning everything had been set in relation to his appearing" (CF § 80.2, 328).

one human being but to the whole of human nature, and thus to form the Kingdom of God. Here, the incarnation in Christ is the means to the final goal, the communication of the divine to all. I believe this latter reading to be the correct one. This is supported by other passages: "When we trace to the divine causality our consciousness of fellowship with God, restored through the efficacy of redemption, we posit the planting and extension of the Christian Church as the object of the divine government of the world," as it reads on the same page.[68] And also: "the divine purpose [has been] set on the union of the Divine Essence with human nature in the Person of Christ, and, as a result thereof, the union of the Divine Essence with the fellowship of believers through the Holy Spirit."[69] This last formulation also squares with the idea of a causal pyramid that I proposed in the section on redemption. Christ is the first with whom God seeks this intimate fellowship, but the ultimate goal is, through him, the fellowship with all. Schleiermacher has philosophical reasons not to refer to the incarnation as the goal thereof.[70] Yet in the end, this is how it functions.[71]

Understanding the incarnation in Christ as a means to the divine impartation to all will be helpful for our next step. Omnipotence I not only determines the place of the incarnation in the divine decree but also determines the place of human sin and divine redemption. Here we encounter the most original aspect of Schleiermacher's approach. For other supralapsarian Christologies, God's dealing with sin is logically subordinated to the divine intention to

68. CF § 164, thesis, 723.

69. CF § 164.2, 724.

70. Schleiermacher gives four reasons why not to apply the terminology of means for God's dealing with creation. Means are external to the goal, but the whole of finite existence is included in the goal of God's action. Means are employed when the agent has to take recourse to something not originating in herself, which in the relation between God and the world is excluded by the world's absolute dependence on God. It is difficult to use means terminology without suggesting a form of choice on the part of the agent, whereas God's acts are not based on choice and deliberation. Finally, a work is esthetically more pleasing when all its parts are an integrated whole than when some parts are identifiable as means used for other parts as their goals (CF § 168.1, 733–34). I think in the end we can take all these caveats into account and still use the means and ends language. Schleiermacher's preference for the terminology of parts and wholes fits again in my notion of a causal pyramid, in which the perfect divine impartation to Christ functions as a crucial part of the larger whole, the divine impartation to humankind.

71. Other texts that support my reading are the references to an unqualified humanity as the address of divine impartation: "if then the pivot of the divine government is redemption and the foundation of the Kingdom of God, involving the union of the Divine Essence with human nature" (CF § 165.1, 726–27); "it is only through him that the human God-consciousness becomes an existence of God in human nature, and only through the rational nature that the totality of finite powers can become an existence of God in the world" (CF § 94.2, 388). See also the affirmation that "every form of the God-consciousness, however imperfect . . . ranks for us as a divine impartation to human nature" (CF § 166.1, 728).

become incarnate. Sin is a human act, not rooted in any divine initiative. In redemption the incarnate One deals with human sin, but without this being part of the primal divine intention. That redemption is necessary is better seen as a sign of how much the original intention has been undermined. However, as we noted before, for Schleiermacher sin is not excluded from the scope of divine causality, but God is the author of sin. This calls for a different place for sin in the divine decree. If sin is the fruit of some form of human initiative, there is no problem with seeing it as counter to the prime divine intention; but if God is the author of sin, this would be illogical. Schleiermacher's solution is to integrate sin and redemption in the prime divine intention. Sin is ordained with an eye to the Redeemer.[72] God wants to impart Godself to humankind. The means thereto is Christ, whom God elects to be united with the divine.[73] The next step is to bring the rest of humanity under Christ's causal influence. But what will make humans receptive to Christ's gifts? For this, God ordains sin: "God has ordained that the earlier insuperable impotence of the God-consciousness shall become for us, as our own act, the consciousness of sin, in order to intensify that longing without which even the endowment possessed by Jesus would have met with no living faculty for the reception of what he communicates."[74]

The order of the divine decree has now become clear. God's primal intention is the most complete impartation of the divine essence to humanity. As a means to this, one person is elected with whom God unites. The instrument by which to impart the divine nature to all is redemption. In order to make humankind receptive to the Redeemer, God ordains sin. To make sin, which is not essential to human nature, nothing but universal and inevitable, God creates human nature in a particular way. Thus, while the last section showed that completion is necessary for redemption, the opposite holds too. Redemption is necessary for completion.

Note that Schleiermacher never crosses the self-imposed boundaries for his theological discourse. Nowhere does Schleiermacher speak about God's motives. The ultimate goal of the decree is the impartation of the divine nature, but no reasons are given why this is God's first intent. The language of causality is the only acceptable framework to analyze God's actions. This holds

72. CF § 65.2, 270; § 80.2, 328; § 81.3, 335–37; § 89.3, 368; § 164.3, 726.
73. On the election of Christ: CF § 120.2,4, 553–57.
74. CF § 89.1, 366.

even when the end of *The Christian Faith* speaks of the centrality of love in God's teleology. Love is then described as "the impulse to unite self with the other and to will to be in the other."[75] This is a description purely in terms of the causal activity and outcome of the action, not of its motivation. Any notion of value or virtue, emotions, will or motivations is excluded from this Christology. The contours of Schleiermacher's supralapsarianism resemble Dionysian reality. It suggests the image of God as the overflowing source of all being, "the Absolute Vitality,"[76] God who necessarily imparts the divine reality to all of that which is not God.[77] What is missing though, is the Dionysian perfect goodness as the driving force motivating it all.

Redemption, Creation, and Eschatological Consummation

In Schleiermacher's schema, sin and redemption are essential parts of our relationship to Christ. We need Christ because of our sin, and only because of our sin. If there were another reason why we relate to Christ, God would not have had to introduce sin in the divine decree. We are connected to Christ only through his redemptive activity. There is no space for a meaningful relationship with Christ that is not marked by this.[78] Furthermore, since sin is accidental to human nature, so is humankind's relationship with Christ. This has important implications for Christ's role in creation and eschatological consummation.

If Christ's relationship to humankind is accidental, he cannot be said to be the mediator of creation. Schleiermacher indeed reinterprets the

75. CF § 165.1, 726.

76. CF § 51.1, 203.

77. "We must therefore think of nothing in God as necessary without at the same time positing it as free, nor as free unless at the same time it is necessary. Just as little, however, can we think of God's willing himself, and God's willing the world, as separated the one from the other. For if he wills himself, he wills himself as Creator and Sustainer, so that in willing himself, willing the world is already included; and if he wills the world, in it he wills his eternal and ever-present omnipotence, wherein willing himself is included; that is to say, the necessary will is included in the free, and the free in the necessary" (CF § 54.4, 217).

78. Cf. this passage from Schleiermacher's sermon "Christ the Liberator": "Even if there were no sin, there both could and would continue to be a great difference among the individuals who all share a common human nature. But only one person could be the most perfect among and above them all. It must be so, in the nature of the case. And this one person would always be Christ. Even if the rest of us did not have or feel sin, he would still be one of the two things he is even now: our Brother, as he counts us worthy to call him. We could and would rejoice in his extraordinary endowment from above even then. But he would not be the other thing that he is: the one in whose name alone salvation is promised to all. Rather, we would have our salvation in our own righteousness. Nor would he be the one to whom all authority is given in heaven and on earth, for no one has any right to such authority over his equals." Friedrich Schleiermacher, *Servant of the Word: Selected Sermons of Friedrich Schleiermacher*, trans. with introduction by Dawn De Vries (Philadelphia: Fortress Press, 1987), 43–44.

New Testament material related to this idea. Notions such as expressed in 1 Cor. 8:6, Col. 1:15–17, and Heb. 1:4, he sees as "very permissible hyperbolical expressions . . . the utterances of a deep, but not properly divine adoration." In reality, Christ's relationship to creation is only teleological: "Creation and preservation are only ascribed to Christ in such a way that it must remain doubtful whether they do not mean that he is active cause only in so far as he is final cause."[79] All things were created for the Redeemer, but not in or though him.

However, in the preceding section we have seen that this last point needs to be qualified. In the end, the Redeemer too is a means for the final goal: the divine impartation to all humankind. We might wonder what Christ's place is in this final consummation. Is there still a need for him once all opposition against the God-consciousness is completely overcome? Schleiermacher never explicitly answers this question. In general, he ventures into eschatology only reluctantly. Eschatological consummation is an event not contained in our current experience of the divine causality. Therefore we lack a basis for theological propositions concerning this.[80] Nonetheless, two aspects of Schleiermacher's theology suggest a negative answer. First, his understanding of the life and meaning of Jesus is radically noneschatological. No change in the influence of Jesus is to be expected from any of the eschata. For Schleiermacher, events like Jesus's resurrection, his ascension, his sitting at God's right hand, his return, and the final judgment are accidental to Christ's redeeming activity. Redemption is based on the perfection of Christ's God-consciousness, and this is not connected to any of these eschatological events. This can best be shown in the life of the disciples, who experienced Christ's salvific influence before his death and resurrection.[81] The same holds for contemporary believers. Like the disciples, we too need, Schleiermacher believes, neither resurrection, ascension, nor second coming to experience the spiritual presence or the enduring influence of Christ.[82]

79. CF § 99, postscript, 424. The immediate context of Schleiermacher's remarks is his discussion of the nature of Christ. If Christ's divinity cannot be understood in ontological, but only in causal terms, it is indeed difficult to conceive how to speak about Christ as mediator of creation. However, one does not need the detour of metaphysics of the incarnation to come to this conclusion. Christ's mediatorship is already excluded by the order of the divine decree.

80. CF § 157.2, 697–98.

81. CF § 99.1, 418.

82. Ibid., and CF § 160.2, 708.

Second, the source of this spiritual presence and influence is not Christ today, but Christ yesterday. It is an "impulse given by his historical life," which shaped a community that still mediates its causal effect.[83] Schleiermacher likens this causal effect to the influence a charismatic lawgiver or a founding father can have on his community years after his death.[84] He sternly rejects the notion that "one can share in the redemption and be made blessed through Christ outside the corporate life which he instituted, as if a Christian could dispense with the latter and be with Christ, as it were, alone." This would disregard that "what owes its origin to divine agency can nevertheless be received only as it appears in history, and also can continue to function only as an historical entity." It would destroy "the essence of Christianity by postulating an activity of Christ which is not mediated in time and space."[85] This construal of Jesus's influence excludes more than the idea of individualistic Christianity. It also excludes the notion of a causal involvement by an ascendant, living Christ in his community today. It only allows for the causal influence issued from "a single point," the historical Jesus.[86] But in that light there is no need for a resumed relation with the living Christ at the end of time. All that is needed is for the causal effect of the historical Christ to exhaust itself. The eschaton is the consummation of his redeeming influence, but without need for his abiding presence.[87]

III. Fault Lines

Redemption and Omnipotence

Consistency is Schleiermacher's hallmark, and our analysis only confirms this. Creative theological reflection on the experience of absolute dependence, modified by the experience of redemption, is the source of both his ontological

83. CF § 88.3, 365.
84. CF § 100.3, 429.
85. CF § 87.3, 360.
86. CF § 117.1, 536.
87. A good illustration of the preceding ideas are Schleiermacher's comments on the resurrection and the ascension. First he gives a noneschatological interpretation of the redeeming content of both events, then he redescribes it such that it can be: "neither the spiritual presence which he promised nor all that he said about his enduring influence upon those who remained behind is mediated through either of these two facts. This may well depend upon his sitting at the right hand of God—by which, however, since the expression may be strictly an impossible one, we must understand simply the peculiar and incomparable dignity of Christ, raised above all conflict" (CF § 99.1, 418).

framework and his supralapsarian Christology. Each argument is carefully built on the preceding one. Every Christian doctrine is imaginatively reformulated to fit Schleiermacher's criteria for theological discourse. Nonetheless, a fault line runs through Schleiermacher's proposal—an inconsistency, not within either his ontology or his Christology, but between them.

The problem lies in the notion of alternative possibilities. As noted above, Schleiermacher denies that these exist. According to omnipotence II, the divine causality is completely present in the totality of finite existence. There are no alternatives for reality as it is. Nonetheless, sometimes Schleiermacher writes as if there are. God "might from the very beginning have arranged the whole march of the human race differently."[88] Had redemption not been ordained, "we have the certainty that from the beginning the whole disposition of nature would have been different."[89] Even more important are two alternatives Schleiermacher does not mention, but which are implicit to his Christology. These two are central to my argument. The first is an alternative to the election of Christ. According to Schleiermacher, Christ's human nature is completely identical to ours.[90] The only difference between him and us is sin; but sin is not an essential part of human nature. Christ's and all our individual human natures are open to the sinless life; in all of us "reside[s] the possibility of taking up the divine into itself, just as did happen in Christ."[91] But if that is the case, God did not have to choose Jesus to be the Redeemer. He could have chosen any of us.

The second alternative is a variation on the *ordo salutis*. The ultimate goal of the divine decree is God's impartation to humankind. The divine decree organizes things so that we all are in need of a Redeemer, whose influence mediates to us the divine impartation. The Redeemer himself receives his power from a direct impartation of the divine. However, since all humans have a potency to receive such impartation, God could have imparted Godself to all of us directly. In this case, the ultimate goal of the decree would have been reached, but without the detour of sin and redemption.

Can these alternatives be dismissed? One could try to read the alternatives Schleiermacher himself mentions as part of a rhetorical strategy.

88. CF § 120.3, 556.
89. CF § 164.1, 723.
90. CF § 94.1, 385; § 89.2, 367.
91. CF § 94.1, 385; § 13.1, 64.

Schleiermacher calls attention to the nature of God's actual actions by contrasting them with alternatives. He does not necessarily claim that these alternatives are real. However, my two Christological alternatives cannot be dismissed so easily. They are both implied by the identity between Christ's nature and ours. To dismiss them would be to deny this identity, which would also undermine the actual *ordo salutis*. Christ's redeeming work implies the completion of human nature and he can only complete human nature by partaking in it. These alternatives are therefore an integral part of Schleiermacher's Christology and anthropology.

I believe the only way forward is for Schleiermacher to change his ontology by giving up omnipotence II. His Christology and anthropology demand greater ontological openness than currently allowed. The implications of such a move are, however, not just philosophical. A change in Schleiermacher's ontology implies a change in his theology. To give up on omnipotence II means to allow for an alternative reality. But if more is possible than the actual, current reality rests on a choice. Given omnipotence I, that choice is made by God. But if God chooses, God must have motivations. To give up omnipotence II is to introduce a divine motivation theory. That would be a radical departure from a theology currently expressed only in terms of causal relations. More than relations of power, it would have to speak of divine psychology.

Absolute Dependence and Divine Motivation Theory

Since Schleiermacher's current system does not know of any divine motivation, it is difficult to speculate what such motivation would entail were it introduced. However, what it must entail is an account of the special preference for Christ, whereas God gives him what any or all could have received. Interestingly, Schleiermacher does face this issue in his discussion of the election of Christ. There he considers the question why precisely Jesus of Nazareth was chosen to be the Redeemer, and not anyone else. His answer is "that time and place [of the divine impartation] were chosen as the absolute best, that is as yielding the maximum effect."[92] But Schleiermacher immediately adds that, given divine omnipotence, God is also responsible for the

92. CF § 120.2, 553.

situation in which the choice of Christ would give maximum efficacy.[93] The question therefore cannot be answered, Schleiermacher concludes.

Could Schleiermacher's system contain the notion of divine motivation? Two different puzzles would need to be solved. For the logical minded among us, the pressing issue is whether the tidily woven structure of Schleiermacher's argument allows for omnipotence II to be taken out and replaced with a motivation that guides omnipotence I. I tried to make conceptual space for this move by arguing that omnipotence I and II are logically independent implications of the notion of absolute dependence. But that does not completely solve the issue. The question is now how strongly absolute dependence and omnipotence II are connected. Some implications are so strong that one cannot give up the consequent without giving up the antecedent. If omnipotence II is strictly implied by absolute dependence, the rejection of the latter would force Schleiermacher to give up the former, and then the whole system would come crashing down.

The second puzzle is for the more theological minded. In Schleiermacher's proposal, the notion of absolute dependence functions in a twofold way. It is both an ontological principle and a methodological rule. It expresses the nature of the relationship between Creator and creation, and it limits the discourse of the creatures about the Creator, by saying that our language about God should never go beyond God's causal working on us. However, by relinquishing omnipotence II and introducing divine motivation, we violate the methodological rule. The question is whether we can do this without also undermining absolute dependence as an ontological principle.

My own intuition is that Schleiermacher's proposal cannot be saved from either difficulty. Two of Schleiermacher's arguments for omnipotence II, as discussed above, draw a close connection between absolute dependence and omnipotence II. If we hold that God can do more than God does, Schleiermacher argues, we go outside the immediate experience of absolute dependence. We also imply self-limitation on God's side, which does the same. To hold that God can do more than God does is therefore to give up on absolute dependence. To save Schleiermacher's proposal, two things would need to be shown. The first is that the arguments just mentioned concern absolute dependence as methodological rule, not as ontological principle. By relinquishing

93. CF § 120.3, 555–56.

omnipotence II, we would give up the former, not the latter. The second thing that needs to be shown is that these two functions of absolute dependence are indeed so loosely connected that we can hold onto the ontological principle even when we give up the methodological rule. Thus, it all comes down to the solution to the second puzzle. Here Schleiermacher's own considerations give us little hope. Defending his methodological rule, Schleiermacher argues for it based on the ontological principle. Knowledge of an object reflects the nature of an object, he states. As the knowledge is composite, the object too must be composite. A composite God cannot be the Whence of the absoluteness of our feeling of dependence. Therefore, no knowledge of God is allowed that would suggest that God is such a composite.[94] However, on Schleiermacher's watch, a theology that accepts divine motivation, deliberation, and choice does exactly that.[95] It suggests a composite God and thereby undermines the foundation of the whole system. If Schleiermacher is correct in this line of argument, it seems his system cannot be saved.

Schleiermacher's Christology has a highly original profile. His supralapsarianism is based on his doctrine of absolute dependence and divine causality. Because absolute dependence of humans on God implies a nonreciprocal relationship between God and creation, the incarnation cannot be conceived as a divine response to human sin. And since everything falls within the scope of divine causality, including sin, Schleiermacher does not construe sin as opposition to the divine initiative, but as part of it. Sin and redemption are the means by which God connects all humankind to Christ, through whom the divine impartation enters the world. Finally, since absolute dependence does not allow our theological speech to go beyond the scope of divine causality, Schleiermacher's construal of God's action is cast only in causal terms, with exclusion of a concept of divine motivation.

The same notions of absolute dependence and divine causality that lead Schleiermacher to his supralapsarianism lead him to hold a form of divine omnipotence that excludes any alternative for reality as it is. However, embedded in Schleiermacher's doctrine of redemption, which is part of his supralapsarian argument, lies the idea of alternative realities. God could have

94. CF § 50.2, 195–56.
95. CF § 54.3, 214–15; § 41, postscript, 156.

ordained redemption and divine impartation to develop differently than they actually do. Careful analysis shows that Schleiermacher will not be able to save his proposals from this inconsistency. On the one hand, to save his Christological construal, Schleiermacher would have to give up part of his conception of divine omnipotence and develop a divine motivation theory. On the other hand, if he were to do this, he would very likely fatally undermine the very notions of absolute dependence and divine causality upon which his Christological construal is built.

3

Dorner's Supralapsarian Christology

Isaak August Dorner (1809–84) is nowadays a little-known German theologian. He did not attract many followers; his influence is hardly recognizable in subsequent theologians.[1] His systematics, *System der Christliche Glaubenslehre,* was published when Albrecht Ritschl and his school already were putting their mark on the theological scene.[2] At the publication of the first volume, Dorner himself wrote to his friend Hans Lassen Martensen: "The book will be like a stranger to the current generation."[3] Dorner might have been right. Ritschlian theology has little patience for the high Christological approach and the ontological arguments that Dorner builds his thoughts upon. But while his *System* was like a stranger to his

1. The two exceptions are his account of divine immutability and his construal of the three trinitarian persons as "modes of being." Both were very influential on Karl Barth. For the account of divine immutability, see Isaak August Dorner, *Divine Immutability: A Critical Reconstruction,* trans. Robert R. Williams and Claude Welch (Minneapolis: Fortress Press, 1994); and Karl Barth, *Church Dogmatics* II.1 (Edinburgh: T and T Clark, 1957), 493. For Dorner's construal of the trinitarian persons, see I. A. Dorner, *A System of Christian Doctrine* I, trans. Alfred Cave and J. S. Banks (Edinburgh: T and T Clark, 1888), 447–53; and Karl Barth, *Church Dogmatics* (Edinburgh: T and T Clark, 1975), 359–60.

2. I. A. Dorner, *System der Christlichen Glaubenslehre,* 1st ed. (Berlin: W. Herz, 1879–81), 2nd ed. (Berlin, 1883). Translated in *A System of Christian Doctrine.* References to this translation of *System der Christliche Glaubenslehre* include the abbreviation SCD, the volume number, and page number.

3. Quoted in Jörgen Rothenmundt, *Personale Synthese: Isaak August Dorners dogmatische Methode* (Göttingen: Vandenhoeck und Ruprecht, 1968), 42–43.

Ritschlian contemporaries, it must have been like an old friend to the previous generation. Dorner was not the first of a new era but the last of an old. Nineteenth-century German theology saw a series of supralapsarian theologians, and Dorner was both their chronicler and systematician.[4] In addition to a five-volume history of Christology, he wrote a two-volume history of German Protestant theology, finally followed by his *System*, a four-volume supralapsarian dogmatics. I read Dorner therefore not so much for his influence on the future but for his roots in the past.[5]

Dorner's root intuition is that the relationship between God and human beings is one of free, mutual love and embrace. That God becomes incarnate is the fullest expression of divine love, inviting and eliciting a human answer. Dorner's theological argument for this intuition takes the form of a long meditation on "the ethical." But other than the Ritschlian moral approach of the ethical, Dorner's approach is ontological. Dorner distinguishes from the natural world "a second world, the ethical, for which nature (the human included) has only the significance of conditioning presupposition. Humanity can fulfill its commission only in a history of freedom, which is essentially conditioned in its successful progression by the fact that the divine self-impartation is increasingly interwoven and intertwined in it."[6] Dorner argues, on the one hand, how this ethical world is rooted in the Trinity, which in itself is the personification of the ethical; and how, on the other hand, this ethical world and its history of human freedom and divine self-impartation are consummated in the incarnation.

One caveat: Dorner presents his argument as a consistent chain of necessary steps, resulting from the very nature of ethical necessity. In doing so, he sides with a long tradition of thinkers, starting with Aristotle, who believe that *scientia* (*Wissenschaft*, or science, as the problematic English tradition has it)

4. For an overview of nineteenth-century German supralapsarian theology and its subsequent discussion, see J. A. Dorner, *History of the Development of the Doctrine of the Person of Christ*, vol. III, trans. Patrick Fairbairn (Edinburgh: T and T Clark, 1978), 237–48.

5. The secondary literature of Dorner is rather slim. Besides the volume by Jörgen Rothermundt, *Personale Synthese*, there are: Christine Axt-Piscalar, *Der Grund des Glaubens: Eine theologiegeschichtliche Untersuchung zum Verhältnis von Glaube und Trinität in der Theologie Isaak August Dorners* (Tübingen: J.C.B. Mohr [Paul Siebeck], 1990); Michael Hüttenhoff, *Erkenntnistheorie und Dogmatik: Das erkenntnistheoretische Problem der Theologie bei I.A. Dorner, Fr. H.R. Frank und R.A. Lipsius* (Bielefeld: Luther Verlag, 1991); Thomas Koppehl, *Der Wissenschaftliche Standpunkt der Theologie Isaak August Dorners* (Berlin: Walter de Gruyter, 1997). The only extensive discussion of Dorner's arguments for supralapsarian Christology is by Jörgen Rothermundt, *Personale Synthese*, 161–68, and in Koppehl, *Der Wissenschaftliche Standpunkt der Theologie Isaak August Dorners*, 145–51.

6. Dorner, *Divine Immutability*, 147.

can only be practiced concerning the necessary.[7] The twentieth century has seen the end of this tradition. Therefore, while I take Dorner's claims concerning the necessity of his thesis seriously, I do not hold it against him when, as I argue in the last section, he will have to part from the necessity of his construal to make his argument work.

As in the case of Schleiermacher, Dorner sees the incarnation as imbedded in and the consummation of an ontological order. Therefore, as in the previous chapter, I devote the first part of my discussion to Dorner's ontological framework. The second part concerns the arguments for supralapsarianism. Since Dorner's work is relatively unknown, it is important to lay out his proposals in detail. In the final part I argue that Dorner's proposals contain several different interpretations of the incarnation. All these share the conviction that the incarnation is not contingent upon human sin; but they differ in their approach to the meaning of the incarnation: its motivation, its end, and its effect. For Dorner to save the heart of his proposal, the incarnation as the consummation of an interpersonal relationship between God and human beings, he will have to give up some cherished parts of his ontology.

I. Dorner's Ontological Framework

The Ethical

With the notion of "the ethical," the starting point of Dorner's argument, Dorner wants to identify the loftiest of all ideas. It is "the absolute highest thought . . . the queen, whose throne is exalted above all else."[8] It is "not merely opposed to unconditionateness, but to everything else, by virtue of its internal worth and its necessity, a necessity infinitely higher than any in the physical sphere, and able to claim the highest honour."[9] The ethical is "that which is valuable in itself and unconditionally."[10] It is "that which is the essentially good, as its own absolutely worthy and positive end."[11]

7. SCD I, 159–84. Cf. for a somewhat idiosyncratic history of the influence of this epistemological rule on the practice of theology: A. Vos, *Kennis en Noodzakelijkheid: Een kritische analyse van het absolute evidentialisme in wijsbegeerte en theologie* (Kampen: Kok, 1981), especially 1–134, 240–78.

8. SCD I, 308.

9. Ibid.

10. Dorner, *Divine Immutability*, 169.

11. SCD I, 311.

These quotations are the closest Dorner comes anywhere to giving a definition of the ethical. Rather than supplying a direct description of the ethical, Dorner contrasts the ethical with other strata of reality. Dorner perceives reality as a multilayered universe, a pyramid in which lower layers point to and find their meaning in higher levels. Dorner draws a particularly stark contrast between the physical and the spiritual layers. The physical is the world of power and causality, as well as "design and order, of beauty and harmony." All of these need the spiritual to give regulative content to their existence—"they have no true absoluteness in themselves . . . everything physical first has its true goodness from the fact that it serves what is positively good, what is ethical, as end."[12] Power, for example, needs value to be regulated. Although as a whole the spiritual realm structures the physical realm, it itself is structured by a ranking order of goods. Justice is part of the spiritual, but not the highest good. Justice without the ethical is empty: "Its absolute right and its necessity it derives from a positive and absolute end, which it protects, but which it does not create, but which must rather be given to it together with its whole empire."[13] Finally, the ethical is also to be distinguished from the good. The good, as Dorner points out, "might be regarded as a mere natural impulse, without freedom,—a work of the Nature in God. . . . But in that case God would not have himself under control,—he would act in a manner purely physical."[14] This is the most important characteristic of the ethical: it can be had only by an act of self-involvement. If it were obtained only by being part of one's nature, it would be no more than a physical attribute, an expression of natural power. The ethical needs to be owned by a free act. As I explain below, this leads to an important antimony in the doctrine of divinity.

The idea of the ethical is necessary, because the structure of reality necessarily needs a final cause, as "that which holds all human life together."[15] As such, it exists not only as idea, but also as being, a being identical to God. Dorner argues for this identification starting from the premise of God as the highest and necessarily existent being, a premise Dorner believes he has earlier proven by a form of the ontological argument.[16] If the ethical is the

12. SCD I, 308; cf. 264–76.
13. SCD I, 304; cf. 276–305.
14. SCD I, 309.
15. SCD I, 311.
16. SCD I, 214–30.

absolute highest and rationally necessary thought, it needs to be identical with God. It cannot receive its existence outside God, since then something absolutely worthy would exist independently of the absolute being that God is. And it cannot exist as a potential idea in God, since to be potential falls short of being absolute, as the idea of the ethical is.[17] Therefore, God and the ethical are one, and "the Deity himself is to be designated as the ethical absolute."[18]

The ethical is part of God's necessary nature. However, it is essential to the ethical "that it be the production of volition, nay, that it have its being in volition."[19] This is what differentiates the ethical from the physical. Therefore, if God "were only fatalistically and compulsorily determined in his being by the law of the ethical, or were he immediately at one therewith without conscious will, he would merely be a necessitated ethical substance."[20] On the other hand, the ethical cannot just be seated in an act of will. If the divine will, undetermined by the divine nature, decides what is ethical, the ethical is ultimately grounded by "something merely physical, a simple assertion of power, a chance." Both an ethical nature without a self-determining will and an ethical act of will without a determining ethical nature are merely expressions of physical power. The antinomy thus disclosed suggests that "the truly ethical consists in the union of the truly necessary and the free."[21] Such union is only consistently conceived, Dorner believes, in the doctrine of the Trinity.[22]

17. SCD I, 312–13.

18. SCD I, 319. Cf. Dorner, *Divine Immutability*, 169: "The ethical is to be posited as primal power in God himself, without which God would not be God; God is to be identified as the ethical itself, as the primal ethical (*Urethische*)."

Dorner could have given an argument for the existence of God based on the idea of the ethical. As the next paragraph suggests, the ethical needs will and consciousness (cf. SCD I, 303, 323). Given the absoluteness of the ethical, its will and consciousness need to be absolute themselves. On the presuppositions of perfect being theology, which Dorner holds onto, absolute will and consciousness are divine. With an argument analogous to the *ratio Anselmi*, which Dorner uses for his ontological argument, the ethical will and consciousness could be shown to exist not only in the ideal but also in reality. Given this line of argumentation, Dorner could have avoided the detour of first developing an ontological argument for the existence of God, followed by an argument for the ethical, after which God and the ethical need to be identified. That Dorner chooses the detour shows that he is concerned with more than establishing the existence of God; he wants to establish the nature of and relationships between the layers of the ontological pyramid.

19. SCD I, 427. Cf. Dorner, *Divine Immutability*, 169.

20. SCD I, 315. Cf. Dorner, *Divine Immutability*, 170.

21. SCD I, 419. Dorner believes this antinomy is to be the same as the problem of whether the good is good because God wills it, or whether God wills the good because it is good. SCD I, 428–32.

22. SCD I, 427–30.

The Trinity

Dorner's solution for the antinomy is to distribute the necessary and the free over the persons of the Trinity. The ethically necessary has an existence in God the Father.[23] He is the first form of being in God, that of "moral law and morally necessary being," the seat "of the eternal truths generally, so of ethical truth."[24] However, the ethically necessary by itself amounts to "nonethical naturalism" or fatalism. Therefore it desires freedom as "the absolute form which is alone adequate or conformable to the ethically necessary."[25] This desire itself is necessary, implied by the self-preserving nature of the ethically necessary.[26] But the result is "the mode of the existence of the spiritual God in the form of freedom," the Son.[27] His nature is to be the "principle of ethical movement out of [the Father], or, as opposed to what is ethically necessary, the principle of freedom as the instrument for his ethical self-production or self-realization so as to ensure his absolute ethical personality and his living love."[28] The Son, in his turn, desires to condition himself by the Father, the ethically necessary. He recognizes in the ethically necessary his own truth and foundation; by renouncing the ethically necessary, the Son would renounce himself.[29] There is thus, on the side of the Father, the ethically necessary, a necessary volition of the free, as the necessary form of the ethically necessary; and on the side of the Son, the principle of freedom, there is a striving back to the ethically necessary, as the constitution of his own being. The agent by whom both divine modes of existence know and will each other Dorner identifies as the Spirit.[30] Through the Holy Spirit, the Son finds in the ethical necessity the volition of the being of the free, that is, himself; and the Father finds in the free the willing of the ethical necessity.[31] The Spirit, as the bond between Father and Son, is thus their mutual

23. SCD I, 432.
24. SCD I, 433.
25. SCD I, 435.
26. Ibid.
27. SCD I, 434.
28. Ibid.
29. SCD I, 436.
30. SCD I, 437.
31. This is one of the reasons why Karl Barth made his much-repeated objection that, in this proposal, the Spirit is "characterized as the real God over against the Father and the Son." Karl Barth, *Protestant Theology in the Nineteenth Century: Its Background and History*, trans. Brian Cozens and John Bowden (Grand Rapids, MI: Eerdmans, 2002), 571. Cf. Axt-Piscalar, *Der Grund des Glaubens*, 183, n.82.

love, "for love is the unity of ethical necessity and freedom, because it wills the ethically necessary as such, that is, with consciousness and absolute desire."[32]

This construal allows Dorner to participate in two contemporary debates on trinitarian theology. On the one hand, Dorner's doctrine of the Trinity is self-consciously differentiated from the proposals of contemporaries who take divine love as the constituting principle of the Trinity.[33] Dorner objects that while love presupposes the loving entities, it does not constitute them.[34] On the other hand, his proposal also allows him to reject the position that God, being love, needs created reality in order to have an object for the divine love.[35] God's love is all-sufficient, completely fulfilled by loving the highest, that is, ethical necessity. But as such, God's self-sufficient love is self-love.[36]

Note that the "freedom" which the Son embodies in this proposal is rather thin. The Son is free in the sense that his embrace of the ethically necessary is not a physical expression of his nature but an expression of "the power to will what it likes."[37] But the Son does not seem to be free to like anything other than he does. To choose differently than what is implied by the ethical necessity is for the Son to renounce himself. Therefore, while the Son acts by will rather than nature, his acts of will are still determined by his nature. And while this nature is necessary, so are his acts. This is confirmed by Dorner's arguments that, as I show below, the two most important acts of the Son, creation and incarnation, are acts of ethical necessity.[38]

Further, an unwelcome implication of Dorner's trinitarian construal is that it is not clear whether any of the trinitarian persons is fully divine. For instance, if "the truly ethical consists in the union of the truly necessary and

32. SCD I, 437.

33. SCD I, 408–12; 426–27. Dorner refers to Ernst Sartorius and Theodor Liebner. Cf. for the historical background, Axt-Piscalar, *Der Grund des Glaubens*, 121–36.

34. SCD I, 426.

35. SCD II, 11. Christine Axt-Piscalar contrasts Dorner here with Richard Rothe: *Der Grund des Glaubens*, 211–19.

36. SCD I, 463–64.

37. SCD I, 435.

38. For creation as a work of the Son rather than the Father or the Spirit: "The Father represents in the Trinity, which has no mere physical and logical but also an ethical necessity, the primary basis, the original truth and the holy nature or the ethically necessary. On the other hand, the Son is the principle of the divine movement, in logical, ideal relation the principle of revelation, objectivation, in ethical relation the principle of freedom, whilst the Holy Spirit as the third principle re-conducts the circle of movement from the opposite to its commencement, and thus becomes in relation to the world the principle of immanent, proper living spirit, intellectually and religiously the principle of internal certainty, ethically the principle of the proper internal sanctification in free conscious loving impulse." SCD III, 291. Cf. also SCD II, 40, and III, 141.

the free," the Father, who is only necessary, cannot be called truly ethical.[39] However, as I noticed above, to be truly ethical is a necessary implication of being divine. If the Father is not truly ethical, he is also not divine. Concerning the Son, he is said to have a nature and since the Son is a necessary product of the Father, his nature is necessary too. Unless this nature can be described as ethical necessity, the Son is not divine either. If this nature can be described as ethical necessity, it is the Son, rather than the Father, who is divine: freely by will, and necessarily by nature, he would embody the truly ethical.

Given these problems of Dorner's trinitarian proposal, it is important to distinguish which parts he actually needs for his overarching argument. The heart of the proposal, the distribution of the necessary and the free over the persons of the Trinity, is introduced as a solution to the perceived antinomy between the ethical as both implied by God's nature and produced by God's will. This part of the proposal, however, does not function any further in Dorner's position concerning the necessity of creation and incarnation. All Dorner takes from his proposal to the next step of the argument is the notion that creation is not necessitated by a need for an object of God's love. While Dorner gains this notion from his particular trinitarian construal, the history of theology shows it can be gained from other construals as well. It should not be too difficult to repair Dorner's overarching argument by an alternative trinitarian proposal with the same assets as his current one, but without the liabilities.

Creation

From the ethical and necessary character of the triune God, Dorner moves to creation as the ethical and necessary product of this God. He rejects the most current models of creational necessity: the Dionysian model of divine superabundance and the more contemporary Hegelian model of the creation of the world as a step in the development of divine consciousness. The latter suggests that the world supplies a defect in God, which runs counter to trinitarian all-sufficiency. It also suggests that the world is a mere element in God, which leaves no room for a relative self-dependence of creation. This would exclude an ethical relationship of freedom between God and creation; and, as Dorner

39. Unless, of course, the Father's willing of the Son is an expression of ethical freedom; but if the Father were able to will in freedom, he would not need the Son. For the quotation, see SCD I, 419.

will argue, it is such an ethical relationship that God is after in the act of creation.[40] Similar arguments can be leveled against the Dionysian model. Dorner rejects images like God as the "overflowing source of all being," pointing out that this suggests that the world is of the same nature as God, with little control of God over how far the divine nature extends.[41] Likewise, Dorner disagrees with Dionysian arguments which suggest that God, given divine love, needs to communicate to and share with others. While these arguments are more attractive, since they built on the ethical category of love, they are still too simplistic. Suggesting that God needs to communicate to others presupposes the existence of what is not God; but if this does not yet exist, there is also no need for communication and sharing.[42]

Dorner's own argument proceeds in two steps. First, he secures the existence of what is not God as a mental object of the divine. God, in divine omnipotence, knows all possibilities as residing in the divine intellect. Omnipotence also knows them to be distinct from the divine self, since the divine actuality is all-sufficient and blessed, and thus not in need of the realization of the possible. While God does not need the possible, the possible needs God for both its possible and actual existence.[43] Dorner wants to protect his doctrine of creation against collapsing in Hegelian conceptual structures, even while both models hold the necessity of creation. Once the existence of the possible is established, Dorner introduces the divine motivation for calling some possibilities into actual reality. "As holy love he is not merely self-affirming personality, he also loves the sentiment of love in itself and absolutely, is *amor amoris*. Thus, not merely is there no reason in him for wishing to make himself the only abode of love, but on the contrary, his love finds its delight in multiplying, aggrandizing the life of love, in forming a kingdom of love."[44] God is a lover of love, and God's motive in creation is to multiply love. This determines the nature of what God creates: "a world of rational beings, who through communication of divine love become themselves capable of love."[45] Somewhat as an afterthought Dorner adds that, while this does not explain all of

40. SCD II, 9–10.
41. SCD II, 10. Cf. SCD I, 309.
42. SCD II, 11.
43. SCD II, 13–14.
44. SCD II, 14. Cf. SCD I, 443, and SCD II, 25: "God is the causal principle of a real existence other than love."
45. SCD II, 15.

creation, God, who not only loves love but also life, also creates nonrational beings: "But there is nothing to prevent divine love desiring also another—nature—in harmony, of course, with its desire for a kingdom of love, and even desiring the existence of another beside love in the world, and imparting to it of its fullness. Love is also a lover of life."[46]

In creating humanity with an eye to multiplication of the life of love, God aims to make human beings both object and subject of love. As I will show, the contours of these two are rather similar. First, God creates human beings to be subjects of love. To be capable of love is to be an ethical being, and to be the latter, one needs to be free. Free beings are "not simply irresistibly determined by the force of his love, but [are] capable of entering into a *spontaneous* communion of love with him"—something that in itself, as Dorner observes, "is a fresh security for the abiding distinctiveness of the creature in relation to God's act of self-communication."[47] All of this means that humans are made in the image of God—who in desiring "free personalities, . . . desires likenesses of himself."[48]

In contrasting free human ability to will and to love with irresistible divine determination, Dorner differs strongly from the conceptual structures of Schleiermacher's anthropology. As noted in chapter 2, Schleiermacher does not deny human freedom, but this freedom is embedded in the experience of absolute dependence on the divine. Human beings are free to do as they choose, but their spontaneous choosing is founded upon and determined by the divine causality. Dorner also uses the notion of absolute dependence, but with a different scope. To be absolutely dependent on God means to be absolutely constituted by God without any creational assistance. However, this goes hand in hand with a notion of freedom vis-à-vis God, in that "in the same divine will, on which we are absolutely dependent in our *being,* is included the willing of our freedom, the willing of the exercise of our powers, by means of which the *character of our being* is at least partially determined."[49]

That human beings are created as subjects of love means that they are created in the image of God. But so does the fact that human beings are objects

46. Ibid.
47. SCD II, 19. Cf. Dorner, *Divine Immutability*, 144–45.
48. SCD II, 20; cf. SCD II, 25.
49. SCD II, 118.

of God's love. They are "designed to be the object of his perfect, unreserving love, and by this means perfect, God's likeness outside God."[50] In loving humans, God communicates Godself to them, makes them mirrors of the triune, gives them the highest God has to give: to become like Godself.[51] The gift of God's love is the gift of the divine image.[52]

The divine image is partly endowment, partly destination.[53] It cannot be otherwise. To be like God is to share in God's holiness, God's goodness, God's love. But these are ethical attributes. They cannot be given as nature; they can only be embraced by an act of will. Human ethical destination requires ethical self-determination. The end of creation is "a rich life of love," but that end can only come through history.[54] Sin is not the primary reason why creation and consummation are not the same, but the very nature of the relationship between God and humans demands it. The ethical goal of creation demands history, a history of the "twofold surrender of God to man, and of man to God."[55] Only thus "is it possible for man in his onward progress to take part in his self-development, and be in God a free, independent personality, in the spirit of Paul Gerhard's saying: 'What is slow in coming is held the faster, and what is long delayed tastes all the sweeter.'"[56]

Religion and Revelation

The technical term for this history of twofold surrender is religion. "Religion is the living, reciprocal relationship of God to man and of man to God."[57] Seen from the side of the creature, religion is the history of human acknowledgment and embrace of its absolute dependence. In religion, humans distinguish between their partial dependence on finite reality, and the absolute dependence of all finitude on God—absolute dependence for its existence, that is. Further, instead of resisting this dependence, the religious person accepts her

50. SCD II, 16. In fact, a creature is "not therefore an object of love to God's self-communication, save in so far as he views it to be a subject of love." SCD II, 19. Cf. SCD II, 25.

51. Cf. just the pages SCD II, 16, 17, 19, 21, 27, 54.

52. SCD II, 77–84.

53. SCD II, 77, 79.

54. SCD II, 25.

55. SCD II, 124.

56. Ibid. Cf. SCD II, 79, 81.

57. SCD II, 114. Cf. SCD II, 77: "With religion the portrayal of God in the personal creature is realized, in order that man may be God's image."

dependence in humility and piety.[58] This acknowledgment is, by its nature, a communal act. Dorner acknowledges that it might seem as if the reciprocal relationship with God can be fully satisfied as enacted between individuals, but two arguments speak against it. First, to embrace one's absolute dependence on God goes hand in hand with an acknowledgment of God as the creator and father of all. To suggest that God is only related to oneself is not religion but egoism. If religion is to accept God as God is, it is to accept God as the Lord of "a vast spiritual kingdom."[59] Second, to accept God as God is implies to accept oneself in the way one is created, that is, as a member of this kingdom. This is not just an extrinsic aspect of humanity but is intrinsic. Humans are created as relational beings, dependent on each other for their development.[60]

Religion needs revelation, however. Without it, religious activity is only "intercourse with the pictures of one's own fancy and the moods of feeling resulting therefrom," and therefore "merely a kind of intercourse with oneself and not religion."[61] Religion presupposes interaction with the divine, but God can only be known by revelation. "In every true act of worship, veils so to speak are removed between God and man; God reveals himself to the good man, the latter becomes conscious of God."[62] As a continuation of the divine self-communication initiated in the act of creation, the content of revelation is not primarily one of propositions, truth, or certainty, but a revealing of Godself.[63] This revelation comes in twofold form. First, there is internal revelation: inspiration, the working of the Holy Spirit on human hearts and minds. Second, there is external revelation, the work of God through mighty acts and miracles.

58. SCD II, 117.

59. SCD II, 126.

60. SCD II, 126–27 and SCD II, 75–77.

61. SCD II, 115; cf. SCD II, 116, 120, 133.

62. SCD II, 134. There are remarkable analogies between Dorner's and Barth's speaking about the nature of divine revelation. Both emphasize that God can only be known by an unveiling on God's part. Both also hold that God can only be known by God, and that human knowledge of God is a form of participation in God's knowing of Godself: "true knowledge of God only arises through a being and self-knowledge on the part of God in us—a being and self-knowledge which originate knowledge and make his thoughts our thoughts—all our true knowledge of God has for its medium the consciousness that we are thought, willed, loved by God" (SCD II, 120). The decisive conceptual difference between these two does not concern the nature of divine revelation, but the nature of human receptivity to God's revelation. While Barth holds that the ontological gap between God and creation can only be overcome by divine miracle, Dorner thinks much less of such a gap, holding that "God's activity in implanting the germs of reason, and with them the ability to apprehend him and become conscious of him" is the fundamental element in divine revelation; SCD II, 116.

63. SCD II, 198. Cf. SCD II, 134: "revelation, being related to man's entire nature, is meant to impart to him a share in the divine life in general, not merely in the divine knowledge."

Internal revelation seems to be the most proper: "that it must perforce be internal is scarcely matter of doubt, religion having reference to an inner act of God on the spirit, an act of communion, so that Revelation in any case only reaches its proper end, when it is internally imparted and made over the spirit."[64] However, purely internal revelations, even if they are really divine, are still "of necessity definite modifications of ourselves."[65] External revelation is therefore necessary. It gives us the external assurance and epistemic certainty that internal revelation lacks.[66] It also makes possible the communal aspect of religion. Purely internal revelation is only accessible to one, but external revelation can be received by all.[67]

II. Dorner's Supralapsarian Christology

The Argument from Revelation

In Dorner's schema, religion, revelation, and piety are not primarily about sin, atonement, and reconciliation. They are the historic and communal expression of humanity's growth into community with God, and thereby the supralapsarian consummation of humanity's essential nature. Religion and revelation have their consummation too: in Christ. This is the final step of Dorner's argument. The idea of the ethical led us to the necessary existence of God, triune and self-sufficient. The ethical nature of the triune God necessarily expresses itself in creation. The goal of creation is to multiply the life of love. God does this by creating human beings who are, on the one hand, created after God's image, that is, who are ethical subjects capable of love, and who are on the other hand objects of love, that is, who are recipients of the self-communication of God. This reciprocal relationship between God and creation is called religion; the divine contribution to this relationship is called revelation. However, revelation, and thereby religion, and thereby the whole relationship between God and creation, are directed toward a final moment of consummation: incarnation. And since revelation and religion are

64. SCD II, 141.
65. SCD II, 143.
66. Ibid.
67. SCD II, 142.

supralapsarian, so is the incarnation. "In the divine world-idea the perfective will, because fixing the ultimate aim, is even antecedent in a logical respect to the redemptive will conditioned only by the Fall."[68]

Dorner has three main arguments to support his supralapsarian Christology—the first two explicit, the last implicit. The first argument holds that revelation, according to both its form and its content, attains its perfection in the incarnation. With respect to the form of revelation, Dorner proposes a ranking order based on how adequately the form can receive, guard, and cultivate revelation. This criterion results in the lower ranking of external and impersonal forms of revelation as revelation through nature, and a higher ranking for internal forms of revelation as inspiration. Even in the case of inspiration, revelation is only accidentally connected to the medium: "In the life of every inspired man there was a period when he was not such, a period which cannot be without after-consequences."[69] One of the decisive factors in this ranking order seems to be the separation of external and internal forms of revelation. Without an internal component, the external form is incapable of ethical reception and cultivation of revelation; without the participation of the external, the internal form has no praxis. The consummation of revelation should therefore be one whose "entire person [is] made an organ of revelation," who "is given at once in inseparable unity external as well as internal revelation and the completion of both."[70] In other words, a "man who, from the first moment of his existence, in his entire person lives in a sphere of being pertaining to revelation and never separated from God."[71] The same conclusion can be reached with respect to the content of revelation. Dorner is less explicit about a ranking order of revelation's content, but the highest ranking is clearly the communication of "the entire fullness of the Godhead."[72] Therefore, "since it is God's will in his eternal love to make an absolute communication of himself as regards his entire communicable being, in the world-idea or world-council he willed not merely the spiritual existence or relative receptiveness for him, but as revealer or λόγος he wills absolutely such cosmic existence as is endowed with perfect receptiveness for him and his presence,

68. SCD II, 210.
69. SCD II, 206.
70. Ibid.
71. Ibid.
72. SCD II, 207.

i.e. he wills the perfect divine image in the form of realization in the world, which again is the Son of his love."[73]

The last move of the argument raises a question. Granted that Dorner has shown that divine incarnation is the absolute form of revelation, higher than all other, relative forms of revelation, which of the preceding steps of the overarching argument calls for such absolute revelation? Dorner has shown that God created the world so as to communicate Godself to it, but why does this necessitate absolute revelation? Would relative revelation not do? Dorner does have an answer to this question, but it is not an answer developed straight from the doctrine of revelation. Dorner's answer is dependent on his doctrine of religion. As we will see below, on Dorner's construal the absoluteness of revelation, that is, the incarnational aspect thereof, is not called for by God's desire for self-communication itself, but by the anthropological requirements to receive revelation. As I argue, this is quite a telling move in Dorner's argument. While it is a possible construal, it was not the only one available to him.

The Argument from Religion

Revelation is the divine component of the reciprocal relationship called religion. Religion is, as I noted in a previous section, a communal affair. Human beings worship God together; not only because God is the God of all, but also because God created humans as relational beings, who are hardwired to act in social cohesion. As social entities, religions are necessarily also historical. And as historical entities, they also have a historical origin. Dorner is a typical nineteenth-century adherent of the "great men theory" of the origin of religions: religions find their origin in the visionary leadership of an inspired personality—a Buddha, a Moses, a Mohammed.[74] Thus the religious life of humankind is broken down in several religions, all embedded in their own culture, all tracing their roots to a different founder. While these communities reflect the divine wish that humans worship God in piety, their diversity also expresses their own human relativity. Relative religions help their adherents come to relative development. But they cannot help them come to the perfection God has in mind for them. Their structures are limited by their historic

73. Ibid.
74. SCD II, 129–31, 143.

and cultural situatedness; their power is curbed by the imperfection of their founders. Their vision falls short of the all-comprehensive vision of God. Absolute religion, on the other hand, as the embodiment of the divine vision of a kingdom of love, is not limited to a particular culture or region but embraces all cultures and all regions. To come to their consummation, to be incorporated in the kingdom of love, individuals need therefore the all-comprehensive consciousness and power of absolute religion.[75]

Absolute religion does not differ from relative religions by tracing its origin to a single founder. Such structure is inherent to the nature of religious communities. The founder of this religion, however, needs to "be of such a character, that before him all distinctions of time and space, all limits of nationality and individuality, vanish, because in him appears the central personality, the personality therefore having equal affinities with all, in which resides power to give unity and perfection to all."[76] The founder needs to be all-embracing in the way absolute religion is all-embracing, and finally, in the way God's ultimate vision for creation is all-embracing. But the only one capable of such embrace is Godself. The only one qualified to found this religion is he who "by God's self-communication to humanity being in him absolute and universal, or by the principle of divine revelation, God as λόγος, issuing forth in him, communicating himself to man, or by the λόγος becoming man in him"[77]—the incarnate One.

Thus, the incarnation, as the absolute revelation of God, is necessitated by the need for an absolute religion. Human beings find themselves consummated in the divine kingdom of love, and only absolute religion can usher in the kingdom. But absolute religion cannot be founded by a human being. Religion may be the "the living, reciprocal relationship of God to man and of man to God,"[78] but absolute religion needs God's input in this relationship to be so strong that Godself becomes its founder.

The Argument from the Ethical Nature of Humanity

Dorner has one more argument for his supralapsarian Christology. It is not, like the two previous ones, part of his official Christological presentation.

75. SCD II, 211–13.
76. SCD II, 211.
77. Ibid.
78. SCD II, 114.

Instead, it is implicit, tucked into his doctrine of sin. Nonetheless, it is an argument based immediately upon his doctrine of the ethical, and therefore at least as helpful to his case as the arguments from revelation and religion.[79]

Human beings are ethical creatures. In distinction from animals, they have more than physical powers but are created for the ethical good. The ethical, however, needs to be owned. If it were obtained only by being part of one's nature, it would be no more than a physical attribute, an expression of natural power. The ethical is only had by free, self-involved act. These acts can also only be made at a certain point in time. Humans do not immediately have the cognitive, voluntative, and emotional powers to make ethical decisions. They need to be developed. Situating oneself vis-à-vis the ethical is, however, essential to being a human personality. Being human therefore entails development through stages of self-consciousness, individuality, and subjectivity, until one reaches the stage of free, personal decision—the stage where one develops from being a mere potential to being an actual personality.[80]

For this final decision two things are necessary. Subjectively, human beings need to be undetermined in their decision, free from binding factors in their environment. In the current postfall situation, where humans are bonded in original sin, this is even more important. Further, objectively, the ethical good needs to "be placed before the eyes in its full clearness and truth, not merely as the voice of consciousness or as γράμμα, but in its most lucid and attractive form as personal love."[81] Both conditions are only fulfilled in divine incarnation. Christ sets people free from their current situation of bondage to sin, so that they can freely make their decision. Only the incarnate One embodies the necessary personal presence of the ethical in invitation and love. "He brings the crisis; his manifestation has it in itself to necessitate every one to decide for or against good itself."[82] In other words: the incarnation is a given because of the ethical nature of humankind. God creates human beings such that they need to choose for or against the ethical in order to become full personalities; but such a choice can only be made in interpersonal interaction with the ethical.

79. This argument is completely absent in any discussion of Dorner's supralapsarianism. See: Rothenmundt, *Personale Synthese*, 161–67, and Koppehl, *Das Wissenschaftliche Standpunkt der Theologie Isaak August Dorners*, 245–51.

80. SCD III, 59–60.

81. SCD III, 70.

82. SCD III, 71.

This last condition is rather interesting. To situate oneself vis-à-vis the ethical, it is not enough to know the ethical. Human beings can know the ethical by their natural cognitive capacities, as Dorner's argument shows. They also learn about the ethical in the context of religion. But what is necessary to encounter the ethical is not knowledge but love; love, which is not expressed by way of any third object, but by the offer of an interpersonal relationship with Godself. As I argue in the last sections, this is a very different conception of the meaning of the incarnation than given in all previous arguments.[83]

Infralapsarian Antinomies

In addition to these three arguments for supralapsarianism, Dorner poses three questions concerning the infralapsarian position, each of them meant to point out an antinomy.[84]

First, assuming that the incarnation counts as the strongest possible expression of divine love, Dorner points out that in the infralapsarian position divine love is more strongly confirmed and more clearly manifested to a sinful humanity than to a sinless one. This seems to slight sinless humanity.

Second, assuming the notion of an absolute religion as the consummation of the relationship between God and humanity, Dorner points out that infralapsarians have to take the relationship between Christ and the absolute religion as contingent. In a sinless universe, consummation is reached by way of Christless absolute religion; in a sinful universe, by way of a Christ-filled absolute religion. But not only is it "repugnant to the spirit of Christian piety" to assign to Christ so subordinate a position, it is also inconsistent with the absoluteness of religion to suggest that it is a contingent matter which religion counts as absolute.

83. The way God and creatures situate themselves vis-à-vis the ethical is both similar and dissimilar. As I noted in the second section, God too is only ethical by an act of self-involvement. This divine act is an act of self-love: the Son, God in the form of freedom, embraces in free obedience (SCD I, 435) the Father, God in the form of ethical truth. Creatures, however, situate themselves vis-à-vis the ethical by an act of love directed at the other: the incarnate God. God, who wants to give humans the *imago dei*, did not create them with the same ethical structure as the divine: a necessarily ethical nature, embraced by a free act of ethical self-love. This suggests the ethical is noncommensurable: human beings can be ethical in an interpersonal relationship with the divine, but cannot have the ethical independently.

84. SCD II, 218–20.

Finally, assuming that in the incarnation the highest crown and honor are given to the humanity of Christ, Dorner points out that infralapsarians at the same time take Christ's human nature to be lower in rank than all others, since all other humans are created for their own sake, but Christ, not being part of the original plan of creation, is created as a means for the well-being of all others. This even seems to suggest that Christ's human nature, at least from the perspective of divine motivation and end, is different from ours, which goes against the Chalcedonean dogma.

None of these arguments is very original in itself; for each of them, related arguments obtain elsewhere in the supralapsarian literature. What is interesting though is how Dorner molds these arguments to fit into his notion of reality as a layered universe. If it makes sense to see reality as a pyramid topped by the absolute, with people, events, or religions all taking their proper place in the ranking order, it is hard not to take the incarnation as the absolute, the top of the pyramid. But if Dorner's take on reality as a multilayered pyramid is not original to him but typical for his day and age, this may explain the sudden popularity of supralapsarian theology in the nineteenth century.

Creation, Consummation, and Redemption

The doctrine of creation is the stepping-stone of Dorner's supralapsarian Christology. The incarnation is the fulfillment of the divine goal: to extend the life of love. At the same time, Dorner spends little time on God's act of creating as an independent moment within the larger story of divine–human relationships. Three structurally interrelated reasons are at play. First, the necessitarian structure of Dorner's argument makes it impossible to distinguish between creating and consummating as conceptually different acts. Such a distinction would turn on the freedom of God to call into being what is not God, without engaging it in a relationship of consuming love. This would give conceptual space for theological reflection on the particular nature of the act of creation, independently of the act of consummation. In Dorner's proposal, God does not have such freedom. The act of creating is a necessary expression of his ethical nature, necessarily aimed at consummation.[85] Second, Dorner's

85. This does not imply, however, that consummation, and in particular incarnation, comes as a natural development of creation. Dorner repeatedly emphasizes the newness of incarnation and consummation vis-à-vis

notion of creation is strictly anthropocentric. As I noted, creation other than humanity is introduced as an afterthought. This is the result of Dorner's strong emphasis on the ethical over all other aspects of creation. By describing the divine motivation as ethical, aimed at a kingdom of love, all aspects of creation not capable of engaging in ethical relationships fall outside the scope of divine attention. Even while Dorner says that God created all nonhuman creatures because God is not just a lover of love but also of life, his strict focus on the ethical bars him from developing a notion of divine delight in all of creation. Third, even while the eternal Logos, as principle of divine movement, is the divine actor in creation, what is decisive for human bliss and woe is the confrontation with the Logos incarnate in history. This includes, as I note later in this section, the idea that real sin is only committed in the context of the incarnation, not yet in the context of creation. But this empties the doctrine of creation of many traditional notions such as goodness, law, and morality.

Dorner's doctrine of eschatological consummation is the extension of the conceptual structures just laid out: a strong concentration on the ethical and the absence of divine delight in other strata of creation. At the same time, because of the emphasis on the ethical, creation and consummation cannot collapse. The relationship of love that God initiates in creation calls for free human participation. Such freedom and participation can only be developed over time. "What is slow in coming is held the faster, and what is long delayed tastes all the sweeter." The decisive point of this development is, as I noted, the confrontation of the human being with the incarnate Christ. Dorner draws from this last point the conclusion that even in a world without sin, Christ would have come twice: "The division of Christ's Parousia into a first and second was not merely necessary on account of the atonement, because the work of redemption required Christ's sacrifice of himself in suffering and death, but was also involved in the necessity of an *ethical* process in those to be redeemed. The glory and the sight of Christ's power could not be the first, because the sight would have corrupted the motive of surrender to Christ, and have injured the ethical character of faith."[86] Dorner's description of the actual

---

creation. Revelation, of which the incarnation is the consummation, "must impart something analogous to the product of creation, something new, not previously existent in the spirit" (SCD II, 135). Cf. SCD II, 136–38. Christ "is not the product of empirical humanity, but of the [divine] idea of humanity destined to perfect every one else" (SCD III, 322).

86. SCD IV, 377.

consumed life is more detailed than traditional eschatology, as he himself points out.[87] This is a direct result of his take on the divine motivation for it all. If God's aim is the establishment of a kingdom of love, the consummation of the ethical, one's eschatological expectation should be allowed to extrapolate from the ethical relationships as one knows them now. The beatified enjoy reunion, mutual recognition, infinitely diversified fellowship, and joy.[88] They shall behold all the great spirits in the history of humanity.[89] Humankind will live in an eternal Sabbath, in which there is neither inactivity nor unrest in the activity. The talents of individuals will not be lost, but raised to higher potency. All will still advance and never want of an arena of satisfying activity.[90] Everyone has "the measure, which one is able to receive," while all share in that which is given to another, through the absolute communion in love binding together the perfected.[91] Above all, of course, they delight in the presence of God and Christ. Their knowing of God is no longer fragmentary, and their loving of God is "blessed contentment. Then will Christ keep the supper anew with us, and the highest solemnities of the present are but a weak foretaste of the powers of the world to come."[92] Over and over Dorner emphasizes the centrality of Christ in the consummation. "Christ's person, conceived in the New Testament as ever actively at work, and in due time again becoming visible, gives colour and impress to every point in Christian eschatology. . . . If theology relegated him to a secondary position in reference to the consummation, it would make him a person of transient importance,—a view which by reflex must necessarily disorganize the whole of Christology and the doctrine of God's self-revelation."[93] Given the supralapsarian nature of the incarnation, Christ is not to fade away even when the redemption has been completed, but central to the life of the beatified.[94]

87. SCD IV, 382.
88. SCD IV, 431.
89. Ibid.
90. SCD IV, 432.
91. SCD IV, 433.
92. SCD IV, 430.
93. SCD IV, 378.
94. Cf. SCD II, 216: "although when the work of redemption is done, he will then lay aside his redeeming office, yet will the world not lose him, its honour and crown. He will still retain his place as the first-born of the household, the head of the church, his existence not being conditioned by sin. Were he removed from the kingdom of God, the church of the saved would lose the eternal object of its gratitude and the source of its salvation. Therefore does the N.T. teach that his kingdom is an everlasting kingdom. He is the administrator of an everlasting priesthood. Out of his fullness, the fullness of the head, God's church receives and lives,

While the ethical will be consummated, the nonethical will be overcome. Dorner's attention is focused on the two categories that govern the physical world: time and space. He characterizes these, rightly, as limitations.[95] These limitations are overcome in "the stage of the absolute consummation of the humanity," the ascension. Now, "in eternal union with him, [humanity] has become henceforth, in its glorified and pneumatic form, the adequate organ of God as the Son. Jesus is now set free from all earthly burden, all narrowing force of matter, from every, even physical, imperfection . . . without limitation of space and time."[96] Space and time are thus not just limitations to created reality, but imperfections. They are overcome in resurrection and ascension, because here God's incarnation has been consummated.[97] In this last point one encounters an important line of thought for Dorner's Christology, but one conceptually independent of his supralapsarianism. Dorner conceives of the assumption of Christ's humanity as not completed in one moment, but as a process developing over time, initiated in conception, but only consummated in resurrection and ascension. With Jesus's growth in humanity comes a qualitative growth of union with divinity. The heart of this union is the ethical, that is, the reciprocal willing and realizing of the union by divinity and humanity. The results of this union is first of all a divine-human personality, as the ethical consciousness of this union, and further, over time, a sharing of Christ's humanity in the prerogatives of his divinity.[98] From mortal, his body becomes immortal, and from being limited by space and time, it partakes in the eternal glory of divinity.[99] All of this is summarized in the Pauline notion of the

---

suffers, prays, and toils. He never becomes useless or superfluous. The organism of glorified humanity and of the spirit-kingdom never loses its head. Whatever lies beyond the religious stage, of which he is the centre, can only be something inferior, a mere Logos-religion, a church without a head homogeneous with itself."

95. SCD IV, 139.

96. SCD IV, 138–39.

97. SCD IV, 132, 138.

98. See SCD III, 283–380. This conception of the metaphysics of the incarnation is, of course, very different from a classical view, in which the one divine person, having an essential set of divine properties and powers, acquires by assumption a second, accidental set of human properties and powers. Both sets are held by one divine person, without the sets communicating properties or powers to each other. Cf. my "The Logic of Assumption," in *Exploring Kenotic Christology*, ed. C. Stephen Evans (New York: Oxford University Press, 2006), 265–90, especially section II. By this account, humanity and divinity, being complete sets of properties and powers, both have their own consciousness, will, and intellect. The problem of this account is that it suggests Christ had a divided mind. To solve this problem, Dorner develops his alternative account, based on the unity of the divine and human in the one personality of Christ. Cf. for the developments of Dorner's Christological thought, Axt-Piscalar, *Der Grund des Glaubens*, 219–55.

99. SCD III, 331; SCD IV, 138.

pneumatic body of the resurrection.[100] In the final resurrection, what holds for Christ holds also for humankind. "Our pneumatic spiritual body shall bear Christ's image."[101] Like Christ's body, it will no longer be restricted by space and time.[102] The material world will be in so intimate a union with spirit "that no place will any longer exist for decay. Without loss of substantiality, matter will have exchanged its darkness, hardness, heaviness, immobility, and impenetrableness for clearness, radiance, elasticity, and transparency."[103]

If Dorner could be shown to be sound in his interpretation of both the metaphysics of the incarnation and the eschatological cosmos, this would be another argument for supralapsarian Christology. If God had decided to usher in the space-time liberated cosmos by way of the pneumatic body of the consummated Christ, this would be a reason for divine incarnation independent of human sin. Christ would be the key to an ontological change of creation, not a change from sinful to sinless, but from a restricted to an unrestricted cosmos.

Finally, human sin itself is a contingent interruption of a necessary divine plot. Divine creation, love, consummation, are all necessary consequences of God's ethical character. By contrast, human response, be it positive or negative, is contingent.[104] This response is, as I noted above, primarily a response to the divine love expressed in the presence of the incarnate One. Human beings situate themselves vis-à-vis the ethical by their choice for or against the incarnate One. However, this causes problems for the doctrine of the atonement. Sin is, in Dorner's schema, the rejection of the ethical. The ethical cannot be truly rejected until God is present in Jesus of Nazareth. This means, on the one hand, that it is difficult to conceive of sin that is different from a rejection of

100. SCD IV, 138, 139. Cf. SCD III, 323.

101. SCD IV, 429–30.

102. SCD IV, 430.

103. SCD IV, 429.

104. SCD I, 178. Given the contingency of sin, Dorner divides his *System* in two parts, the first concerned with necessary theology (God, Trinity, Incarnation), and the second concerned with contingent theology (sin, atonement, justification). Interestingly, Dorner never discusses what the scientific status of the second part is, a question important in a model of academic research in which only necessary states of affairs count as accessible for *scientia*. In emphasizing the contingency of sin, Dorner rejects Schleiermacher's model of supralapsarianism, without mentioning him by name: "Just as little, certainly, can the mode of demonstrating the necessity of the God-man be approved, according to which sin is associated with humanity, and redemption with sin, so that the necessity of the God-man would depend on the necessity of sin. If God ordained sin, or made it inevitable by refusing the gift of his Spirit, this would tell against the *holiness* of his love" (SCD II, 217).

Christ. On the other hand, a rejection of Christ falls outside the scope of the atonement.[105] If this were different, the free ethical choice of the human being would not be respected, but if this is true, it is hard to see whether there is any serious sin left for which Christ can be said to atone. Dorner aims to solve this problem by making a distinction between two kinds of sin. One kind is generic, participated in by all of humanity, but not yet amounting to personal guilt. This is the sin that puts humanity in need of atonement. The other kind is individual, an expression of personal responsibility, and deciding on the person's ultimate fate.[106] It seems, however, that this solution undermines the desired Christological account of sin. The central difficulty of Dorner's account here is that the scope of sin is wider than the "scope" of the incarnate One. An alternative construal would be to hold onto the Christological account of sin, but to extend the scope of the incarnate One by providing a thicker Christological understanding of creation than Dorner does. If creation were embedded in Christology, every sin in creation could be understood within a Christological context. Such will be the move made by Karl Barth.

III. Diverging Lines

Incarnation: Ontological or Interpersonal

Supralapsarian Christology is an umbrella term, referring to a family of interpretations of the incarnation. All these interpretations share the conviction that the incarnation is not contingent upon human sin; but they differ in their approach to the meaning of the incarnation: of its motivation, its end, and its effect. In this last section, I argue that Dorner's proposal embodies a number of diverging supralapsarian interpretations of the incarnation. I raise three questions concerning the incarnation, suggesting for each question two different answers. I argue that Dorner's proposal never consistently answers these questions, for his answers waver between the two options. However, each option amounts to a different supralapsarian profile, in need of a distinct set of arguments. By not facing these questions, Dorner's proposal loses much of its strength.

The first question I pose is this: is the God–human relationship, established in the incarnation, primarily ontological or interpersonal? To incarnate

105. SCD IV, 94.
106. SCD III, 54.

is a relational act. In becoming incarnate, God relates to what is not God. Incarnation is not the only way in which God relates to what is not God; God relates also in creating and in forms of revelation other than incarnation. Clearly, by assuming a human nature, God intends to form a specific relationship with his creatures, only attainable by this particular act. What is the nature of this relationship?

Supralapsarianists have traditionally answered this question in two different ways, and Dorner's work contains both answers. One answer is that God aims at establishing an interpersonal relationship of mutual love and commitment. Such is the answer implied by the largest part of Dorner's proposal. God's aim is a kingdom of love, of people being subject and object of love. God becomes incarnate to establish this kingdom, either by facilitating absolute religion as the means by which the kingdom is fostered, or in the form of a suitor, pursuing an answer of his beloved.

Another answer to the question is that the nature of the relationship is not primarily interpersonal but ontological. By assuming a human nature, God is able to change and complete the ontological structure of reality. Dorner has this answer too, in his eschatology. In the incarnation, God joins divinity to humanity in such a way that the latter's time-space limitations are overcome. In the eschaton, the beatified's humanity will mirror Christ's humanity, and they will no longer be subject to the limitations of time and space.

The difference between these two answers lies in the way they conceive of the address of the gift of incarnation. The first conceives of the incarnation as a gift given to human persons: by assuming a human nature, God makes Godself available for interpersonal interaction from one human being to the other. The second conceives of the incarnation as given to human nature: by assuming human nature, God is able to change the ontological status of humanity from the inside out.

Dorner wants both: by assuming human nature God changes the assumed nature in divinizing it, overcoming its time-space limitations, and God becomes present to human persons in the form of a suitor, pursuing their love. Once these humans answer the divine lover, to their natures happens what happened to Christ's: they are divinized.

However, these latter eschatological expectations presuppose more than an interpersonal relationship between Christ and the beatified. That Christ's humanity is no longer subject to time and space is attributed to the ontological unity of divinity and humanity in the one consummated personality of the

God-man. For other persons to share in this feature implies more than that their bodies become simple mirror images of Christ's body, but that they share in the ontological changes of Christ's humanity brought about by its ontological union with his divinity. This suggests Christ and the beatified are ontologically related themselves. Rather than an interpersonal relationship, this would, in Dorner's terms, be a physical relationship.

Dorner nowhere gives an account of how such a physical relationship between Christ and the beatified should work. He emphasizes that Christ is "the principal or central beginning of a new humanity, which, born of the heart of God, is in a position to be the power of union for dissevered humanity."[107] At the same time, he also emphasizes that "the true conception of Christ as the head or representative of humanity bears an ethico-religious character."[108] Christ unites a new humanity, not by physical power, but by ethical invitation. Interpreting the relationship between Christ and the beatified as ontological rather than interpersonal seems therefore to go against the ethical grain of Dorner's overall argument.

Incarnation: Means or End?

The second question I pose is this: how does the incarnation relate to God's ultimate goal? Is the incarnate One identical with God's ultimate goal or only a means thereto? In the previous chapter I analyzed an example of the latter construal. For Schleiermacher, God's ultimate goal is the impartation of the divine to all, fellowship with the believers through the Spirit. Christ is the first with whom God seeks this, but the ultimate goal is, through him, the fellowship with all. Some of Dorner's proposal contains the same notions, but other parts tend in the opposite direction.

Central to this issue are Dorner's three arguments for supralapsarianism: incarnation is the perfection of revelation, needed to establish absolute religion, and necessary to establish an ethical relationship with humankind. All of these arguments imply an interpersonal relationship forged by the incarnation: each argument turns around the personal presence of and interaction with the divine in human form. They differ, however, on whether the incar-

107. SCD III, 322.
108. SCD III, 321.

nation functions as means or as end to God's ultimate goal. For the third argument, the incarnation is explicitly an end. The act of incarnation is the embodiment of God's love for humankind. There is no other goal to this act than its consummation, no other consummation than for it to be accepted and returned. But for the second argument, the incarnation is a means. The end of creation is "a rich life of love," but that end can only come through history. The ethical nature of love demands development in freedom, a history of "twofold surrender of God to man, and of man to God." This twofold surrender is expressed in religion. Religion adequate to the divine goal is absolute religion. Religion, by its very nature as a historical phenomenon, needs a founder. Absolute religion needs an absolute founder. Therefore, in order to establish absolute religion, God appears in human form. Incarnation is thus a means to a later end. Ambiguous on this argument is the role of the incarnate One once the goal is reached and the kingdom of love ushered in. This ambiguity has repercussions for one's eschatology. I noted this in Schleiermacher's Christology: for him the eschaton is the consummation of Christ's redeeming influence, but without need for Christ's abiding presence. By contrast, Dorner emphasizes the lasting importance of and communion with Christ in the eschaton. But without a clear account of the incarnation as an end, and not as a means, the theological foundation under such a proposal is shaky. Finally, Dorner's first argument for supralapsarianism betrays the same ambiguity. The incarnate One is the absolute form of divine revelation, communicating "the entire fullness of the Godhead," and appropriating a human nature to be God's own. On Dorner's construal, God is motivated to absolute revelation by the need for an absolute religion. Thus the incarnation is a means to a final good. However, as I indicated above, this is not the only way Dorner could have presented his argument. He could also have construed it along the lines of his third argument for supralapsarianism: God, aiming at a relationship of love with humankind, is motivated to absolute revelation because this is the only form of revelation implying the full presence of Godself—absolute revelation, divine presence, not because of a higher goal, but as an end in itself.

Why this ambiguity? My thesis is that Dorner's wavering between these two options is embedded in another issue. Dorner's proposal is ambiguous on the function of the incarnation because of a deeper-lying ambiguity. Decisive for whether one takes the incarnation to be means or end is what one takes to be the divine motivation behind it. For Dorner, the motivation for incarnation is embedded in the motivation for creation. Here is the most troubling ambiguity of Dorner's system.

Incarnation: The Ultimate Motive

According to Dorner, God creates because God is *amor amoris,* a lover of love: "As holy love he is not merely self-affirming personality, he also loves the sentiment of love in itself and absolutely, is *amor amoris.* Thus, not merely is there no reason in him for wishing to make himself the only abode of love, but on the contrary, his love finds its delight in multiplying, aggrandizing the life of love, in forming a kingdom of love."[109] However, the love expressed in the notion *amor amoris* is not particular, but general. To be a lover of love is not the same as to be a lover of a particular individual. If one is a lover of a particular individual, one loves that individual for its own sake. If one loves a particular individual because one is a lover of love, one loves that individual not for its own sake but for love's sake. What this proposal says is not that God creates Adam because God is motivated by a particular love for Adam, but that God is motivated by a general love for loving relationships. Adam and his family are being created and loved, not for their own sake but as a means to a general end. They are instrumental for the greater good, created as instances of subjects capable of love, potential inhabitants of the divinely intended kingdom.

This construal has enormous impact on Dorner's proposals concerning divine–human relationships. I suggest the ambiguity exposed above concerning the meaning of the incarnation is a direct result thereof. When, in his first and second supralapsarian arguments, Dorner construes the incarnation as a means to another end, "a rich life of love," he treats the divine involvement in the divine–human relationship in the same instrumental way as human involvement. The incarnate One is not an end in itself but a means by which the kingdom of love is ushered in—just as human beings are not ends in themselves but are created as instruments by which the kingdom is realized. Another place where the *amor amoris* argument works through is in Dorner's construal of human beings as objects of divine life. As I pointed out before, Dorner takes the gift of God's love to be the gift of God's image. Humans are "designed to be the object of his perfect, unreserving love, and by this is meant

109. SCD II, 14.

perfect, God's likeness outside God."[110] By this gift, they are made capable of being not just objects, but subjects of love. However, to take the gift of the divine image as the highest expression of "unreserving" love only makes sense when human beings are loved not for their own sake but for love's sake, as potential subjects of love. If human beings were loved for their own sake, the highest expression of love would not be for them to be made like God, but to be brought into relationship with God. The grandest gift of love would be love itself.

Most of what Dorner says suggests he wants the latter: an ethical relationship between God and human beings, a kingdom of love, in which humans are not loved as a means to a general end, but for their own sake. It would fit well with Dorner's third supralapsarian argument: the incarnate One is the suitor, whose only goal is to be accepted. However, such construal demands a far-reaching change in Dorner's overarching proposal: if God loves particulars for their own sake, this love cannot be construed as necessary but needs to be understood as contingent. Here is why: if God's love for particulars were necessary, the objects of God's love would also need to be necessary. To hold that these particulars are necessary, one needs to embrace one of two ontological models. The first model is Schleiermacher's ontology, according to which the possible and the actual are identical, and thus the actual is necessary. Dorner explicitly rejects such ontology.[111] The second model is an ontology in which there are more possible particular objects of divine love than the ones that are actualized, but in which God's actualizing love for the ones loved is nonetheless necessary. But why would God necessarily love this rather than that possible particular? If, as Dorner holds, nothing necessitates God other than the ethical necessity, what ethical necessity would necessitate God to create and love me, but not to create and love my possible, but not actual younger brother?[112] It seems that nothing in the ethical necessity suggests that God should love this rather than that set of particulars. Therefore, God's love and the objects of God's love are contingent.

But if this is true, and if it is true that God creates for love's sake, then the act of creating is contingent as well. For Dorner to embrace a contingent act

110. SCD II, 16.

111. SCD I, 333.

112. Cf. SCD I, 458. Dorner contemplates why God does not create more people than God does. His answer is that as many are created as necessary for the end, the life of love (SCD II, 26). This line of argument suggests that Dorner accepts that more creatures are possible than the ones actually created.

of divine creation changes his proposal completely. In the proposal, it is the necessity of God's creative act that sets everything else in motion. God's ethical necessity is expressed in the act of creation; given the nature of the ethical necessity, creation will be brought to consummation; given the same ethical necessity, this will be done by way of incarnation. None of this follows, though, when the act of creation is a contingent act. Of course, it could still be argued that God leads creation to consummation, and that the incarnation is central to consummation. In such a scenario, the governing divine act would not be given with God's nature, but would be the result of a free act of God's will. And if creation were embedded in God's will rather than God's nature, it would be better to start one's theological account thereof not at the beginning but at the end of God's work: What goal had God in mind when God freely called creation into being? What motivated God to create? Systematically this means that the argument for supralapsarian incarnation should not be embedded in the doctrine of creation but in eschatology.

4

Barth's Supralapsarian Narrative

If Dorner's proposal were to be revised along the lines I suggested at the end of the previous chapter, his proposal would amount to a supralapsarian argument embedded not in the doctrine of creation but in eschatology; the incarnation read as an expression not of God's necessary nature but of free motivation. Karl Barth's theology is an example of such an eschatological approach. His supralapsarian argument is developed within his doctrine of election, but election is for Barth the eschatological category per se. As the first divine decision, it decides about the goal of all reality. In the beginning is the end.

In addition, Barth gives priority to narrative over ontology. For the two preceding authors, the incarnation functions as a consummation of a preconceived ontological order. Barth's understanding of the incarnation is embedded in the narrative of scripture. That is not to say that Barth has no ontology; his is no "God without Being" (Marion). But the ontology is established in Jesus's history. Therefore, this chapter is devoted to Barth's narrative; in chapter 5 I discuss its ontological implications.

The Election of Jesus Christ

In the beginning was Jesus Christ. In the beginning, before anything else was determined, formed or realized, was he. For Barth, the story of God and humankind is the story of the being, life, and work of Jesus Christ. But this story did not just start in the Palestinian deserts or the fields of Bethlehem. The being, life, and work of Jesus Christ do not have their beginning in time: they have their beginning in eternity.

Like Schleiermacher, Barth narrates the story of God and humankind from the perspective of God's eternal election. Everything that is and happens traces its origin to these first decisions of the divine council. And at the beginning of these was Jesus Christ:

> In the beginning, before time and space as we know them, before creation, before there was anything distinct from God which could be the object of the love of God or the setting for his acts of freedom, God anticipated and determined within himself (in the power of his love and freedom, of his knowing and willing) that the goal and meaning of all his dealings with the as yet non-existent universe should be the fact that in his Son he would be gracious towards man, uniting himself with him. . . . This choice was in the beginning.
> As the subject and object of this choice, Jesus Christ was in the beginning. He was not at the beginning of God, for God has indeed no beginning. But he was at the beginning of all things, at the beginning of God's dealings with the reality which is distinct from himself. Jesus Christ was the choice or election of God in respect of this reality. He was the election of God's grace as directed towards man. He was the election of God's covenant with man.[1]

A close reading of this passage in the larger context of Barth's doctrine of election helps us to identify six characteristics of God's elective actions. These characteristics, some inferentially connected, all closely interrelated, together form a pattern that governs all further divine activity: God's election of Jesus

1. Karl Barth, *Church Dogmatics*, Vol. II.2 (Edinburgh: T and T Clark, 1956–75), 101–2. Hereafter, *Church Dogmatics* is cited as CD, followed by volume and part number, and page numbers.

Christ is primal in order, self-giving in nature, graceful in its motivation, creative in its effect, all-inclusive in its scope, and supralapsarian in character.

God's election of Jesus Christ is primal in order—"at the beginning of God's dealings with the reality which is distinct from himself." When God decides to reach outside of Godself, to call into being what is not God, the first he establishes is Jesus Christ. He is "the beginning of God before which there is no other beginning apart from that of God within himself. Except, then, for God himself, nothing can derive from any other source or look back to any other starting point. He is the election of God before which and without which and beside which God cannot make any other choices."[2]

God's election is self-giving in nature. "God anticipated and determined . . . that . . . he would be gracious towards man, uniting himself with him." God's first decision has a twofold determination. It is a choice of the other, an election that chooses "the other to fellowship with himself." But it is also and foremost "a self-election [by God] in favor [of] this other."[3] God "determines man for himself, having first determined himself for man."[4] God determines "that he should not be entirely self-sufficient as he might be," to reach out to what is not God, and the character of this divine reaching out is one of self-giving. "He constitutes himself as benefit or favour."[5] God determines to unite Godself with the other, the embodiment of which is the incarnation.

God's election is graceful in its motivation. Jesus "was the election of God's grace as directed towards man." God does not elect out of necessity. It is an act of grace, in that "God owes his grace to no one, and no one can deserve it. . . . [G]race cannot be the subject of a claim or a right on the part of the one upon whom it is directed."[6] The structure of God's graceful acts is not such that something outside of God relates to God and triggers a graceful response in and from God; it works the other way around. God, in divine freedom and love, decides to elect, and as such establishes a relationship with what is not God. "God in his love elects another to fellowship with himself. First and foremost this means that God makes a self-election in favour of this other. He ordains that he should not be entirely self-sufficient as he might be.

2. CD II.2, 94.
3. CD II.2, 10.
4. CD II.2, 91.
5. CD II.2, 10.
6. CD II.2, 10–11.

He determines for himself that overflowing, that movement, that condescension. He constitutes himself as benefit or favour. And in so doing he elects another as the object of his love."[7] Love precedes election; election precedes the elect.

The consequence thereof is that God's election is creative in its effect. "In the beginning, . . . before there was anything distinct from God." In establishing a relationship with what is not God, God does not just establish a relationship but also establishes the very entities that are at the receiving end of this relationship. The structure of election is not one in which God, from a range of already existing entities, elects some and rejects others. Election is not a function of a more general relationship God has with the world, but every further relationship God has with the world finds its starting point in the act of election.[8] In other words: the relationship God establishes in election with what is not God precedes the relationship God has with what is not God in creation. This latter point underscores the freedom of God's grace expressed in election: "Free grace is the only basis and meaning of all God's ways and works *ad extra*. For what *extra* is there that the ways and works could serve, or necessitate, or evoke? There is no *extra* except that which is first willed and posited by God in the presupposing of all his ways and works. There is no *extra* except that which has its basis and meaning as such in the divine election of grace."[9]

God's election is all-inclusive in its scope—"the goal and meaning of all his dealings with the as yet non-existent universe." Given the priority of election over creation, all that God's creative act establishes is included in God's election. This should, however, not be understood as if "man as such" or "the human race as a whole" is the object of election, "nor indeed a large or small total of individual men." Election is particular. Elected is "the one man Jesus and the people represented in him. Only secondary, and for his sake, is it 'man,' and 'humanity' and the whole remaining cosmos."[10] In other words, election is addressed and applied to every individual, but "every 'individual' in himself and as such would be rejected if it were not that his election is incorporated in that of Jesus Christ."[11]

7. CD II.2, 10.
8. See CD II.2, 78.
9. CD II.2, 95.
10. CD II.2, 8.
11. CD II.2, 351.

Finally, God's election is supralapsarian in character—"As the subject and object of this choice, Jesus Christ was in the beginning." God's electing act is supralapsarian in the twofold sense of the word. It is supralapsarian, both predestinatarian and Christological. Divine predestination is not a first step in a divine response to human sin, and neither is the incarnation. Although the foregoing would already be enough ground to draw this conclusion, Barth adds a new element. Christ is not only the object of the election—not even the premier object of divine choice—but he is also its subject. To say that Jesus Christ was in the beginning does not only mean that he is the object of God's decree, but also that he is "himself the plan and decree of God, himself the divine decision with respect to all creation and its history whose content is already determined."[12] He is both elected and elector—"from the very first he participates in the divine election; that election is also his election; it is he himself who posits this beginning from all things; it is he himself who executes the decision which issues in the establishment of the covenant between God and man."[13] In fact, Barth believes that all of the preceding characteristics call for this last step. Deciphering the logic of this last claim will therefore be central to understanding the supralapsarian nature of Barth's Christology.

The Subject and Object of Election

At least since Augustine, theologians have spoken about Christ as the object of election. They have done so in two ways. For some, Christ's election is an illustration of our election. On the doctrine of the two natures, Jesus's human nature is assumed by the divine Word. This nature is thus brought into fellowship with God. Pure grace motivates this act: nothing the human nature was or did earned this honor. If election is understood as determination to eternal bliss, choosing this nature to be united with the divine Word can be taken as an exemplary form of election. There is no higher bliss than to be assumed by the divine.[14] For others, Jesus's election is not only an illustration of election, but also the foundation on which all other divine acts of election are

12. CD II.2, 104.
13. CD II.2, 105.
14. See Augustine, *De praedestinatione sanctorum liber ad Prosperum et Hilarium primus*, XXX.xv.

founded. That God graciously chose to unite this human nature with the divine Word is not only exemplary of the way in which God chooses other beings, it is also the cause of God's graciously relating to other elects.[15]

Some supralapsarians see in the notion of Christ as object of election the starting point for a supralapsarian argument. If election is determination to eternal bliss, it has to be supralapsarian in nature, Duns Scotus argues. Eternal bliss is the primal goal of life, the reason for which humans are created. As the motive of creation, it precedes everything else, including human sin and divine response thereto. But if Christ too is elected, the same holds for him. In fact, since the bliss to which Christ's soul is predestined is the highest bliss of all, it needs to precede all other acts of election. God's election of Christ's human nature is thus the first action in the divine relating to what is not God.[16]

Barth underwrites the notion of Christ as object of election.[17] Jesus Christ is the elected man. He also underwrites the notion of the centrality of Christ's election. Jesus Christ is the elect of God, the one who "from the very beginning (from eternity itself) as elected does not stand alongside the rest of the elect, but before and above them as the one who is originally and properly the elect. From the very beginning (from eternity itself), there are no other elect together with or apart from him, but, as Eph. 1:4 tells us, only 'in' him."[18] Nonetheless, the supralapsarian character of Barth's thought is not founded upon the idea of Christ as the object of election. To build a supralapsarian argument on the notion of Christ as object of election conceptualizes Christ primarily as the beneficiary of the gift of incarnation.[19] For Barth, Christ is primarily the benefactor. Central to Barth's argument is that not only is Christ the first elected human, but he is this precisely because he is also the electing God. "Jesus Christ is not merely one object of the divine good-pleasure side by side with others. On the contrary, he is the sole object of this pleasure, for in the first instance he himself

15. For the discussion about this approach among the Reformed scholastics, see: Richard Muller, *Christ and the Decree: Christology and Predestination in Reformed Thought from Calvin to Perkins* (Durham: Labyrinth, 1986).

16. See the texts and commentary in Allan Wolter, "John Duns Scotus on the primacy and personality of Christ," in *Franciscan Christology: Selected Texts, Translations, and Introductory Essays*, ed. Damian McElrath (New York: St. Bonaventure, 1980, 1994), 139–82.

17. CD II.2, 118–20.

18. CD II.2, 116.

19. Compare for a critique of Scotus's argument along these lines: Nico den Bok, "Liefde op zoek naar een geliefde: Over persoon-zijn in Augustijns-Franciscaanse zin, belicht vanuit christologie en verkiezingsleer," *Kerk en Theologie* 49 (1998): 184–98.

is this good-pleasure, the will of God in action."[20] Jesus Christ is, from the beginning, with the Father and the Spirit the subject of election.[21]

To establish this point, Barth develops four arguments. Two arguments are exegetical, two more theological. The exegetical arguments are explicitly developed in Barth's doctrine of election; the theological arguments are implicit, imbedded in the notions of divine self-giving and divine self-revelation. In this and the next section I lay out Barth's exegetical arguments.

Barth's exegetical arguments are based on three groups of biblical passages, each group representing a particular pattern of thinking about Christ. Together these patterns form a cumulative case for Barth's position.[22] The first pattern is found in a cluster of texts that refer to Jesus Christ as active subject from before the foundation of the world. In the context of his doctrine of election, Barth refers to Ephesians 1:4, 1:11, and 3:11, as well as Romans 8:29ff. and Colossians 1:15.[23] Later, in his doctrine of creation, Barth focuses on texts that refer to creation as in or through Christ: John 1:3ff., Hebrews 1:2ff., and Colossians 1:15ff.[24] In his doctrine of time, Barth returns to the issue with reference to the same texts, and in addition 1 Peter 1:20 and Revelation 13:8.[25] Finally, the same issue and the same texts are treated in the context of the doctrine of reconciliation.[26] Barth's exegesis of these texts consistently highlights two features. First, Barth emphasizes that none of these texts makes a distinction between the Son as λόγος ἄσαρκος, the preincarnate Word, and as Jesus Christ, the embodied Word. The one in whom all are elect and created, the one who is in the beginning, the one who is from before the foundation of the world is not referred to as λόγος ἄσαρκος, but as Jesus. An exegesis that does not take this point into account erodes the content of these texts.[27] Second, Barth interprets the role of Jesus in these texts as one of an active agent. This receives particular emphasis in those texts that speak of an activity δἴ αυτο or εν αυτω as divine acts of election and creation. Barth does not interpret these phrases as "through him"

20. CD II.2, 104.
21. CD II.2, 101, 105, 107.
22. For an extensive discussion of this material and the relationship of Barth's exegesis to historical-critical scholarship, see: Mary Kathleen Cunningham, *What Is Theological Exegesis? Interpretation and Use of Scripture in Barth's Doctrine of Election* (Valley Forge, PA: Trinity Press International, 1995).
23. CD II.2, 60.
24. CD III.1, 51–56.
25. CD III.2, 483–84.
26. CD IV.2, 33–34.
27. CD II.2, 107; III.1, 54; III.2, 483; IV.2, 33.

or "in him," but in the stronger sense of "by him." On this reading, Jesus is not just instrument but active subject in election and creation. "'In him' does not simply mean with him, together with him, in his company. Nor does it only mean through him, by means of that which he as elected man can be and do for them. 'In him' means in his person, in his will, in his own divine choice, in the basic decision of God which he fulfils over against every man."[28]

Whereas these texts indeed give Barth good grounds to reject an interpretation of their object as the λόγος ἀσαρκος, Barth has a harder case defending his strong reading of the δἵ αυτο and εν αυτω He legitimates this last move by his exegesis of the second and third cluster of texts. The second cluster concerns texts from the Prologue to the Gospel of John. Barth argues that the notion of Logos functions in the entire Prologue as a placeholder, "a preliminary indication of the place where later something or someone quite different will be disclosed," namely Jesus.[29] He supports this reading by an exegesis of the clause in John 1:2, "The same was (ούτος ήν) in the beginning with God." Barth suggests that this clause is not a recapitulation of verse 1, but a reference forward to the declaration of John the Baptist in verse 15, who, with use of the same expression ούτος ήν, says: "This was he of whom I said, 'He who comes after me ranks ahead of me because he was before me.'" The "he" the Baptist refers to is clearly Jesus, the incarnate Logos; and if verse 2 of the Prologue refers forward to the same "he," so must, given the flow of the argument in this section, the "he" of verse 1, who was "in the beginning," and the "he" of verse 3, "through whom all things were made."[30]

The third cluster of texts concerns those passages that speak of Jesus as the one who elects his disciples: John 13:18, 15:16, and 15:19. Barth insists that these texts should not be understood "loosely" but in the "strictest and most proper sense: the electing of the disciples ascribed to Jesus must be understood not merely as a function undertaken by him in an instrumental and representative capacity, but rather as an act of divine sovereignty, in which there is seen in a particular way the primal and basic decision of God which is also that of Jesus Christ."[31] This too would support Barth's strong reading of the δἵ αυτο or εν αυτω in the first cluster of texts.

28. CD II.2, 116–17; cf. CD III.1, 54.
29. CD II.2, 96.
30. CD II.2, 98.
31. CD II.2, 106.

Finally, in addition to these readings, Barth puts forward an exegetical argument of somewhat different nature. This argument aims to bring out the logical presuppositions of the notion of Christ as the object of election and the Pauline formula that we are elected "in Christ." The Pauline formula means that Christ is more than a mere illustration of election; he is its focal point and the head of all the elect. But for him to have such standing before God and such power among humankind, he needs to be more than the object of election. "For where can Jesus Christ derive the authority and power to be the Lord and Head of all others, and how can these others be elected 'in him,' and how can they see their election in him the first of the elect, and how can they find in his election the assurance of their own, if he is only the object of election and not himself its subject, if he is only an elect creature and not primarily and supremely the electing Creator?"[32]

Barth himself does not put much weight on the latter argument; it is presented, almost in passing, in the context of the other exegetical considerations. However, I believe it deserves more attention since it is logically independent of Barth's exegetical argument. Even if Barth's preceding exegesis were less convincing, one still has to engage this argument as suggesting an important presupposition of the Pauline formulation.

"In Him"

Having thus established the nature of the "him" in whom we are elected, Barth is now ready to turn to the nature of the "in." Just as he reads the "him" in the strongest way possible, so does he read the "in": "From the very beginning (from eternity itself), there are no other elect together with or apart from him, but, as Eph. 1:4 tells us, only 'in' him. 'In him' does not simply mean with him, together with him, in his company. Nor does it mean only through him, by means of that which he as elected man can be and do for them. 'In him' means in his person, in his will, in his own divine choice, in the basic decision of God which he fulfills over against every man.... And so they are elect 'in him,' in and with his own election... his election is the original and all-inclusive election."[33] Barth

32. CD II.2, 116.
33. CD II.2, 116–17.

describes the relation expressed by the word "in" as participation: "What can this election be . . . but . . . a participation in the grace of the One who elects, a participation in his creatureliness (which is already grace), and a participation in his sonship (which is eminently grace)?"[34] In later volumes, Barth unpacks the "in him" in terms of an ontological connection. There is "an ontological connection between the man Jesus on the one side and all other men on the other," because "an ontological declaration about their own being under his sovereignty" was made. "It belongs to the distinctive essence of the Jesus Christ of the New Testament that as the One he alone is he is not alone, but the royal representative, the Lord and Head of many," because they are "in him."[35]

"In him" becomes thus virtually a technical term.[36] In conformance with the logic of election, it suggests that we are before we come to exist. We are objects of election, participating and ontologically—in being—connected in and to Christ before we receive embodied existence. The relationship God establishes, in election with what is not God, precedes the relationship God has in creation with what is not God. Note also how the relationship between Christ and those elected in him mirrors the relationship between God and Christ. When God decides to give Godself to what is not God, that which is not God is established: Jesus Christ. He does not yet have embodied existence, but he still was in the beginning with God, "beyond time and beyond the nexus of the created world and its history," in "the sphere where God is with himself, the sphere of his free will and pleasure."[37] Likewise, Christ establishes those who are elected in him, and who now have existence in him "before they were."[38]

Divine Self-Giving

Election, divine self-giving, and divine self-revelation are in Barth's theology intimately related. The notions of divine self-giving and self-revealing are ex-

34. CD II.2, 121.

35. CD IV.2, 275.

36. Cf. George Hunsinger, *How to Read Karl Barth: The Shape of His Theology* (New York: Oxford University Press, 1991), 114–16.

37. CD II.2, 100.

38. CD III.3, 88.

plications of the content and form of God's election. The decisive moment in God's election is God's determination to give Godself. This self-giving takes the form of self-revelation. The content of divine self-revelation is self-giving.[39]

Divine self-giving and divine self-revelation are also strictly parallel in their internal structure. They both turn on God's self-involvement in relating to what is not God, a self-involvement expressed in the incarnation. They are both motivated by the free, mysterious grace of God. They both conceptualize a contingent divine activity *ad extra* as extension of an essential divine activity *ad intra*. Finally, they both conceive of the incarnation as a supralapsarian divine gift.

At the heart of Barth's understanding of God's self-giving stands the Dionysian image of God as the overflowing source of glory, goodness, and love—an image hardly ever mentioned in the literature on Barth, but on careful reading very much at the center of how Barth conceived and experienced God. When God turns to us, this is "an overflow of his essence."[40] God determines for Godself "overflowing, movement, condescension."[41] "His inner glory overflows and becomes outward."[42] Or, in a longer passage:

> The fact that God makes this movement, the institution of the covenant, the primal decision "in Jesus Christ," which is the basis and goal of all his works—that is grace. Speaking generally, it is the demonstration, the overflowing of the love which is the being of God, that he who is entirely self-sufficient, who even within himself cannot know isolation, willed even in all his divine glory to share his life with another, and to have that other as the witness of his grace. This love of God is his grace. It is love in the form of the deepest condescension. It occurs even where there is no question of claim or merit on the part of the other. It is love which is overflowing, unconstrained, unconditioned.[43]

39. Cf. for the interrelatedness between election, self-giving, and self-revelation, among other places: CD II.1, 53, 54, 59, 104, 309, 450. Given these relationships, it is wrong to read Barth's construal of the work of Christ as only revelational and void of ontological content. The content of divine revelation is always divine self-giving, which is an ontological event. Contra Alister E. McGrath, "Karl Barth als Aufklärer: Der Zusammenhang seiner Lehre vom Werke Christi mit der Erwählungslehre," *Kerygma und Dogma* 30 (1984): 273–83.

40. CD II.1, 273; cf. CD II.1, 274: "The blessings of his Godhead are so great that they overflow as blessings to us, who are not God."

41. CD II.2, 10.

42. CD II.2, 121.

43. CD II.2, 9–10.

The Dionysian picture suggests a twofold divine movement. First, there is the movement *ad intra*—no overflowing without an internal source. Barth conceptualizes this by speaking about God as an event. God, in Godself, is a being in act.[44] The nature of that act is the *perichoresis* of God's own self-differentiated modes of being. God is one who is essentially one in loving community. It is God's nature to love, and this love is "the love of the Father, the Son, and the Holy Spirit."[45] God *ad intra* is not one who exists in solitude—"On the contrary, He is Father, Son and Holy Spirit and therefore alive in his unique being with and for and in another."[46] This inner love of God is necessary, not in the sense that God would be forced to it by an outside force, but in the sense that it is essential to God's nature.[47] It is also self-sufficient: God's love does not need an object different from Godself in order to fulfill this essential part of God's being.[48] God is Godself a completely satisfying object of love.

It is only given the self-sufficiency of God's act *ad intra* that the movement *ad extra* has the character of an overflow. If God's work *ad extra* were an expression of a need or resulted in a gain, the metaphor of overflowing would not be apt. Instead, "God has without his work, what he seeks and creates in his work."[49] But what God has *ad intra*, without God's work, is fellowship. It is fellowship that God now also seeks *ad extra*. God's reaching out to what is not God is therefore an act of divine self-involvement: God makes Godself to be "both benefactor and benefit."[50] By loving us, "God does not give us something, but himself; and giving us himself, giving us his only Son, he gives us everything."[51] This is the content of the divine act of election: supralapsarian incarnation. The love that characterizes the trinitarian nature is thus extended in the incarnation, and "our being loved by him is our being taken up into the fellowship of his eternal love, in which he is himself for ever and ever."[52]

44. CD II.1, 257–72.
45. CD II.1, 279.
46. CD II.1, 275.
47. CD II.1, 280.
48. Ibid.
49. CD II.1, 273.
50. CD II.2, 10.
51. CD II.1, 276.
52. CD II.1, 280.

Divine Self-Revelation

Modern theology tends to characterize divine revelation as self-revelation, but not everyone means thereby the same. Dorner, for example, conceives self-revelation as a form of manifestation of God, opposite to a communication of propositions. Presumably, the opposition Dorner tries to get at is one of revealing truths about God, versus a revelation of Godself.[53] For Barth, however, these are not real contradistinctions. Barth too conceives of revelation as a manifestational event, but at the heart of this event we find the God who speaks.

> [S]peech, including God's speech, is the form in which reason communicates with reason and person with person. To be sure it is the divine reason communicating with the human reason and the divine person communicating with the human reason. The utter inconceivability of this event is obvious. But reason with reason, person with person, is primarily analogous to what happens in the spiritual realm of creation, not the natural and physical realm. The Word of God—and at this point we should not evade a term so much tabooed today is a rational and not an irrational event.[54]

Furthermore, Barth is not afraid to speak of divine revelation as being "authentic information about God."[55] "By the Word and Spirit we are told that God is and who he is, what he wills and does and will do, and what this means for us."[56] There is no opposition between communication of truths about God versus communication of Godself, if we conceive of revelation as "God speaking about himself."[57]

The underlying issue in this debate is that for Dorner, the notion of "self" in self-revelation refers primarily to the content of the revelation. For Barth, the emphasis is different. God is the content of divine self-revelation; but this

53. I. A. Dorner, *A System of Christian Doctrine*, Vol. II, trans. Alfred Cave and J. S. Banks (Edinburgh: T and T Clark, 1891), 134, 198.

54. CD I.1, 135.

55. CD II.1, 210.

56. CD II.1, 211.

57. CD II.1, 48.

cannot be unless God is also its subject and object. Unpacking these claims leads us right into the heart of Barth's understanding of revelation—and puts us, once again, on the road to supralapsarianism.

Barth's doctrine of revelation is based on two correlated arguments concerning our inability to know God. Both arguments combine an ontological principle with an epistemological premise. The ontological principle is, for both arguments, the absolute otherness of God. The first argument combines this principle with the epistemological premise that like is only known by like.[58] The conclusion is that divine revelation can only happen mediately. Humans cannot know God directly, since God is completely unlike creatures. Only a medium that is alike to creatures can reveal God. The second argument combines the ontological principle with the epistemological premise that knowledge of an object equals power over the object.[59] This combination leads to the conclusion that God can only be known if Godself gives God to be known. God, as the complete other, falls outside the scope of creaturely power. Only God is master over Godself.

Barth himself suggests that these two epistemological premises amount to the same content.[60] This is where Barth is mistaken, as is clear simply from the different results of these two arguments. The first argument amounts to a need for incarnation. If only a creature can reveal God, divine self-revelation calls for God to assume creaturely form. Such form would unveil God, but also veil God. It would unveil, because God makes Godself an object of human knowledge; it would veil, because it would reveal God mediately, "under the sign and veil of other objects different from himself."[61] The second argument amounts to a need for the Holy Spirit. Only God has power over who will hear God's revelation. "The Lord of speech is also the Lord of our hearing."[62] Nonetheless, the two arguments are intimately related. While the two epistemological principles are not identical, the first principle can be read as an implication of the second. If to apprehend an object means to have power over an object, no creature can be expected to apprehend an object that is of a transcendental order.

58. Or, in Barth's terms, "we resemble what we can apprehend," CD II.1, 188.
59. Or, in Barth's terms, "to apprehend certainly means to possess," CD II.1, 189.
60. See CD II.1, 188–89.
61. CD II.1, 16.
62. CD I.1, 182.

By these arguments, the only one who knows God is Godself. What precedes our knowledge of the divine is God's knowledge of Godself. Before God gives Godself to be an object for us, God is an object for Godself.[63] It is a knowledge embedded in the divine existence of self-differentiated modes of being—it is triune: "First of all, and in the heart of the truth in which he stands before us, God stands before himself; the Father before the Son, the Son before the Father. And first of all and in the heart of truth in which we know God, God knows himself; the Father knows the Son and the Son the Father in the unity of the Holy Spirit. This occurrence in God himself is the essence and strength of our knowledge of God."[64] Since only God can know God, our knowing of God will therefore have to take the form of participation in God's triune self-knowledge.[65] In divine self-revelation the Father addresses us in the Son, and the Holy Spirit receives this address in us.

That God unveils Godself by way of veiling is partly due to our sinfulness, but not wholly.[66] The ontological and epistemic principles that govern divine revelation are not a result of sin, but given with the nature of Creator and creation. Incarnation, as the necessary means of divine self-disclosure, is therefore a supralapsarian event, and revelation "will remain a miracle to all eternity of completed redemption."[67]

63. CD II.1, 16.
64. CD II.1, 49.
65. CD II.1, 181.
66. For attribution to the "state of fallen man," see CD I.1, 166.
67. CD I.2, 245. For the study of Barth's development, it is important to note that in *The Göttingen Dogmatics* Barth takes the incarnation still to be an infralapsarian event: "Revelation, or, more precisely, incarnation . . . is the divine answer to the human question concerning the overcoming of the contradiction of human existence . . . it takes place because of the *fall*, to reverse the fall, to redeem us from evil, from guilt and its penalty. . . . Man as God created him, paradisal man, needed no divine revelation or incarnation." Karl Barth, *The Göttingen Dogmatics: Instruction in the Christian Religion* (Grand Rapids: Eerdmans, 1991), 155. This is remarkable, since the ontological and epistemic principles at work in the *Church Dogmatics* predate *The Göttingen Dogmatics*, to the second edition of his *The Epistle to the Romans*. Based on these principles, Barth could have developed a supralapsarian Christology much earlier; in reality, he does so only in the context of the Christological doctrine of election of the *Church Dogmatics*. What is decisive in the *Church Dogmatics* is not even its supralapsarian nature; the doctrine of election in *The Göttingen Dogmatics* is already supralapsarian rather than infralapsarian (466–68). Decisive is the exegetical and theological concentration on Christ as the subject of election. See for the ontological and epistemic premises at work in *The Epistle to the Romans* and *The Göttingen Dogmatics*: Bruce L. McCormack, *Karl Barth's Critically Realistic Dialectical Theology: Its Genesis and Development* (New York: Oxford University Press, 1995), 207–8, 245–66, 269–70, 327–28, 350–67, 371–74.

Consummation, Redemption, and Creation

Election is an eschatological category, and the eschaton is first in order of the divine decrees. Election is to creation's eternal bliss, the establishment of the covenant between God and humans, and the incarnation. These are the divine goals, that to which all God's work is directed. But what is final "cannot be a second or later thing. It can only reveal the first thing. What takes place here is the accomplishment and therefore the revelation of the original and basic will of God."[68] The end is thus in the beginning: the eschaton precedes everything else.

Previously, we noted that election precedes creation. The incarnation of Jesus Christ establishes the community between God and humans, the covenant; creation calls the elect into existence. Barth expresses the relationship between covenant and creation as one of mutual grounding. Creation makes the covenant possible;[69] it forms the stage for covenant's story.[70] As such, it is the external basis of the covenant. The covenant in its turn is the internal basis of creation.[71] Creation does not exist for itself. "Its creatureliness is pure promise, expectation and prophecy of that which is in [God's] grace, in the execution of the will of his eternal love, and finally and supremely in the consummation of his Son, God plans for man and will not delay to accomplish for his benefit. In this way creation is the road to the covenant."[72] At the same time, creation does not oblige God. The covenant is not implied by God's creative acts. "We might not be at all, and we might be without being the objects of his love. God does not owe us either our being, or in our being his love."[73] In this, Barth's account of creation and its eschaton differs from an approach like Dorner's. For Dorner, the eschaton is implied by the very nature of creation. For Barth, the eschaton is "an act of faithfulness, constancy, and self-

68. CD IV.1, 36.
69. CD III.1, 42.
70. CD III.1, 44.
71. CD III.1, 231.
72. CD III.1, 231.
73. CD II.1, 281. Cf. CD III.3, 110; IV.1, 10.

affirmation on the part of God," the fulfillment of God's original will, but not something owed to creation.[74]

The priority of the covenant shapes Barth's understanding of sin. To sin is to reject the grace given in election.[75] It is the desire to be one's own eschaton.[76] However, since humans are elected, that is, ontologically connected to Christ, even before they were created, to sin is "an ontological possibility for man. We are actually with Jesus, i.e. with God. This means that our being does not include but excludes sin. To be in sin, in godlessness, is a mode of being contrary to our humanity. For the man who is with Jesus—and this is man's ontological determination—is with God. If he denies God, he denies himself. He is then something which he cannot be in the counterpart in which he is. He chooses his own impossibility."[77] On the other hand, for "man *in abstracto*," that is, for the human being "apart from the merciful will of his Creator primarily directed towards him," the fall and original sin "are an ontological necessity." This because man *in abstracto* is "a being hopelessly exposed to the threat of surrounding non-being."[78]

This dialectic between the impossibility and necessity of sin brings out an important feature of Barth's theology. A theology that prioritizes the eschaton over creation might be expected to place sin and reconciliation in a third place in the schema of divine ordinances. First God elects; then God creates; then God deals with human resistance and sin. However, this would suggest that creation can be conceived as free from sin. In Barth's theology, this is not the case. In Barth's narrative, creation is from its beginning under threat. God's election of the good is from the beginning accompanied by the existence of evil, and humans are from the beginning susceptible to evil's temptation. Creation never knew a golden age; Adam's fall was an event never preceded by any other. The first human was from the beginning the first sinner.[79] And "in himself and as such man will always do as Adam did."[80] I say more about this part of Barth's proposal below. For the moment, it is clear how such a reading

74. CD IV.1, 36, 37.
75. CD III.3, 306–9.
76. CD IV.1, 10.
77. CD III.2, 136.
78. CD III.2, 146. See on the notion of "man *in abstracto*" also: CD II.2, 306, 317, 318, 322, 449.
79. CD IV.1, 508.
80. CD II.2, 122.

influences the structure of the narrative. Creation in itself needs, from the beginning, redemption. Electing this creation is therefore to choose the path of reconciliation even before anything has been created. The incarnate One is "the Lamb slain, and the Lamb slain before the foundation of the world."[81] The covenant is thus both eschatological and salvific. In the Barthian reading, the eschaton is essentially salvific in content, and salvation is essentially eschatological in form.[82] What God "effects and does and reveals by becoming man—for us—is much more than the restoration of the *status quo ante* . . . God makes himself the means of his own redemptive will, but he is obviously more than this means. And in making peace by himself he obviously gives us more than this peace, i.e., more than a *restitution ad integrum*, more than the preserving and assuring to us of our creaturely being and this as our opportunity for salvation. For when God makes himself the means of his redemptive will to us, this will and we ourselves attain our goal. What is at first only God's gracious answer to our failure . . . is nothing more nor less than the coming of salvation itself, the presence of the *eschaton* in all its fullness."[83] Salvation brings the consummation of threatened and sinful creation: "Salvation, fulfillment, perfect being means—and this is what created being does not have in itself—being which has a part in the being of God, from which and to which it is: not a divinized being but a being which is hidden in God, and in that sense (distinct from God and secondary) eternal being."[84]

Creation, theater of the covenant, is thus last in the divine plan. Its purpose is to make possible the history of the covenant. In the strict eschatological reading of Barth though, purpose, meaning, and value collapse. If the purpose of creation is the covenant, so is its meaning.[85] And if the meaning of creation is the covenant, so is its value. The biblical judgment " '[i]t was very good' means concretely that it was adapted to the purpose which God had in view."[86] Creation's goodness is not derived from being created by Christ.[87] It only

81. CD II.2, 123.

82. If, as I argued before, divine self-giving and self-revelation form the content and form of divine election, and the eschatological covenant is the expression of divine choice, this means that in Barth's reading divine self-giving must be salvific, and divine self-revelation eschatological. This is indeed the case.

83. CD IV.1, 13.

84. CD IV.1, 8.

85. CD III.1, 42; III.3, 36; IV.1, 50.

86. CD III.1, 213. Cf. CD III.1, 99, 332.

87. CD III.1, 53.

derives its goodness from its future.[88] Creation as such is ambivalent and empty.[89]

At the heart of Barth's supralapsarianism lies thus his reading of the biblical narrative as a narrative of election. Election is an eschatological category; and the eschaton is the first in order of the divine decrees. Object and subject of these decrees is Jesus Christ—not the Son as λόγος ἄσαρκος the preincarnate Word, but the Son as Jesus Christ, the incarnate Word. The incarnation stands thus at the very beginning of God's relating to what is not God.

Barth supports this reading of the biblical narrative with a series of detail exegetical excursuses. He also has several theological and philosophical arguments at his disposal, but these are guns that are never brought into position independently of the exegetical case. In fact, biographically, Barth could have drawn these arguments from his theological presuppositions long before he came to his supralapsarian Christology, but he never did. His reading of the biblical reading had—at least biographically—a decisive priority over all other considerations.

Human beings are incorporated in the narrative of election because they are elected "in" Christ. They are objects of election, participating and ontologically—in being—connected in and to Christ before we receive embodied existence.

This is the narrative—but what about the ontology? What does it mean that Christ—not the λόγος ἄσαρκος but Jesus of Nazareth—is both object and subject of election? And what does it mean that human beings receive being in him, before they have embodied existence? It is to these questions that I turn next.

88. Compare CD II.1, 113–14, where Barth wonders how "nature Psalms" like Psalms 8 and 104 can speak of a world in which the divinity, wisdom, and goodness of the Creator are readily recognizable: "Can we rightly understand Ps. 104 even for a single moment without the commentary of Rev. 21:1–5: . . . 'Behold, I make all things new.' "

89. C. van der Kooi develops an important critique on this part of the Barthian heritage in a comparison with Calvin, for whom all of reality still was filled with the sacramental presence of God: *As in a Mirror: John Calvin and Karl Barth on Knowing God* (Leiden: Brill, 2005).

5

Barth's Supralapsarian Ontology

For a long time, a chapter title like the one above would have been interpreted as an oxymoron, if not a theological offense. "The Holy Spirit is the declared enemy of all metaphysics," wrote Barth, and judgments like these have earned Barth the reputation of resisting all philosophical analysis in the context of theological discourse.[1] In Barth we do not find an ontology, says Manfred Josuttis.[2] And if we do, it goes against the spirit of the master, adds Barth's old friend Otto Weber.[3] Barth prefers the category of praxis over one of ontology, declares Friedrich-Wilhelm Marquardt.[4]

In recent years, the tide has turned. Eberhard Jüngel's work on the ontological implications of Barth's doctrine of the Trinity, once

1. "Der Heilige Geist . . . ist der abgesagte Feind aller Metaphysik." Karl Barth, *Christus und wir Christen* (München: Christian Kaisar, 1948), NF Heft 11, 1948), 9; quoted in Wilfried Härle, *Sein und Gnade: Die Ontologie in Karl Barths Kirlicher Dogmatik* (Berlin: Walter de Gruyter, 1975), 1, n.1.

2. Manfred Josuttis, *Die Gegenständlichkeit der Offenbarung; Karl Barths Anselm-Buch und die Denkform seiner Theologie* (Bonn: H. Bouvier, 1965), 15; quoted in Härle, *Sein und Gnade*, 2.

3. See Eberhard Jüngel, *God's Being Is in Becoming: The Trinitarian Being of God in the Theology of Karl Barth*, trans. with a new introduction by John Webster (Grand Rapids: Eerdmans, 2001), 77 n.5.

4. Friedrich-Wilhelm Marquardt, *Theologie und Sozialismus: Das Beispiel Karl Barths* (Munich: Kaiser Verlag, 1972), 321; quoted in Härle, *Sein und Gnade*, 3, n.5. Cf. the discussion in Jüngel, *God's Being Is in Becoming*, 125–39.

the exception to the antiontological rule, is now hailed as a classic.[5] George Hunsinger's guide to reading Barth's work, while not devoting extensive attention to Barth's ontology, speaks without reluctance about the ontological implications of Barth's theological proposals.[6] John Webster has written on Barth's moral ontology, and Bruce L. McCormack tries to work out Barth's "covenantal ontology."[7]

Antiontological interpretations of Barth are problematic because Barth himself speaks freely about the ontological implications of his theology. Humanity is ontologically determined in its relationship to Christ.[8] Christ has an ontological significance.[9] What the New Testament says about the being of Christ has an ontological character.[10] The covenant has an ontological setting.[11] Barth rejected, with more or less success, the influence of philosophical presuppositions on theological conceptualization. This is why he rejects metaphysics as the construction of human wisdom opposite to divine revelation.[12] But ontology is simply the doctrine of being, and "we must not yield to a revulsion against the idea of being as such" but "take up the concept... with complete impartiality."[13] However, the theologian should "put ontology under the critique and control of theology, and not the other way around."[14]

In this chapter, I analyze the ontological implications of Barth's supralapsarian narrative. I argue that two theological theses govern these implications. The first thesis is that Christ is the subject of election. As we have seen, Barth's supralapsarian narrative contains an extensive argument for this the-

5. See, for example, Alan Torrance, "The Trinity," in *The Cambridge Companion to Karl Barth*, ed. John Webster (Cambridge: Cambridge University Press, 2000), 85 [72–91].

6. George Hunsinger, *How to Read Karl Barth: The Shape of His Theology* (Oxford: Oxford University Press, 1991), 117, 129, 136, 153, 228.

7. John Webster, *Barth's Ethics of Reconciliation* (Cambridge: Cambridge University Press, 1995), 214–30. Bruce L. McCormack, "Grace and Being: The Role of God's Gracious Election in Karl Barth's Theological Ontology," in *The Cambridge Companion to Karl Barth*, ed. John Webster, 92–110; and Bruce L. McCormack, "The Ontological Presuppositions of Barth's Doctrine of the Atonement," in *The Glory of the Atonement: Biblical, Historical, and Practical Perspectives*, ed. Charles E. Hill and Frank A. James III (Downers Grove, IL: InterVarsity Press, 2004), 346–66.

8. Karl Barth, *Church Dogmatics*, Vol. III.2 (Edinburgh: T and T Clark, 1956–75), 132. Hereafter, *Church Dogmatics* is cited as CD, followed by volume and part number, and page numbers. Cf. CD IV.2, 275.

9. CD III.2, 133.

10. CD IV.2, 281.

11. CD IV.1, 45.

12. Cf. CD I.1, 36–38.

13. CD II.1, 260.

14. Karl Barth, *Das Geschenk der Freiheit* (Zollikon-Zürich: Evangelische Verlag, 1956), 25, quoted in Härle, *Sein und Gnade*, 2, n.3.

sis. Its ontological implication is that Christ existed from all eternity. The second thesis is what I call the thesis of creational entropy. It suggests that creation, in and by itself, will necessarily lapse into evil. Barth's narrative does not contain an argument for this thesis, nor do we find much of an argument for it elsewhere in his oeuvre. It does, however, have huge implications for the shape of his narrative. Because of creational entropy, in order to uphold creation God needs to anchor creation in divine being itself: creation needs to be divinely assumed.

I. The Subject of Election

As we have seen, the notion that Christ is not just the object but also the subject of election is central to Barth's supralapsarianism. The implication thereof is that Christ existed not only in time, but also in eternity. "Jesus Christ was in the beginning with God," "before time and space as we know them." Not merely as an intentional object in the plan and decree of God, but as "himself the plan and decree of God," "the will of God in action," himself "the electing God."[15] There is, suggests Barth, "between the eternal Godhead of Christ . . . and his elected humanity . . . a third possibility. . . . And that is the being of Christ in the beginning with God."[16]

What does Barth mean by this third possibility, the eternal existence of Jesus Christ? We can ask two sets of questions: on the one hand, as it were "downstream" from the eternal moment of election, how does Christ's presumed eternal existence relate to his existence in time? On the other hand, "upstream" from the moment of election, if Christ is himself the electing God, what does this tell us about the divine being and identity? In this part I discuss four possible interpretations of Barth's notion of the eternal being of Christ. The first two are concerned with the questions downstream from election; the last two concentrate on the questions upstream. I analyze these interpretations in terms of both their internal consistency and their consistency with other parts of Barth's overall proposal. Three of the four I find wanting; for the fourth interpretation I suggest what I think is something close to what Barth was up to.

15. CD II.2, 104, 101, 104, ibid., 103.
16. CD II.2, 107.

Christ's Eternal Existence as Preemption of the Temporal

The first interpretation is one put forward by some of Barth's oldest interlocutors, such as his old friend Emil Brunner and the Dutch theologian Cornelius Berkouwer. They read Barth as moving salvation history's center from time to eternity. If Christ was in the beginning with God, if he is "the Lamb of God slain before the foundation of the world,"[17] then what is decisive for salvation history does not take place in the hills of Judea and the streets of Jerusalem, but in the realms of eternity. It is not so much the life of the historical Jesus but of the eternal Jesus that we should heed.

This interpretation comes with implied criticism. If the core of salvation history is thus moved from time to eternity, the meaning of Jesus's earthly life and work is jeopardized. "If the eternal pre-existence of the God-Man were a fact," writes Emil Brunner, "then the Incarnation would no longer be an *Event* at all; no longer would it be the great miracle of Christmas."[18] In fact, this objection not only concerns the event of the incarnation, but can be extrapolated to Barth's dealing with history as a whole. On Barth's proposal, Berkouwer suggests, there is no conceptual space for what Berkouwer calls the stepwise character of God's work.[19] Everything has already been decided. All that is left for time is to reveal what already has been determined in eternity: "the decisiveness of history can no longer be fully honored."[20]

17. CD II.2, 123.

18. Emil Brunner, *Dogmatics I: The Christian Doctrine of God*, trans. Olive Won (Philadelphia: Westminster Press, 1949), 347.

19. G. C. Berkouwer, *The Triumph of Grace in the Theology of Karl Barth*, trans. Harry R. Boer (Grand Rapids: Eerdmans, 1956), 252.

20. Ibid., 255. Cf. also Robert W. Jenson, *Alpha and Omega: A Study in the Theology of Karl Barth* (Edinburgh: Thomas Nelson, 1963), 85–86, and 162–63: "Jesus Christ is the eternal decree of God before all time. Jesus Christ is the history in Palestine which reveals this decree. Barth does not separate these two; his concept of revelation and knowledge is far too rich. But we must still ask: Which is the prior definition? Barth defines the history in time as the revelation and analogy of eternal history and so gives his answer. And with this answer he puts himself in danger of removing reconciliation itself, the inner reality of Jesus['s] life, from our history." This charge resonates with the wider claim that Barth's notion of salvation is spelled out in epistemological terms, a charge classically made by Gustav Wingren in *Theology in Conflict: Nygren-Barth-Bultmann* (Philadelphia: Muhlenberg Press, 1958), and repeated by contemporary writers such as Alister E. McGrath, "Karl Barth als Auflärer: Der Zusammenhang seiner Lehre vom Werke Christi mit der Erwählungslehre," *Kerygma und Dogma* 30 (1984): 273–83; and Kathryn Tanner, "Jesus Christ," in *The Cambridge Companion to Christian Doctrine*, ed. Colin E. Gunton (Cambridge: Cambridge University Press, 1997), 264–68 [245–72]. I believe the arguments developed below against the criticism of Brunner and Berkouwer hold also against this wider claim.

It is no accident that we find this interpretation in the earliest of the literature on Barth, because a prima facie case can be made for such a reading. Barth does talk about the incarnation as eternal,[21] and he does talk about the events of Jesus's life as a revelation of things previously determined. However, the critique implied in this reading misses two important parts of Barth's overall proposal, which qualifies these notions of determination and revelation. First, on Brunner's and Berkouwer's interpretation, revelation is an event posterior to divine election and self-giving. However, for Barth, divine revelation is not the revelation of things previously determined, but the revelation of God by way of God's self-presentation. The incarnation, as the expression of God's election, is both God's self-revelation to what is not God and God's self-giving to what is not God. As we saw in the previous chapter, divine self-revelation and divine self-giving relate herein as content and form.[22] It is for this reason that Barth can speak, somewhat later in *Church Dogmatics* II.2, of what took place in the temporal life of Jesus Christ as "the eternal will of God temporally actualized and revealed."[23] On Brunner's and Berkouwer's interpretation this would not make sense. Revelation, yes, but not actualization.

Second, Brunner's and Berkouwer's interpretation misunderstands the role Barth assigns to time and history. In the reading of Brunner and Berkouwer, time is only an add-on to an all-decisive eternity. But not so for Barth. Time is, like the whole of creation of which it is a part, "what makes the history of God's covenant with man possible."[24] Eternity is the realm of God's initiatives, but time is the realm of humanity's response. As Barth says at the end of his discussion of the election of Jesus Christ:

> Such is God's activity in predestination in so far as he is its subject. But it is not the whole of this activity. In it there begins the history, encounter and decision between himself and man. For the

21. CD II.2, 108.

22. Cf. the opening sentences of the section on "The Election of Jesus Christ": "Between God and man there stands the person of Jesus Christ, himself God and himself man, and so mediating between the two. In him God reveals himself to man. In him man sees and knows God. In him God stands before man and man stands before God, as is the eternal will of God, and the eternal ordination of man in accordance with this will.... In him God has joined himself to man" (CD II.2, 94).

23. CD II.2, 179. See also, among many places, in Barth's anthropology: "the man Jesus is the... realization and revelation in the creaturely world" of the will of God (CD III.2, 144); and in the Christology: Christ's humanity is "the execution and revelation... of the will of God" (CD IV.2, 31); "the execution and revelation... of the election of Jesus Christ" (CD IV.2, 32).

24. CD III.1, 42.

> fulfillment of the election involves the affirmation of the existence of elected man and its counterpart in man's election, in which God's election evokes and awakens faith, and meets and answers that faith as human decision. The electing God creates for himself as such man over against himself. And this means that for his part man can and actually does elect God, thus attesting and activating himself as elected man.[25]

In eternity God elects humanity, but only temporally existing humanity can elect God in return. As with eternity, the central subject of this temporal act of human response is Christ. This is probably best illustrated by Barth's discussion of Jesus's prayer at Gethsemane, which he calls "a remarkable historical complement to the eternal decision taken in God himself."[26] Salvation in Christ hinges on both forms of election, since it hangs not on a partial, but on the complete history of Christ.

Christ's Eternal Existence as Reflection of the Temporal

The second possible interpretation is almost the mirror image of the first reading.[27] In response to the critique implied in the first reading, this interpretation proposes to look at the eternal existence of Christ as a reflection of his earthly existence. The conceptual key to this proposal is Barth's doctrine of eternity. Barth holds that God relates to time in a threefold way: in preceding time's beginning, in accompanying time's duration, and in existing after time's ending. However, Barth applies to these three ways of divine relating to time a Boethian notion of eternity. While God relates to time's movement and change, Godself lives in an eternity that is characterized by simultaneity. In God's eternity there is no past, present, and future; everything is all at once—including God's threefold relating to time. But this means that the temporal events of Jesus's life should not be thought of as happening after the eternal election and

25. CD II.2, 177.

26. CD IV.1, 238–39; see for Barth's discussion CD IV.1, 264–73. Cf. the reference to the same event in the passage referred to above, describing Christ's election of God: "All that this man can and will do is to pray, to follow, to obey . . . 'not my will, but thine, be done'" (CD II.2, 177).

27. I believe the following is or comes close to what John Colwell wants to argue in his *Actuality and Provisionality: Eternity and Election in the Theology of Karl Barth* (Edinburgh: Rutherford House Books, 1989), 241–46.

existence of Jesus Christ. If God lives in simultaneous duration, and if this simultaneity includes God's relating to time, then God's eternal election and Jesus's eternal existence on the one hand, and Jesus's temporal existence on the other hand, are all simultaneous as well.

In fact, if we use the logic of divine foreknowledge, that which is foreknown by God has ontological priority over God's foreknowing of it—"God foreknows event x because it will obtain," not "event x will obtain because God foreknows it"—we could argue that the ontological basis for eternal election and Jesus's eternal existence lies in the temporal events of Jesus's life, and not the other way around: Jesus exists in eternity, because Jesus exists in time.[28] This would create the conceptual space for the decisive importance of the obedience of the temporal Jesus.

However, like the previous interpretation, this reading is not consistent with other parts of Barth's proposal. First, while Barth holds that the three ways of God's relating to time—pretemporal, supratemporal, and posttemporal—all obtain simultaneously, he does ascribe a different logic to each way of relating. Posttemporally, God relates to time in judging it. Supratemporally, God relates to time in preserving it. Pretemporally, God relates to time in determining it. And it is within the logic of this pretemporal relating of God to time that Barth situates election and Christ's eternal existence.[29] While it does not make sense to talk about a temporal priority of the eternal existence of Christ over his temporal existence, there is a logical and ontological priority.

Further, this interpretation cannot explain the presence of Christ in eternity as an active subject of election. It does tell us how Christ and his temporal existence are simultaneously present to God in eternity, but as God's intentional objects—objects of divine knowing and willing. This, however, does not tell us how Christ is present in eternity as an active subject, "himself the electing God."[30]

28. Such a reading could argue from passages like CD III.2, 484: "the event of the particular life of Jesus . . . [was] foreseen and resolved, and to that extent had already taken place." Cf. CD III.2, 476–77 and CD IV.2, 33: Jesus is before all things, "because this is what God knows and wills." Colwell does not make this last move, maintaining an identity of "the temporal history of Jesus Christ" and "the eternal decision of God," arguing that "the ontic basis of election is to be simultaneously located in both the primal history of God's decision and the temporal event of Jesus Christ" (*Actuality and Provisionality*, 244, 245).

29. CD II.1, 622; see also CD II.2, 53: the eternal decree "precedes everything temporal"; and CD II.2, 175: the eternal decree is "prior to all external events."

30. Mary Kathleen Cunningham defends a variation on the second interpretation. She argues that Barth offers diverse conceptualizations of the eternal being of Christ, depending on their doctrinal settings. Within the

Christ's Eternal Existence as Divine Self-Constitution

What discussing these two interpretations thus teaches us is that, on the one hand, election and Christ's eternal existence should not be read as preempting history and jeopardizing the temporal existence of Jesus Christ; on the other hand, that the identity of Jesus Christ and the meaning of his eternal existence cannot be understood "downstream," from the perspective of temporal reality, but only "upstream," from their relationship to eternal God. In a number of articles, Bruce L. McCormack explores the latter option.[31]

According to McCormack, Barth's notion of Christ as the subject of election has at least two implications. First, it means that the *Logos asarkos*, the Logos in his nonembodied state, never existed just in and for himself, but was always already *incarnandus*, the Logos who will become incarnate. "There is no mode of being or existence in the triune life of God above and prior to the eternal act of self-determination in which God 'constitutes' himself as 'God for us' and, therefore, there is no such thing as an 'eternal Logos' in the abstract."[32] Only such a reading "would make it clear that it is 'Jesus Christ' who is the subject of election and not an indeterminate (or 'absolute') *Logos asarkos*."[33] This in turn implies, second, that in God's eternal life "the triunity of God is a function of the divine election."[34] If Trinity were to precede the divine decree of election, Barth

---

context of the doctrine of election, Barth describes the eternal Christ as active subject; but in later contexts, such as the doctrine of creation and of reconciliation, Barth wants to avoid depreciating the reality of Christ's historical lifetime and therefore describes the existence of the eternal Christ as a presence in God's intention. Mary Kathleen Cunningham, *What Is Theological Exegesis? Interpretation and Use of Scripture in Barth's Doctrine of Election* (Valley Forge, PA: Trinity Press International, 1995), 39–43. However, while in these later contexts Barth does use terminology deriving from divine intentionality, all passages referred to by Cunningham, with one exception (CD IV.2, 21–32), also describe the eternal Christ as an active subject (CD III.1, 50: it is "the Son of God as the Son of Man, the Word made flesh," who is the subject of the "specific creative causality" through which all is created; CD III.2, 477: "He is the one who comes: coming in the eternal council of the Father; coming in the work of creation; coming in the history of the divine covenant with Israel; and coming finally in the hiddenness of his pre-Easter life"; CD IV.1, 50: "Jesus Christ is in truth the first, i.e., the content and subject of that first divine will and purpose and resolve which underlies the beginning of the creaturely world and is therefore superior to it"). The suggestion that the content of Barth's doctrine changed over time is therefore not correct.

31. McCormack, "Grace and Being," 92–110; Bruce L. McCormack, "Barth's grundsätzliche Chalkedonismus?" *Zeitschrift für Dialektische Theologie* 18 (2002): 151–57 [138–73]; McCormack, "Ontological Presuppositions," 356–61; and Bruce L. McCormack, "Seek God Where He May Be Found: A Response to Edwin Chr. van Driel," *Scottish Journal of Theology* 60 (2007): 62–79. This last article is a response to my critical discussion of McCormack's proposals in "Karl Barth on the Eternal Existence of Jesus Christ," *Scottish Journal of Theology* 60 (2007): 51–56 [45–61]. What follows above is meant as a continuation of our conversation.

32. McCormack, "Seek God Where He May Be Found," 66.

33. McCormack, "Grace and Being," 95.

34. Ibid., 103; McCormack, "Seek God Where He May Be Found," 67.

would posit exactly such "mode of existence in God above and prior to God's gracious election," which, in McCormack's interpretation, is excluded by Christ's eternal existence.[35] Therefore, God's triunity, nature, and attributes should all be logically posterior to the decree of election:

> the eternal act of self-differentiation in which God is "God a second time in a very different way" (CD 1/1, 316, 324) and a third time as well, is *given* in the eternal act in which God elects himself for the human race. The *decision* for the covenant of grace is the ground of God's triunity. . . . The works of God *ad intra* (the trinitarian processions) find their ground in the *first* of the works of God *ad extra* (viz. election).[36]

One caveat: when McCormack speaks about the modes of divine existence prior or posterior to election, he talks about not a temporal, but a logical and ontological ordering. If God is eternal, as previously discussed, there is no temporal differentiation in God. But there still might be a logical and ontological differentiation in the divine being.

McCormack's reading of Barth is motivated by two concerns. The first is an ontological concern: if the Logos was not always *incarnandus*, "how is it possible for God to become, to enter fully into time as One who is subjected to the limitations of human life in this world, without undergoing any essential (i.e. ontological) change?"[37] The second is a more a spiritual concern: how do we know that in the incarnation God is not just playing a role, but that we have to do with real divine self-involvement, other than if the incarnation is essential to God?[38]

The debate triggered by McCormack's proposal justifies a closer analysis.[39] It will be helpful to distinguish between three different set of questions: questions of interpretation (Is this what Barth says?); questions of motivation (Is this what Barth should have said given his other theological commitments?); and

35. McCormack, "Grace and Being," 102.
36. Ibid., 103.
37. Ibid., 96–97.
38. Ibid., 97.
39. See for other responses to McCormack: Paul D. Molnar, *Divine Freedom and the Doctrine of the Immanent Trinity: In Dialogue with Karl Barth and Contemporary Theology* (London: T and T Clark, 2002), 62–64, 81; Kevin W. Hector, "God's Triunity and Self-Determination: A Conversation with Karl Barth, Bruce McCormack and Paul Molnar," *International Journal of Systematic Theology* 7 (2005): 246–61; Paul D. Molnar, "The Trinity, Election, and God's Ontological Freedom: A Response to Kevin W. Hector," *International*

questions of evaluation (Is the proposed reading of Barth internally coherent?). I argue that the answer to all three kinds of questions is negative.

On McCormack's reading, Barth's work on the election entails a radical shift in his doctrine of God. In the previously written volumes of the *Church Dogmatics*, Barth presented God's activity *ad extra* as a contingent overflow of an essential and trinitarian divine activity *ad intra*. The fellowship God seeks with us God already has without us, that is, "in his being and therefore his act as Father, Son and Holy Spirit."[40] It is because of the fullness and sufficiency of the divine life in itself that God can subsequently turn to what is not God. Barth unfolds this idea by describing each of the divine attributes as a basis for God *ad extra*, the incarnation. God can enter into time, because God has time in Godself.[41] God can enter into space, because God is spacious in Godself.[42] God can reach out to creation in love, because in Godself God has all the love God needs.[43] Each of these divine preconditions of the incarnation is Trinitarian in nature. God's own time is the time of the Trinitarian processions.[44] God's own space is the space of Trinitarian coexistence.[45] God's own love is "the love of the Father, the Son and the Holy Spirit."[46] And "our being loved by him is our being taken up into the fellowship of this eternal love, in which he is himself for ever and ever."[47] On this model, election is thus a contingent function of an essential Trinitarian life.

Journal of Systematic Theology 8 (2006): 294–306; Paul Helm, "John Calvin and the Hiddenness of God," in *Engaging the Doctrine of God*, ed. Bruce L. McCormack, 67–82 (Grand Rapids: Baker Academics, 2008); and George Hunsinger, "Election and the Trinity: Twenty-Five Theses on the Theology of Karl Barth." *Modern Theology* 24 (2008): 179–198. McCormack's reading received support in two dissertations written by his students: Adam Neder, " 'A Differentiated Fellowship of Action': Participation in Christ in Karl Barth's *Church Dogmatics*" (dissertation, Princeton Theological Seminary, 2005); Matthias Gockel, *Barth and Schleiermacher on the Doctrine of Election: A Systematic-Theological Comparison* (Oxford: Oxford University Press, 2006); and in Paul Dafydd Jones, "The Humanity of Christ in Karl Barth's *Church Dogmatics*" (dissertation, Harvard Divinity School, 2006).

40. CD II.1, 273. Barth continues: "It implies so to speak an overflow of his essence that he turns to us. We must regard this overflow as itself matching his essence, belonging to his essence." Cf. CD II.1, 257: "He is this loving God without us as Father, Son, and Holy Spirit, in the freedom of the Lord, who has his life from himself"; and 280: "He loves us and the world as he who would still be the one who loves without us and without the world . . . this overflowing is conditioned by the fact that although it could satisfy itself, it has no satisfaction in this self-satisfaction, but as love for another it can and will be more than that which could satisfy itself."

41. CD II.1, 611–12.

42. CD II.1, 470–71. Cf. CD II.1, 612.

43. CD II.1, 273, 280.

44. CD II.1, 615.

45. CD II.1, 463.

46. CD II.1, 279.

47. CD II.1, 280.

This radically changed, according to McCormack, with the publication of Barth's doctrine of election.[48] Here the trinity becomes a function of divine election. All that precedes the act of election is "[God's] existence itself," but "*how* he exists, how his being is structured, is . . . a function of his will and decision."[49] Divine election is not an expression of a preceding inner Trinitarian love, but "God gives to himself his own being as Father, Son and Holy Spirit" in "the eternal act in which God chooses to be God in the covenant of grace with human beings."[50]

Barth himself does not interpret his doctrine of election as a radical shift vis-à-vis his earlier work. On the contrary, the doctrine of election in *Church Dogmatics* II.2 is presented within the same conceptual framework that governed *Church Dogmatics* II.1: God's activity *ad extra* is a contingent overflow of an essential and Trinitarian divine activity *ad intra*:

> God did not stand in need of any particular ways or works *ad extra.* He had no need of a creation. He might have well been satisfied with *the inner glory of his threefold being,* his freedom, and his love [emphasis added]. The fact that he is not satisfied, but that his inner glory overflows and becomes outward, the fact that he wills the creation,

48. In earlier publications, McCormack had located the change of Barth's position in the years 1936–37; in "Seek God Where He May Be Found" he corrects himself and locates the change in the winter semester of 1939–40 when Barth began to work on CD II.2 (63–66).

49. McCormack, "Seek God Where He May Be Found," 67. McCormack calls God's existence "absolutely necessary" and the outcome of God's will and decision "contingently necessary." Since he does not comment further on his modal semantics, it is hard to say whether we should read these terms as "necessary" versus "contingent," or whether both aspects of God are said to be necessary, being that the former is part of God's nature or essence, and the latter subject to a (necessary or essential) act of the divine will. In an earlier publication, I argued that McCormack seemed to hold the latter ("Karl Barth on the Eternal Existence of Jesus Christ," 53). However, I argued, if divine election and incarnation are the result of a necessary act of God's will, one cannot avoid the conclusion that creation is necessary to God. After all, "Election is God's self-determination to be with human beings. It is the establishment of Jesus Christ, the God-man. If election is an essential act of God, so is the incarnation. But incarnation implies creation: it implies humanity" (54). McCormack seems to have read this argument as concerned with creation "other than Jesus Christ," since he replies that my critique does not follow because "only that is 'essential' to God, and therefore 'constitutive' of the divine being, which God has determined *himself* to be, not what he has determined the world to be"—after which he continues to argue, correctly, that while for Barth humanity participates in Jesus Christ, there still is an ontological distinction between humanity and Jesus Christ ("Seek God Where He May Be Found," 69–70). However, my argument does not concern creation "other than Jesus Christ," but that creation which is Jesus Christ, who is after all God as well as the firstborn of all creation. If God's determination to be Jesus Christ is essential and constitutive of the divine being, then Christ's—created—humanity is constitutive of the divine being.

50. McCormack, "Seek God Where He May Be Found," 66.

> and the man Jesus as the first-born of all creation, is grace, sovereign grace, a condescension inconceivably tender.[51]

Election is the contingent expression of the essential "glory of his threefold being": Trinity precedes election. The latter point is also expressed when Barth, describing what he means by Jesus Christ as the subject of election, argues, "Of course, the fact that Jesus Christ is the Son of God does not rest on election. What does rest on it is the fact that as such he becomes man. . . . Between the eternal Godhead of Christ which needs no election and his elected humanity, there is a third possibility . . . and that is the being of Christ in the beginning with God, the act of the good-pleasure of God."[52] And again, speaking of Christ as the electing God and electing man: "It is true, of course, that even as God he is elected: the elected of his Father. But because as the Son of the Father he has no need of any special election, we must add at once that he is the Son of God elected in his oneness with man, and in fulfillment of God's covenant with man."[53]

Furthermore, this conceptual framework governs not only Barth's presentation of the doctrine of election but also the later volumes of theological anthropology and the doctrine of reconciliation, as is witnessed by Barth's endorsement of the notion of a *Logos asarkos*, which Barth calls "indispensable for dogmatic enquiry and presentation."[54] In the light of McCormack's proposal, a passage at the beginning of Barth's doctrine of reconciliation is especially interesting. Having spoken of election and covenant, Barth wants to emphasize that "the first and eternal Word of God, which underlies and precedes the creative will and work as the beginning of all things in God, means in fact Jesus Christ"—and not "the eternal Son or the eternal Word of God in abstracto, and therefore the so-called λόγος ἄσαρκος." The latter, "the second 'person' of the Godhead in himself and as such," is "the content of a necessary and important concept in trinitarian doctrine when we have to under-

51. CD II.2, 121. See for the image of God's elective action as an overflow of God's being in and for Godself, also the beginning of Barth's presentation of the doctrine of election: "The fact that God makes this movement, the institution of the covenant, the primal decision 'in Christ,' which is the basis and goal of all his works—that is grace. Speaking generally, it is the demonstration, the overflowing of the love which is the being of God, that he who is entirely self-sufficient, who even within himself cannot know isolation, willed even in all his divine glory to share his life with another, and to have that other as the witness of his glory. . . . It is love which is overflowing, free, unconstrained, unconditioned. . . . He determines for himself that overflowing, that movement, that condescension" (CD II.2, 9–10).

52. CD II.2, 107.

53. CD II.2, 103.

54. CD III.1, 54. Cf. CD III.2, 147; CD IV.1, 52.

stand the revelation and dealings of God in the light of *their free basis* in the inner being and essence of God" (emphasis added). But once we are dealing with the content of "the revelation and dealings of God, and in particular with the atonement, with the person and work of the Mediator, it is pointless, as it is impermissible, to return to the inner being and essence of God and especially to the second person of the Trinity as such."[55] Without any problem Barth holds it here together: that the eternal Word of God is identical with Jesus Christ, and that there nonetheless is a *Logos asarkos*, an eternal Word of God in Godself. The latter should not be given up for the sake of the other, because Barth believes that without the notion of a *Logos asarkos* he cannot say what he wants to say: that while the content of God's revelation is that God wants to be God-for-us, the basis of God's revelation and dealings is that God's inner being and essence are free from what is not God.[56]

McCormack frankly admits that his proposals go against Barth's own interpretation of his doctrine of election. He believes "that Barth either did not fully realize the profound implications of his doctrine of election for the doctrine of the Trinity, or he shied away from drawing them for reasons known only to himself." Therefore, McCormack's reading is not so much a reading of the full Barth as "a critical correction against Barth," the goal of which is to remove an inconsistency in Barth's thought.[57]

Barth, however, was usually neither ignorant of nor shy about those changes in his thinking that forced him to abandon old projects. *Römerbrief I* was followed by a very different *Römerbrief II*; the *Christliche Dogmatik* was aborted for a new *Kirchliche Dogmatik*. Therefore, McCormack's frank admission notwithstanding, the fact that Barth himself sees no difficulty with developing the notion of election and ensuing doctrines within the conceptual framework of *Church Dogmatics* II.1 counts as a prima facie argument against McCormack's interpretation.

If neither before nor after his doctrine of election Barth himself ever embraced anything like McCormack's position, the persuasiveness of the latter's proposal depends completely on the concerns that motivate him: could it

55. CD IV.1, 51–52.

56. The same conceptual framework also determines Barth's account of the innertrinitarian relationship between the Father and the Son in CD IV.1 (187–88 and 201–4). I discuss these texts below.

57. McCormack, "Grace and Being," 102; cf. McCormack, "Seek God Where He May Be Found," 77.

be that Barth should have said that which he did not say, given his other theological commitments down the road?

McCormack's first concern is rooted in Barth's treatment of the relationship between divine immutability and the obedience and humiliation of the incarnate one. Barth believes that if we want to hold to the former, and understand the latter as the obedience and humiliation not just of Christ's humanity but of Godself, we have to say that obedience and humiliation are grounded in God's being: "in equal Godhead the one God is, in fact, the one and also another, . . . a first and a second, one who rules and commands in majesty and one who obeys in humility."[58] McCormack proposes his correction of Barth in order to preserve this understanding of the godhead: in God there is a first who commands and a second who obeys because this is how God constituted Godself to be in the act of election.

McCormack's correction is, however, not necessary to safeguard Barth's position. That the incarnate One lives in humiliation and obedience to the Father could also be said to be a perfect expression of who God is in and for Godself, an expression of an over-againstness in God which logically and ontologically preceded the act of election.[59] This is how Barth sees it himself: it is

> essential to the being of God . . . that there is in God himself an above and a below, a *prius* and a *posterius*, a superiority and a subordination. . . . In order not to be alone, single, enclosed within himself, God did not need co-existence with the creature. . . . Without the creature he has all this originally in himself, and it is his free grace . . . if he allows the creature to participate in it.[60]

In fact, it is only this position, and not McCormack's correction, that can safeguard Barth's understanding of divine obedience and humiliation. If incarnation is an expression of the divine "other's" obedience, and incarnation is established in the act of election, then the one who is obedient needs to be logically and ontologically prior to the act of obedience. Incarnation and election cannot be acts of obedience of the divine other, if the other is only begotten in

58. CD IV.1, 202.

59. McCormack registers this himself ("Grace and Being," 96–97), without explaining why this interpretation is not satisfactory.

60. CD IV.1, 201. Cf. 187–88, 202–4.

these same acts. But this is exactly the case in McCormack's correction: for him, the one who is obedient is constituted as a function of the act of election.[61]

McCormack's second concern is that if the second person of the Trinity precedes rather than is established by the act of election, "the decision to assume flesh in time could only result in something being added to [his] already completed identity; an addition which has no effect upon what he is essentially." And this would mean that "being the Redeemer . . . is merely a role he plays, something he does."[62]

Indeed, in Barth's own conceptual structures, the incarnation is, ontologically speaking, not an essential divine property. But why would this mean the incarnation is "only a role he plays"? For example, when two people decide to get married, their decision is accidental to their ontological essences. They could have decided not to get married; they could have decided to marry other people. But it would be vastly inadequate therefore to call their marriage merely a role-play.

McCormack's worry is only convincing if one signs up for an unspoken essentialist premise: that only those things are "real" which are ontologically "essential." It is not surprising to see such a premise at work: it is a premise in the background of much Western thought, starting with Plato and Aristotle. What is surprising is to see a Christian theologian adhere to it, since the only strand in Western thinking that has consciously rejected this premise is Christian theology. From the Christian point of view, there is too much "real" that is nonetheless not ontologically "essential": love, sin, grace, forgiveness.

Once the essentialist premise is dropped, there is no reason to call election and incarnation a role-play, even if it is not part of God's essence. All that is necessary is that these acts imply divine self-involvement. But for Barth that is exactly what, as I argued in the previous chapter, God's election is: an act of self-revelation and self-giving. As such, God's election is not essential, but it is

61. By contrast, for Barth the begetting by the Father of the Son is logically and ontologically prior to their relationship of commanding and obeying. At the end of his discussion, in the context of an excursus on the use of the term *Son* for the second Trinitarian mode of being, he writes: "But the term cannot bring out the ontological necessity in which this Father has this Son, and this Son this Father, the perfection in which this Father and this Son are one, i.e., are the different modes of being of one and the same personal God, the eternity of the fatherly begetting and of the being begotten of the Son, *which is the basis of their relationship*, their free but also necessary fellowship and love in the activity of the Holy Spirit as the third divine mode of being of the same kind, the self-evident fulfillment of that determination of a son to his father, the actual rendering of a perfect obedience, the ceaseless unity of the one who disposes and the one who complies, the actual oneness and agreement of that which they will and do" (emphasis added; CD IV.1, 209–10).

62. McCormack, "Grace and Being," 97.

nonetheless part of the divine identity: God's narrative identity, that is, the set of contingent acts and events that shape the direction of one's life.

McCormack's proposal is thus not convincing as an interpretation of Barth's doctrine of election. But what if we were to read his proposal not as an interpretation of, but as a variation on Barth: as the beginning of a supralapsarian theology in its own right? Other than for Barth, God's supralapsarian election would here constitute the divine being.

I believe even as a supralapsarian theology in its own right, McCormack's proposal runs into insurmountable difficulties, in this case difficulties of incoherency. I want to point out two such difficulties.

First, in McCormack's proposal, what makes election and incarnation possible? For Barth it is, as we have seen, the Trinitarian nature of God, and the divine attributes established in and by this Trinitarian nature. How is that for McCormack? If election and incarnation logically and ontologically precede the triune nature and God's attributes, then what makes it possible for God to elect and to give God to what is not God?[63] One would think that at least there has to

63. When I raised this question in "Karl Barth on the Eternal Existence of Jesus Christ" (54), McCormack accused me of leaving "Barthian soil" and refused to answer, saying that "any attempt to look away from the God of electing grace revealed in Jesus Christ in an effort to find a ground of the possibility of election must inevitably open the door to natural theology. That is a door I chose not to open. What God in fact *does* is clearly possible for him; more than that I cannot say" ("Seek God Where He May Be Found," 73). I think McCormack's refusal to engage my question is surprising as well as unfortunate.

It is surprising because I am not asking McCormack to find a ground for God's election and incarnation outside God's revelation; I am asking him what, in his reading of it, the actuality of the revelation tells him about the capacity of the Revealer. In other words, I ask him to make exactly the same move as Barth makes when he develops his Trinitarian doctrine. Barth argues that we come to the doctrine of the Trinity by starting with the actuality of the revelation, from which we then conclude that there is a corresponding intradivine possibility—the immanent Trinity. For example, concerning the Father: "God can be our Father because he is Father in himself, because fatherhood is an eternal mode of being of the divine essence" (CD I.1, 390); "from the fact that in Jesus and Jesus alone he is manifest as the Creator and therefore as our Father it follows that he already is that which corresponds thereto antecedently and in himself" (391); there is "an intradivine possibility in virtue of which God can be manifest to us as the Creator and as our Father" (393). Concerning the Son: "His sonship on the basis of which he can be the revealer, the mediator, the reconciler" (414). Concerning the Spirit: "The intra-divine two-sided fellowship of the Spirit ... is the basis of the fact that there is in revelation a fellowship in which not only is God there for man but in very truth ... man is also there for God" (480). My question is: if McCormack were to make the same move, what kind of intradivine possibility would he find that corresponds to the revelation as he understands it?

My question is, of course, motivated by the suspicion that if McCormack were to attempt to answer this question, he would end up with an intradivine possibility that is inconsistent with his reading of revelation—that is, he would end up with a "mode of being or existence in the life of God above and prior to the eternal act of self-determination in which God 'constitutes' himself as 'God for us.'" McCormack's refusal to engage my question is unfortunate in that it robs him of the opportunity to prove my suspicion wrong.

be divine willing, and also divine power. But what would make it the case that these, unlike all other divine properties, precede the divine choice, instead of following it? And what should be said about their nature, if these are not, like all other divine properties, constituted and determined by Jesus Christ?

This leads to the second problem: not only what properties, but also, what subject precedes the divine choice? In McCormack's proposal, the Trinity—Father, Son, and Holy Spirit—logically and ontologically follows divine election. Remember, though, that the proposal was meant to explain the idea that Jesus Christ is the subject of election. How can he be the subject of election if his existence is also a function of that very election? Throughout his writings McCormack has wrestled with this problem.[64] In his original essay he proposed a solution by appealing to the notion of divine eternity. To think of a divine decision as involving a subject that precedes the decision is to think too anthropomorphically, McCormack suggests. God's decision is an eternal one, and therefore the divine act does not follow the divine subject as in some temporal sequence of events.[65] This reply will not do, however. I am happy to grant that in God there is no temporal sequence of events, but the problem does not concern a temporal before or after, but a logical and ontological one.

For his second solution, McCormack appeals to the doctrine of the Trinity itself. Indeed, "in the strictest sense, it is the 'Father' who is the subject of election," and not Jesus Christ.[66] It is the Father who in the act of election determines himself to be "God 'for us'" as well as Father, Son, and Holy Spirit.[67] McCormack declares himself of one mind with the ancient Trinitarian view that saw the Father as *autotheos, fons deitatis,* and *fons et origo* of the other two Trinitarian persons—albeit, that for the church fathers the Trinitarian relationships logically and ontologically preceded subsequent acts of God *ad extra,* while for McCormack these are "one and the same act."[68] However, Father, Son, and Spirit are the same divine subject. God is "one divine subject three times" over: God exists in threefold repetition. And that means that "all that the Father is, we

64. McCormack, "Grace and Being," 104; McCormack, "Barth's grundsätzlicher Chalkedonismus," 156–57; McCormack, "Seek God Where He May Be Found," 67, 71–73, 76–77.

65. McCormack, "Grace and Being," 104.

66. McCormack, "Seek God Where He May Be Found," 73.

67. Ibid., 66, 67.

68. Ibid., 67, n.17.

might say, he gives to the Son." Given this logic, it is thus also the Son, Jesus Christ, who is the subject of election, McCormack concludes.

This argument will not do either. First of all, given the logic of the argument, it is no more correct to say that the Father is the subject of election than to say it is the Son: both Trinitarian persons are a function of election. The subject of election is an undetermined God, who only becomes Father, Son, and Holy Spirit in the divine act. More important, it is exactly at the point where the argument wants to be innovative—in positing God's activity *ad intra* and *ad extra* as one and the same—that it breaks down. To see this, it is helpful to introduce some traditional distinctions. In classical theology, one makes a distinction between *processiones* and *missiones*. *Processiones* are the inner Trinitarian relationships between the divine persons: the Father begets the Son; the Father (and the Son) brings forth the Spirit. *Processiones* are said to be personal properties (*opera Dei personalia*) of the individual Trinitarian persons: for example, only the Father begets the Son, not the Spirit or the Son. Likewise, only the Spirit is being brought forth by the Father, not the Son or the Father himself. *Missiones* are the activities of Trinitarian persons in the world: the incarnation of the Son, the descent of the Holy Spirit. McCormack's proposal amounts to an identification of *processiones* and *missiones*, of divine activity *ad intra* and *ad extra*, of immanent and economic Trinity: when the Father begets the Son, he does not beget a *Logos asarkos*, but Jesus Christ. The father does so in the act of election. The question was: how can Jesus Christ be the subject of election, if his identity as Jesus Christ is also said to be a function of election? McCormack's answer is: because even while originally the Father is the subject of election, "all that the Father is, he gives to the Son," including being the subject of election.

But here is the problem: one thing the Father is, is "the subject who begot the Son." If the Father gives to the Son everything the Father is, the Father also gives to the Son to be the subject of his own begetting, and that cannot be. Could it maybe be said that the Father only gives to the Son to be the subject of his own *missio*, the incarnation, but not of his *processio*? This would be in line with classical Trinitarian theology. But McCormack cannot say this, since it is crucial to his proposal that the *processiones* and *missiones* are identified. McCormack will have to choose. If the *processiones* and *missiones* are identical, then it can only be the Father, and not the Son, who is their subject. Or it is indeed the Son who is the subject of election and the *missio* of incarnation, but then this must be preceded by a separate *processio*. If McCormack were to choose the former, he could hold to his proposed reversal in the logical and ontological order of Trinity and election, but at the price of giving up his original starting point: Jesus Christ as the subject of election. If he chooses the former, he could hold to his original starting point, but he would have to give up the heart of his proposal: the unity of *processiones* and *missiones*.

Christ's Eternal Election as Divine Self-Determination

Even while I think my arguments show that the notion of divine self-constitution is incoherent, McCormack is not without grounds in pursuing this line of interpretation of Barth. In the end, the problem lies, I think, not so much in McCormack's reading as in an ambiguity in the formulations of Barth himself. To see this, let us return to his statement that "Christ is the subject of election." The problem is that this says too much. In Barth's proposal, the term *election* encompasses a number of divine acts: first, the divine self-determination in which God determines Godself for community with humanity; second, the election of Jesus Christ; and finally, the election of all other human beings.[69] Barth does not always distinguish between these, because for him they are all ontologically connected, since all are elected "in" Christ, and Christ is identical with the divine self-determination. Nonetheless, these three objects of election are logically distinctive, as is clear when we reformulate the statement "Christ is the subject of election" by adding any of these three objects. If we do that, we get three statements with three different meanings.

> Christ is the subject of election of all humanity

implies the priority of incarnation over election, and the fact that it is not an unknown God, but God Incarnate who elects all of us. But

> Christ is the subject of the election of Jesus Christ

and

> Christ is the subject of the divine self-determination

69. Cf. for a passage where all of these are side by side: "how can we regard as absolute and autonomous the choice by which God decides for the existence and nature of the creature? How can we even understand this choice except as it is included in the choice by which God (obviously first) decides for himself, i.e., for this self-ordination, this being under the name of Jesus, this being in Jesus Christ?" (CD II.2, 101).

mean something different, and lead to the incoherencies of McCormack's proposal.

When we look at statements concerning the eternal being of Jesus Christ, other than this one—"Jesus Christ is the subject of election"—they imply something like the first extended sentence, but not the second or third extended sentences. We can see this by reading the following quotations from *Church Dogmatics* II.2:

> Jesus Christ is . . . God in his movement towards man. (II.2, 7)
>
> Jesus Christ is the decision of God in favor of this attitude or relation. (II.2, 7)
>
> He is himself the relation. (II.2, 7)
>
> He is the election of God before which and without which and beside which God cannot make any other choices. (II.2, 94)
>
> He is himself the divine election of grace . . . God's Word, God's decree, and God's beginning. (II.2, 95)
>
> Jesus Christ was the choice or election of God in respect of this reality. (II.2, 102)
>
> Himself the plan and decree of God, himself the divine decision with respect to all creation and its history whose content is already determined. (II.2, 104)
>
> . . . the divine freedom itself in its operation *ad extra*. (II.2, 104)

What all these sentences have in common is that in each sentence the name Jesus Christ picks out, not a subject, but an act and determination of divine willing; and it describes this act and determination of divine willing as the being of Jesus Christ. Jesus Christ is "God in his movement towards man," he is "the decision of God in favor of this relation," he is "himself this relation." What Barth does here is not to give a redescription of the ontological identity of God; instead, he gives a description of the identity of Christ. And this identity is described by way of a verb, an action. Between the *Logos asarkos* and the embodied Christ born in Bethlehem is the divine choice, the divine act and determination to give Godself to what is not God, and this divine determination is the Christ.

If this is what Barth means, we can see how he is thinking when he suggests that "Christ is the subject of election." His point is that when God elects, when God decides about eternal bliss and eternal woe, this act of election is not a *decretum absolutum*, an absolute decree the content of which is hidden in God's sovereignty; but that the act of election is logically preceded by God's self-determination to be God-for-us, God in the mode of self-giving, God who reached out to what is not God. God in God's movement toward humanity performs the act of election.[70] And this "God in God's movement towards man" we can pick out with the name Jesus Christ. However, none of this line of thought suggests that Barth now wants us to take a further step and say that what can be picked out by the name of Jesus Christ not only establishes the act of election, but also constitutes the divine being—even while the statement "Jesus Christ is the subject of election," read in and by itself, has such an implication. My suggestion is therefore that, in interpreting Barth's doctrine of election, we do not start with the statement "Jesus Christ is the subject of election" but that instead we give interpretative priority to all these other statements, and read the idea of Christ as the subject of election in the light thereof.

One way to test this proposal is to see what ontological implications such an interpretation would have, and to compare these to the ontological consequences Barth himself draws out of his position. If I am right, Barth's doctrine of election has no ontological consequences for the notions of immanent Trinity, *Logos asarkos*, or God-in-Godself. Instead of "upstream" of election the consequences will be "downstream," in Christology and anthropology.

What especially will be challenged is the way classical Christology speaks of the metaphysics of the incarnation. Classical Christology analyzes Christ's divine and human nature in terms of sets of attributes, powers, and agency. However, if Christ's being is identical to the act and determination of the divine willing, "God in God's movement towards man," this understanding of Christ's nature is not the most adequate. Rather than an understanding of nature in terms of agency and powers, one would have to think about nature in terms of actions. And indeed, this is the move that Barth makes. His term of choice is *history*. In his anthropology, Barth had introduced a distinction between being in a state and being in a history. Being in a state is being determined by one's given properties and powers. Being in history, by contrast, is to exist in encounter with something that transcends one's own existence: "The history of a being begins, continues and is completed when something other

70. See especially CD II.2, 100–101.

than itself and transcending its own nature encounters it, approaches it and determines its being in the nature proper to it, so that it is compelled and enabled to transcend itself in response and in relation to this new factor."[71] Note that *history* becomes here a technical term, different from its use in common language. A being that is "in a state," determined by its own properties and powers, can still have a history in the common sense. But being "in history" in Barth's technical sense is to have an existence that is determined in an encounter with a transcending power. Such is, Barth suggests, the "nature" of Christ's humanity. Concerning Christ's human nature, there is nothing that suggests a being "in a state"; his humanity is an existence which is completely identical with an encounter with the transcendental:

> The existence of the man Jesus is this history. It is nothing more. It has nothing behind it but the eternal will and counsel of God. It has no other foundation. Thus, apart from the eternal will and council of God, Jesus exists only in this history, i.e., in this history of the covenant and salvation and revelation inaugurated by God in and with the act of creation. Jesus is, as this history takes place.[72]

Christ's "human nature" is thus not a set of properties and powers but is an encounter, an encounter between the divine willing and what is not God.

If this is what Barth means by the eternal being of Christ, an important observation needs to be made. Barth does not want to supplement the traditional understanding of divinity and humanity in terms of natures with one in terms of history; he wants to replace it.[73] Barth would be correct to supplement the traditional understanding since, in the way he construes the identity of Christ, Christ does not start out as a set of properties, powers, and agency. Christ starts out as the act and determination of the divine willing. But Barth would not be correct to replace the traditional understanding, since at a point in time when Christ receives embodied existence he does obtain sets of properties, powers, and agency. In this sense, history precedes nature in the same way that

71. CD III.2, 158.

72. CD III.2, 160.

73. As he says in his doctrine of reconciliation, he wants to "re-translate the whole phenomenology [of traditional Christology] into the sphere of a history" (CD IV.2, 106).

covenant precedes creation—but just as covenant needs creation for covenant to be possible, history needs nature. It needs agents and powers to respond to the preceding action of God in history. While Christ might be said to start out as history, the history of divine willing, this cannot be all there is to his ontological constitution. At a point in time he becomes a responsive agent. But with the changed understanding of human nature—from properties, powers, and agency to an encounter with the divine—it is unclear what the ontological character of human agency is. All acts analyzed so far are divine acts, not human acts. Jesus exists in the history of divine willing, the divine reaching out to what is not God. His human nature is established in that very act. But what this leaves unexplored is how Jesus's human agency participates in this covenantal history. When, in the next section, we move from Jesus's humanity to all of humanity, we will see the same neglect of human agency.

II. The Object of Election

If one becomes a history rather than a state when one is confronted by something that transcends one's history, then every human being is a history—because every human being is confronted by Christ. "To be a man is to be with Jesus," as Barth famously explains in his anthropology.[74] However, humanity's being with Jesus does not originate in first-century Palestine. While Jesus's earthly life is "the execution and revelation" of the eternal election of Jesus Christ, the latter's beginnings lie in eternity.[75] Human beings are included in this election by being elected "in him," as we have seen in chapter 4. Barth understands this "in" as an ontological connection. Humans are objects of election, participating in and ontologically connected to Christ before they received embodied existence.[76] They existed long before they received creational powers and agency: their history with Jesus therefore precedes their being a state.

In this section, I am interested in the nature of humanity's ontological participation in Christ. I argue that this relationship is governed by the logic of assumption: in being elected "in" Christ, humans are assumed "in" Christ.

74. CD III.2, 145.
75. For Jesus's life as the execution and revelation of election, see CD III.2, 145.
76. CD III.3, 88.

I make my case by presenting three soundings of ontological aspects of Barth's narrative. I present these as three relatively independent exercises, each focused on a different aspect. However, as I point out at the end, these three soundings express a similar problematic pattern of relationship between God and creation. I first unpack the relationship between Christ's history and our history, between Christ's human nature and our human nature. I argue that when Christ assumes human nature, it is not just his own individual human nature that he assumes, but "in" this individual human nature is included every human nature. Second, I unpack the relationship between eternity, history, and time. I argue that in Barth's proposal our history is established before time began and will also be preserved after time's ending. The former is our beginning in God's eternal election, the latter our ending in God's eternal eschaton. Time is thus an intermezzo. However, whereas time's function is to allow an active interaction between God and humanity, time's eschatological ending will also entail the end of this interaction. In the eschaton our history is preserved, but our agency is not. Third, I question how Barth's eschatological vision relates to the resurrection. If Christ's resurrection sets the pattern for all of humanity's resurrection, and the resurrected Christ has agency and actively interacts with the disciples, does this not suggest the eschaton contains more than the preservation of our past history? As we will see, Barth says it does not: the resurrection is not a continuation of life, but a preservation of the lived life.

The problem with applying the logic of assumption to the relationship between Christ and other human beings is that assumption negates the interpersonal over-againstness between the assumer and the assumed. The human nature that Christ assumes is only a nature, not also a human person: the human nature receives personhood in Christ. However, if Christ's assumption of his human nature implies his assumption of our human nature, this leaves our human agency out. Hence, I believe, the conceptual structure of Barth's eschatology.

To apply the logic of assumption to the relationship between Christ and the believer is not inconsistent with Barth's supralapsarian thesis. However, it is also not applied by it. Barth could have presented his supralapsarian Christology combined with a very different understanding of its meaning for elected human beings. Therefore, I conclude in a fourth and last subsection, Barth must be driven here by a theological idea other than supralapsarianism. This conclusion leads into the third and final section of this chapter.

Humanity

Greek substance metaphysics makes a distinction between two kinds of substance: primary substance and secondary substance. Primary substance is the individual entity, for example, "a human being." Secondary substance is the general entity, for example, "humanity." The topic of an age-old debate is how these two forms of substance relate, and which one has ontological priority. Does the secondary substance have ontological priority, and are individual primary substances, for example, human beings, instantiations of the general secondary substances, for example, humanity? In that case, the conclusion is easily reached that all individual human beings are ontologically related by participating in the same general secondary substance, humanity, while being individuated by other features, as embodiment. Or do the individual primary substances have ontological priority, and is the general secondary substance truly secondary, an abstraction from the individual primary substances? This debate has an important theological counterpart. When God becomes incarnate, we could take this to be an assumption of an individual primary substance, in which case God assumes an individual human nature among many others. But we could also take the incarnation to be an assumption of the general secondary substance, in which case God assumes the general human nature in which all participate. Each of these options leads to a different theological conceptualization of the relation between the incarnate One and his fellow human beings.

Barth may "re-translate the whole phenomenology [of substance metaphysics] into the sphere of a history,"[77] but the distinctions between primary and secondary substances, with the subsequent theological implications, are still applicable to his proposal. And while his language is not always consistent, it is the latter of the two possibilities that Barth embraces: God assumes "humanity," which is like a secondary substance, and all human beings participate in this assumed humanity.

I will illustrate this by two fragments from Barth's Christology. Barth presents his Christology in three parts. Each part discusses first an aspect of Jesus's life and work and then contains several sections applying this aspect to

77. CD IV.2, 106.

the life of all human beings. In each part there is also a transitional section laying the foundation for the move from Christology to anthropology. I take a first fragment from one of these transitional sections, titled "The Direction of the Son."[78] In this section Barth explains how all of humanity is included in "the homecoming of the Son of Man . . . his elevation and exaltation to fellowship with God, to the side of God, to participation in his lordship over all things."[79] Barth first talks about this homecoming in terms of history. It was a history, "not a private history, but a representative and therefore a public history." Christ's history took place in the place of all human beings, and therefore it is a history "in which all participate . . . the history of this One is world history."[80] But for Barth, history is ontology. And thus, without further explanation, in the next sentence Barth no longer writes about history, but about essence: "In this One humanity itself, our human essence, was and is elevated and exalted." Does Barth mean to speak here of humanity as a primary substance, that is, an individual essence that is like our individual essences, or does he speak of humanity as a secondary substance, an essence in which all of us participate? If it is a primary substance, a human being like us is elevated and exalted. If it is a secondary substance, all of us, participating in humanity, are elevated and exalted. Barth first describes the essence as a primary substance: it is an essence like ours. "It is in perfect likeness with us, as our genuine brother, that he was and is so unique, so unlike us as the true and loyal man. To that in which a man is like all others, and therefore a man, there now belongs brotherhood with this one man."[81] But then, in the next sentence, the meaning of the word *essence* changes to that of a secondary substance: "To human essence in all its nature and corruption there now belongs the fact that in the one Jesus Christ . . . it has now become and is participant in this elevation and exaltation. There is no human life which is not also (and primarily and finally) determined and characterized by the fact that it can take place only in this brotherhood."[82] In the next paragraph Barth continues in this vein. The Christian message, he says, tells us:

78. CD II.2, 264–377.
79. CD IV.2, 269.
80. Ibid.
81. Ibid.
82. CD IV.2, 270.

> that in the union of God with our human essence which then took place uniquely in the existence of this man, prior to our attitude to it, before we are in any position to accept or reject it, with no need for repetition either in our soul or elsewhere, we today, bearing the same human essence and living at a particular point in time and space, *were* taken up (quite irrespectively and even in defiance of our own action and merits) into the fellowship with God for which we were ordained but which we ourselves had broken; and that we *are* therefore taken up into this fellowship in Him, this One.... Primarily and finally we ourselves *are* what we are in *Him.*[83]

For a second fragment I turn to the section in the *Church Dogmatics* most directly devoted to the metaphysics of the incarnation, titled "The Homecoming of the Son of Man."[84] This section forms the foundation for the section that was the source of the fragment I discussed above. We see here the same pattern: the human nature assumed by God is like a secondary substance, a general essence in which all human beings participate. Barth unpacks the notion of incarnation in four steps, respectively in terms of becoming, existence, essence, and exaltation. That God becomes incarnate means that God becomes human. The object of this act of becoming is

> not merely "a man" but the *humanum*, the being and essence, the nature and kind, which is that of all men, which characterizes them all as men, and distinguishes them from other creatures. It is not the idea of the *humanum*.... It is the concrete possibility of the existence of one man in a specific form.... But in this form it is that which is human in all men.... Because it is our being and essence, our nature and kind, which the Son of God willed to realize and has in fact realized in this one concrete possibility of human existence determined and elected and prepared by him, his existence as a human existence, as this one man, has a direct relevance for all other men, and in all the uniqueness in which it is an event in

83. Ibid.
84. CD IV.2, 44–116.

> Jesus Christ his incarnation signifies the promise of the basic alteration and determination of what we all are as men.[85]

While Barth refers to the "being and essence" of human beings in terms which suggest he thinks of secondary substance—*humanum*—he is also clear that in the incarnation we have to do with one concrete possibility of existence, which suggests he thinks of primary substance. This one concrete possibility has, however, a direct ontological relevance for all human beings, in that it "signifies the promise of the basic alteration and determination of what we all are as men." The nature of this relevance is explained in the second step of his explanation of the notion of incarnation, on existence. That God becomes incarnate means that God's existence becomes also the existence of a man. But this man is not "One who is alone as such, who became this man and existed in this way for himself. When we say Jesus Christ we say Jesus Christ and his own—those who are co-elected by him as the Son of God and in him as the Son of Man."[86] In Christ we can distinguish two forms of existence, Barth writes, namely a heavenly and an earthly-historical form. The first form Christ has for himself. But the second he has "in and with his body, his people, his community." The relationship between these two forms of existence is "not so much comparable as indirectly identical to the relationship between himself as the eternal Son of God and his being as man"—in other words, the relationship between Christ in his singular, heavenly being and Christ in his corporate, earthly-historical being is one of assumption. The logic of assumption governs not only the relationship between the Son of God and his human nature, but also the relationship between the Son of God and all of humanity:

> As we have seen already, the human nature elected by him and assumed into unity with his existence is implicitly that of all men. In his being as man God has implicitly assumed the human being of all men. In him not only are we all as *homines*, but our *humanitas* as such—for it is both his and ours—exist in and with God himself.[87]

85. CD IV.2, 48–49.
86. CD IV.2, 59.
87. Ibid.

In the third step of his explanation, on essence, Barth argues that if the existence of the Son of God becomes the existence of the Son of Man, then the divine and human essence must now be united—"the real exaltation of our human essence as it has taken place in Jesus Christ."[88] Finally, in the last, fourth step, on exaltation, Barth repeats the third step as the conclusion of it all: "as the Son of God became and is man, as he caused his existence to become that of a man, as he united divine and human essence in himself, he exalted human essence into himself, and as very God became very man. . . . We refer to the essence common to all men." By and in itself, the last sentence could be read, again, as ambivalent between referring to something like a primary or a secondary substance, but from the aforementioned it is clear: the human nature assumed by God in Christ is not like ours, but is ours. Our humanity participates in Christ's humanity; his humanity is our humanity, and therefore, in Barth's terms, his history is our history. The logic of assumption thus governs the relationship between Christ and other humanity.

Eternity, Time, and History

For a next sounding of Barth's ontology, I turn to his account of eternity and time. According to Barth, God has time. It is eternal time, but time nonetheless. The difference between eternal and created time is the relationships among their parts. Both eternal time and created time have beginning, middle, and end. In created time these are all distinct, even opposed, as past, present, and future. But in eternal time these are all simultaneously present.[89] God's time and its parts are constituted by inner divine multiplicity and movement. It is "the inner movement of the begetting of the Father, the being begotten of the Son and the procession of the Spirit in both." In this inner movement "there is order and succession. The unity is in movement. There is a before and an after. God is once and again and a third time."[90] Yet, this movement takes place in the *nunc aeternitatis*. There is "origin, movement, and goal" in and for

88. CD IV.2, 60.
89. CD II.1, 608.
90. CD II.1, 615.

Godself, but without "separation, distance, or contraction."[91] This "is his time, the absolute real time, the form of the divine being in its triunity."[92]

While our time is characterized by succession, God's relating to our time is still governed by simultaneity. As I noted earlier, God relates to time by preceding, accompanying, and following it, but this threefold relating shares in the simultaneity of divine eternity.[93] The problem with this notion is how to conceive of simultaneously relating to events that themselves do not obtain simultaneously. Followers of this idea of the relationship between eternity and time explain their view with the help of spatial metaphors: as a mountain climber sees the whole of a river, so God sees the whole of time; or as the center of a circle is present to all of the circle's circumference, so God is present to all of time—even while a person standing at the riverbank would see only part of it, and a point on the circumference is only present to what immediately went before and after. While Barth does not offer an explanation of how God's eternity can be simultaneously related to time's past, present, and future, he would probably be sympathetic to these kinds of examples. His own account of eternity and time is interspersed with spatial metaphors. I already noted that eternity's time is constituted by the "movements" of the trinitarian processions. God and eternity are further said to "embrace time on all sides."[94] They "must be understood as the element which surrounds time on all sides and therefore includes its dimensions."[95] Time's "whole extension from beginning to end . . . [is] in eternity like a child in the arms of its mother."[96] The problem with these metaphors is that they try to explain the relationship between God's eternity and creation's time by drawing an analogy between space and time exactly at the point where space and time differ. Space in front of or behind the space I occupy is still simultaneous to me, because it exists at the same time as I do. But time before or after the time which I experience as "now" is not simultaneous to me, because it does not exist at the same time as I do. Barth never offers a solution to this problem.

91. CD II.1, 612, 608.

92. CD II.1, 615. Note that, while in God's eternity beginning, middle, and end are established by the movement of the Trinitarian *processiones* (CD II.1, 615) and relate in a way analogous to the Trinitarian *perichoresis* (CD II.1, 640), there is no one-to-one relationship between beginning, middle, and end and Father, Son, and Spirit, because each Trinitarian person is "all at once in his own essence undividedly beginning, succession, and end" (CD II.1, 615).

93. CD II.1, 640.

94. CD II.1, 613, 623.

95. CD II.1, 619.

96. CD II.1, 623.

The spatial metaphors for the relationship between eternity and time are nonetheless important, since they suggest how time once was not, and once no longer will be. I noted earlier in the chapter that as creation makes covenant possible, so time facilitates the history of the covenant.[97] Time functions as a theater for history.[98] Time allows for the interaction between God and human beings, and human beings among themselves.[99] But time is limited. Time comes to an end, both the times of individual creatures and the time of creation as a whole. "Time will come when the created world as a whole will only have been. . . . Its life will then be over, its movement and development completed, its notes sounded, its colors revealed, its thinking thought, its words said, its deeds done, its contacts and relationships with other creatures and their mutual interaction closed, the possibilities granted to it exploited and exhausted."[100] The creature will no longer be, and therefore time, as mode of its existence, will no longer obtain. The creature will "not need any continuance of temporal existence."[101]

That time comes to an end does not imply there is no eschatological future for the creature. But this future is no continuation of the creature's temporal life; it is a preservation of the life lived.[102] The lived life, in its particular, limited time span, is as such preserved by being allowed to share in God's eternity.[103] Eternity's embrace does not end with time's ending. The gift of the eschaton is

97. "The aim of creation is history. . . . He wills and creates it for the sake of that which in his grace he wills to do to it and with it by his Son or Word in the Holy Spirit. The execution of this activity is history. What is meant is the history of the covenant of grace instituted by God between himself and man; the sequence of the events in which God concludes and executes this covenant with man, carrying it to its goal, and thus validating in the sphere of the creature that which from all eternity he has determined in himself; the sequence of the events for the sake of which God has patience with the creature and with its creation gives it time—time which acquires content through these events and which is finally to be 'fulfilled' and made ripe for its end by their conclusion" (CD III.1, 59).

98. CD II.1, 465.

99. "Time, then, is willed and created by God as the form at any rate of human existence. . . . It is willed and created to be our dimension, corresponding to his. This must obviously mean that God willed and created time as the dimension of the life he ordained for us when we were willed and created, and therefore as the dimension of a life in communion with himself as the eternal and living God, and also in relationship with our fellow-men, to whom he has given that same dimension for the same life in communion with himself. Time was in fact willed and created in order that there might take place his dealings in the covenant with man, which finds its counterpart in the relationship between man and his fellows" (CD III.2, 527).

100. CD III.3, 88.

101. Ibid.

102. It is not "an extension of this life in a continuation of time, but a life in communion with the eternal life of God himself" (CD III.2, 614).

103. "[W]hen the totality of everything that was and is and will be will only have been, then in the totality of its temporal duration it will still be open and present to him, and therefore preserved. . . . Everything will be

the continuation of eternity's embrace, being that in the eschaton the object of the embrace no longer is the living life, but the life lived.[104] The most important implication of this is that while the creature will still exist, it will no longer be in the mode of an active subject. God will still relate to the creature, but the creature will no longer relate to God. As the creature once was, he is again—history.[105]

Resurrection Time

Is the notion of the creature's eschatological future as the preservation of the lived life not inconsistent with resurrection? Barth is quite adamant that Christ's resurrection was a bodily event, taking place "before the gates of Jerusalem in the days of Tiberius Caesar," and therefore "in the place and time which are also ours, in our sphere.[106] But a bodily resurrection implies a continuance of temporal existence. This in turn suggests the continuance of the agency of the subject which is resurrected. If Christ's resurrection is a key to understanding the eschatological resurrection at large, this undermines the conceptual structures of Barth's eschatological expectation as sketched in the previous section.

There are indeed a few places where Barth describes the eschatological future of the creature as an active interaction with its creator.[107] They cannot be explained within Barth's ontological framework of time and eternity. If the

present to him exactly as it was or is or will be, in all its reality, in the whole temporal course of its activity, in its strength or weakness, in its majesty or meanness. He will not allow anything to perish, but will hold it in the hollow of his hand as he has always done, and does, and will do" (CD III.3, 89–90).

104. "Even in eternal life he [the creature] will still be in his time. For he will then be the one who, when there is no time but only God's eternity, and he is finally hidden in God, will have been in his time" (CD III.2, 521).

105. "This preservation is an eternal preservation. It does not end with the ending of the existence of the creature, just as it did not begin with that existence and is not limited by its limitations. In the eternal counsel of God it was applied and assured to the creature before creation itself. Similarly it is still applied and assured to it even when the creature has completed its appointed course, even when it does not exist any longer" (CD III.3, 88). Cf. CD III.2, 522: "That he loves and elects me, that he wills and intends me, that he calls, punishes, accepts, delivers, preserves and rules me, that he is my Light, my Commander, my Succor, my Comfort, and my Hope—all this is history, and has its time, and refers to me in this time of me, even in God's eternity before I was and when I shall have ceased to be."

106. CD IV.3.1, 298. See also, among other places, CD IV.1, 333 and CD IV.2, 143.

107. For example: "After time, in post-temporal eternity, we shall not believe in [the kingdom of God]. We shall see it" (CD II.1, 630); "He predestinated them to be a witness of his glory, and therefore to blessedness and eternal life" (CD II.2, 169); the creature "will find the essence of all creaturely glory in serving [Jesus Christ], actively siding with him and helping him and in this way . . . being clothed with all the honor and also with all the joy and peace of the eternal life" (CD IV.1, 152).

creature's eschatological future is not the continuation of its temporal life but only the preservation of the life lived, there can be no further interaction between Creator and the creature as an active subject. Barth himself does not register this discrepancy.

Barth's interpretation of Christ's rather than the general resurrection is, however, completely consistent with his ontological framework. For Barth, the meaning of Christ's resurrection lies not in an eschatological continuation of his embodied existence but in a revelation to those who still live in time of what his preresurrection life entailed. That life itself needed neither resurrection nor ascension: when Christ reveals himself in his resurrection,

> the significance of this event . . . is not to be found in a continuation of his being in a changed form which is its fulfillment. The being of Jesus Christ was and is perfect and complete in itself in his history as the true Son of God and Son of Man. It does not need to be transcended or augmented by new qualities or further developments. The humiliation of God and the exaltation of man as they took place in him are the complete fulfillment of the covenant, the complete reconciliation of the world with God. His being as such was and is the end of the old and the beginning of the new form of this world even without his resurrection and ascension.[108]

All that Christ's preresurrection life is lacking is "the men to see and hear it as the work and Word of God. . . . It is here that his resurrection and ascension came in, and still come in. . . . The resurrection and ascension of Jesus Christ are the event of his self-declaration. . . . Thus the resurrection and ascension add to what he was and is and to what took place in him—they add to what was to be seen in him—only the new fact that in this event he was to be seen and was actually seen as the one he was and is. . . . As his self-revelation, his resurrection and ascension were simply a lifting of the veil."[109] The resurrection is not the inauguration of a new phase in Jesus's temporal existence but a revelation of the lived life. As the one who once came, he comes now afresh—but it is still the coming of "'Jesus Christ yesterday' (Heb. 13:8)" who comes today

108. CD IV.2, 132–33.
109. CD IV.2, 133.

"in all his being and action of yesterday."[110] He is present today "as the man he had been (had been!)."[111]

Resurrection is the revelation of what happened on the cross—"the realization of the final depth of humiliation, the descent into hell of Jesus Christ the Son of God, but also of his supreme exaltation, the triumphant coronation of Jesus Christ the Son of Man."[112] This humiliation and exaltation could not be revealed at an earlier stage since, although it was determined from all eternity, "it was only in his death on the cross that it was actually and effectively accomplished and completed."[113] On the other hand, now that he has died, it is possible for him to become present at all times and in all places, since on his death "his being . . . became and is as such his eternal being and therefore his present-day being every day of our time."[114] The same is signified by the ascension: "a sign of his exaltation to the right hand of God, to eternal life and rule; of his transition to a presence which is eternal and therefore embraces all times."[115] Resurrection, ascension, and Christ's forthcoming return—the last moment of time and history[116]—are not the inauguration in time and space of the new era, but the "anticipation" of the mode of eternity in the mode of time.[117]

To see what Barth's position amounts to, it might be helpful to anticipate my argument and compare Barth to a proposal I will make in the next two chapters. I will propose that we understand the incarnation as a divine offer of interpersonal relationship. God becomes human in order to be physically present to God's creatures. The resurrection is the inauguration of this embodied eschatological reality. Resurrection thus implies the start of a new phase of life. In Barth's scheme, such a proposal could not be made—it is

110. CD IV.3.1, 291.

111. CD IV.1, 301. To emphasize that for Barth Christ's resurrection is only revelatory is not to deny that this revelation has, as R. Dale Dawson has rightly argued, an ontological pendant: R. Dale Dawson, *The Resurrection in Karl Barth* (Aldershot: Ashgate, 2007), 178–79. As I argued in chapter 4, for Barth divine self-revelation is always the form of divine self-giving. However, that which is ontologically given in Christ's resurrection is nothing beyond what is already established in Christ's death.

112. CD IV.2, 141.

113. CD IV.2, 140.

114. CD IV.1, 313.

115. CD IV.3.1, 318.

116. CD IV.1, 333.

117. CD IV.3.1, 327.

precluded by his understanding of the resurrection as the revelation of no more than the lived life.

Supralapsarianism and the Eschaton

It is time to draw the three preceding sections together. My first sounding of the ontological character of humanity's being as history focused on humanity's beginning; my second sounding focused on humanity's ending. While thus being directed at different phases of humanity's history, the similarities in ontological structure of these two phases are striking. At both moments, humanity is ontologically incorporated: in the beginning, in Christ, in the end, in God. In both cases, this happens at the expense of human ontological independence and agency. In the end, humans are no longer agents, but they are preserved as histories. In the beginning, they are assumed by Christ—and, on the creedal understanding of assumption, part of an assumed nature's ontological character is that it does not have its own personifier, but that it is personified by an external ontological subject. Barth's theory of human agency is not explicitly based on this latter fact, but it is an interesting point against the background of the criticism Barth has drawn for not giving enough conceptual space to human agency.[118]

Not only are the topics of these two soundings similar in structure, they are also causally connected. The creature itself does not have an eschatological future. Its time is limited; its creational existence ends at its death. It is only because and as far as the creature is elected in Christ, ontologically connected to him by partaking in the nature he assumed, that it has an eschatological future. It is Christ's humanity which is elevated; it is his humanity which is given to share in God's eternity, and therefore and thereby all humanity is given an eschatological future. Election is an eschatological category, I argued in chapter 4, and here is the reason why. The end of all humanity is in the beginning.

Barth's understanding of election "in Christ" is thus perfectly consistent with the rest of his narrative. Consistency, however, is not the same as

118. It is also interesting that those who do defend Barth's account of agency and ethics do not engage Barth's notion of Christ's assumption of all humanity. See, for instance, the absence of this notion in John Webster, *Barth's Ethics of Reconciliation* or in his *Barth's Moral Theology: Human Action in Barth's Thought* (Grand Rapids: Eerdmans, 1998).

implication. While it is consistent with humans' beginning as history "in Christ" to say that human beings will end as history "in" God, it is not implied by such a beginning. Why, for instance, could humanity not start out in eternity, but end in time? Why could human beings not start out as history, but end as agents? In other words, why are time and space not carried into the eschatological consummation, other than as that which once was? Why is creation only an intermezzo and not the continued active partner over against God? Nothing in Barth's supralapsarian narrative answers these questions. Barth's proposals must therefore have another motive than his supralapsarianism. This motive we find, I believe, when we introduce one last element of Barth's doctrine of election: rejection.

III. The Object of Rejection

Das Nichtige

Barth holds that, in addition to the Creator and creation, there is a third kind of being: *das Nichtige.*[119] Its existence cannot be explained from the positive will and work of either God or creature.[120] It nonetheless exists, as a force that opposes both God and creation "as an enemy, offending God and threatening his creature."[121] *Das Nichtige* is not identical to the negative side of creation. There is in creation itself a negative as well as a positive side, the dark as well as the bright, tears as well as laughter, death as well as birth. All of these are, however, part of the goodness of creation.[122] Admittedly, it is in the negative that creation experiences that it exists "as it were on the frontier of nothingness and orientated towards it."[123] Nonetheless, the negative is not *das Nichtige* itself, nor has it any connection to it.[124] *Das Nichtige* is also not identical with the sinfulness of creatures. To sin is, indeed, to be seduced by *das Nichtige.* "Sin

119. I prefer to use the German *das Nichtige* over the English translation "nothingness." The German term expresses the causal force embodied by *das Nichtige* much more than the English translation does.

120. CD III.3, 292.

121. CD III.3, 354.

122. CD III.3, 297.

123. CD III.3, 296.

124. CD III.3, 350.

is the concrete form in which nothingness is active and revealed."[125] However, *das Nichtige* is neither established nor exhausted by human sin.[126]

As is the case with all that is not God, *das Nichtige* has its "ontic context" in God's activity in election.[127] It is nonetheless not established by an act of God's election, but in an act of God's election, by an act that necessarily accompanies election, rejection:

> God elects, and therefore rejects what he does not elect. God wills, and therefore opposes what he does not will. He says Yes, and therefore says No to that to which he has not said Yes. . . . Both of these activities, grounded in his election and decision, are necessary elements in his sovereign action. It is only on this basis that nothingness "is," but on this basis it really "is."[128]

When God elects, this necessarily implies that God passes over an "infinite range of possibilities which he . . . with good reason did not realize."[129] In election, God allots to the elect being, and to the nonelect nonbeing. The latter is a form of existence nonetheless: existence as "an alien factor," a "third way of existence," but still an existence with power and activity.[130] "What God has eternally denied, constitutes that which is not."[131] And as such, it forms a menace, "an enemy which is superior to created being, a threatening destroyer . . . [which] possesses . . . its own ponderable reality . . . that which may and can seduce and destroy the creature."[132]

Given this menacing, threatening aspect of *das Nichtige*, it is not sin but *das Nichtige* and its power that is the main focus of God's saving work in Christ:

> The saving and preserving will of God is not primarily directed against sin. With a higher and deeper aim, it is directed against the nothingness affirmed in sin. It hastens to help being against nonbeing in order to destroy the power of the latter, to free the creature

125. CD III.3, 305.
126. CD III.3, 310.
127. CD III.3, 351.
128. Ibid.
129. CD III.3, 77.
130. CD III.3, 289; CD III.3, 349.
131. CD III.3, 76.
132. Ibid.

> by negating its negation, to avert its threat, to constitute a humanity and a world which have nothing more to fear from those frontiers because the abyss of evil has lost its power to attract, and in which God alone is King in his kingdom, as is only meet.[133]

Das Nichtige is not power without limits. It is constituted and upheld by God's act of rejection, but therefore it also only exists "because and so long as God is against it."[134] In other words, "when he no longer [says no], that which he negates no longer exists."[135] But when could God stop saying no to *das Nichtige*? When *das Nichtige* no longer menaces creation. God rejects what threatens creation, but once the threat is averted, there is no longer grounds for rejection. The nature of God's saving work is therefore to safeguard threatened creation from the abyss of *das Nichtige*. It is to go one step further than creation, one step further than to call forth being and nonbeing: "The Creator who gave [creation] being can go further and give it a being secure against non-being."[136] This happens in the incarnation. By becoming present in creation, God overcomes the menacing power of *das Nichtige*. Barth reaches for the *Christus Victor* imagery to describe the confrontation between the incarnate One with *das Nichtige*:

> Nothingness had power over the creature . . . But it was impotent against the God who humbled himself, and himself became a creature, and thus exposed himself to its power and resisted it. Nothingness could not master this victim. It could neither endure nor bear the presence of God in the flesh. It met with a prey which it could not match and by which it could only be destroyed as it tried to swallow it. The fullness of the grace which God showed to his creature by himself becoming a threatened, even ruined and lost creature, was its undoing.[137]

Thus *das Nichtige* is overcome. While creation starts out accompanied by *das Nichtige*, in the eschatological victory of Christ only God and elected creature are left: "it is true that in humbling himself in the man Jesus God had to do not

133. CD III.2, 143.
134. CD III.3, 353.
135. CD III.3, 362.
136. CD III.2, 144.
137. CD III.3, 362.

only with his creature, but with nothingness for the sake of his creature, it is also true, and even more so because definitively and conclusively, that in the exaltation of the same man Jesus God has to do only with his creature and no longer with nothingness."[138]

Supralapsarianism and das Nichtige

If this is Barth's account of divine rejection and *das Nichtige,* a number of questions remain: First, why is it that God's rejection causes its objects to exist? Further, why do these rejected objects not only have existence but also power? Third, why is this power evil? And finally, what exactly happened in the incarnation that led to the undoing of these objects' power? Answering these questions will not only clarify Barth's doctrine of *das Nichtige,* it will also reveal the second motive of Barth's narrative.

Barth says little or nothing to answer the first two questions, other than that "even on his left hand the activity of God is not in vain. He does not act for nothing. His rejection, opposition, negation, and dismissal are powerful and effective like all his works because they, too, are grounded in himself, in the freedom and wisdom of his election."[139] It might, however, be helpful to point out that Barth, like Schleiermacher, rejects a Platonic pantheon of *possibilia* existing independently of God. Barth takes *possibilia* to be under God's control.[140] Since Barth holds that *das Nichtige* is established by "the infinite range of all the possibilities which [God] passed over and with good reason did not actualize," we could think of God's act of establishing all *possibilia* as preceding God's act of electing and rejecting from these *possibilia.*[141] However, in such a scenario God's establishing of all *possibilia* would precede the divine election, whereas Barth adamantly presents the election as the first act of God concerning all that which is not God. It is therefore better to read Barth as wanting to identify both divine acts, such that God establishes the *possibilia* in the act of election and rejection. In this act, some *possibilia* are established as elected and

138. Ibid.

139. CD III.3, 351–52.

140. CD II.1, 535–36. It is difficult to characterize Barth as either a Cartesian voluntarist or a theistic activist (see for these positions above, 14, n24), since he makes no distinction between voluntary and intellectual divine control over the *possibilia.*

141. CD III.3, 77.

others are established as rejected. While this interpretation still does not answer the question why the rejected *possibilia* should be thought of as endowed with causal power, it does incorporate Barth's idea that even God's act of rejection is not in vain.

Barth's answer to the question of where the evil in the rejected *possibilia* originates is even more implicit than his answers to the other questions, but all the more important. A superficial reading of Barth suggests that he holds that *possibilia* are rejected because they are evil. God has, after all, "good reason" not to actualize them. A closer reading reveals, however, that Barth holds the opposite: the *possibilia* become evil because they are rejected. "The character of nothingness derives from its ontic pecularity"—and not the other way around.[142] And elsewhere: "what makes non-being a menace, an enemy which is superior to created being, a threatened destroyer, is obviously not its mere character as non-being, but the fact that it is not elected and willed by God the Creator but rather rejected and excluded."[143] But why do *possibilia* become evil once they are rejected? They become so, I suggest, because all of what is not God necessarily lapses into evil unless God incorporates it into God's own being. Only one form of existence, divine existence, is equivalent to the good. No other form of being is good or will obtain the good, unless it comes to participate in divine being. Not even God can create such a being—all God can do is to safeguard the being God created by giving it a share in the divine life. Creational life itself is governed by entropy.

Barth never explicitly formulates this thesis of creational entropy, but when we assume that such a thesis is in the background we can make sense of a number of related issues in Barth's thinking that are so far unaccounted for. Creational entropy explains why *das Nichtige* exists: it is that which never was to participate in goodness. But it also explains Barth's doctrine of the necessity of sin: creation on its own cannot obtain the good. It explains his eschatological vision: for creation to receive a share in God's life. It explains his take on incarnation and the cross: they are the way in which God incorporates creation in God's own life. And finally, it explains why creation, time, and human agency are only an intermezzo of the history of God and creation: if they were not assumed into the divine life, they would never be free of *das Nichtige*. But if

142. CD III.3, 353.
143. CD III.3, 76.

all of this is true, this is the thesis we were looking for—the thesis which not only explains *das Nichtige*, but which also gives Barth's supralapsarian narrative its shape.

Let us have a closer look at each of these elements of Barth's narration. First, what God elects is not realized as creation *in abstracto*. It is from the beginning elected "in" Christ: it has its being by being assumed by him. Not so with the rejected *possibilia*, however. They receive being, but not "in" Christ. They are "denied the benefit of his preservation, concurrence, and rule."[144] That is why they are immediately subject to creational entropy.

However, the same logic holds for elected *possibilia*. Barth holds, as I have noted in chapter 4, that sin is an impossibility for a human being determined by its electing "in" Christ. On the other hand, for "man *in abstracto*," that is, the human being "apart from the merciful will of his Creator primarily directed towards him," the fall and original sin "are an ontological necessity." This is true because "man *in abstracto*" is "a being hopelessly exposed to the threat of surrounding non-being." [145] Here we have the doctrine of creational entropy in a nutshell: creation in and by itself lapses into evil by ontological necessity.

But why is this? In order to overcome the threat of creational entropy completely, God gives creation "to share in his own life, a life which is quite unthreatened because it is self-grounded and self-renewing."[146] Note Barth's formulation: God's life is not threatened by entropy, because God's life is "self-grounded and self-renewing." Whether a being is subject to sin, evil, and the threat of *das Nichtige* depends on whether it is self-grounded or not.

Das Nichtige forms a threat for non-self-grounded creation as long as creation exists as an ontological entity outside of God. For God to overcome *das Nichtige* is therefore to give it a "share in his own life"—that is, to assume creation in the divine life. This is what happens in the incarnation. When the incarnate One confronts *das Nichtige*, the latter, as always, threatens the created nature it detects in Christ. But creation is now safely embedded in the divine life. *Das Nichtige*, in all its menacing power, may lead to the humiliation of God, but in this humiliation the exaltation of the creature takes place: the

144. CD III.3, 289.
145. CD III.2, 146.
146. CD III.3, 80.

creature is brought home. When this happens, *das Nichtige* is overcome. God no longer has to fight it, to say no to it, because the creature is safe—"in" God.

Finally, creational entropy explains why in the eschaton creation cannot see a restoration of human agency. This would imply an ontological "over-againstness" between the Creator and the creature; but it is exactly such over-againstness that gives space for creation's entropy. Only if the creature exists no longer in its own being and agency, but is incorporated in the divine life, is it safe.

This, then, is what explains the peculiar shape of Barth's supralapsarian narrative. This is why he takes creation to begin and end in God. This is why creation is only an intermezzo. This is, also, why the threefold relating of God to creation is presented in the order of consummation, reconciliation, creation. Creation cannot take second place, because it is never free from sin. It is, by its nature of not being self-grounded—that is, by its nature of being created, destined to lapse into evil.

But why is this? Why does the absence of self-grounding necessitate a lapse into evil? What supports the thesis of creational entropy? That is a question Barth never answered or faced. Clearly, the idea of creational entropy is deeply ingrained in Barth's fundamental understanding of the nature of God and creation; but never in his work is the idea brought out in the open or presented for theological scrutiny.

6

Supralapsarian Christology: Conceptual Structures

Infralapsarianism and *supralapsarianism* are both family names. Neither of these names stands for a particular theory; they stand for two families of ideas. Infralapsarians agree that God became human in order to take care of the sin problem, but they disagree widely on the reason why. The result of this disagreement is a variety of atonement and reconciliation models. Likewise, supralapsarians agree that the incarnation is not contingent upon human sin; but they differ widely on the reason why. The result of this disagreement is a variety of supralapsarian approaches concerning the meaning of the incarnation.

In the preceding chapters, I discussed three supralapsarian proposals, by Friedrich Schleiermacher, Isaak Dorner, and Karl Barth. I laid out their arguments, examined their internal logic, and exposed, where necessary, their incoherencies. Each of these three proposals I discussed in their particularity. But each also functions representatively: each proposal represents a branch of the supralapsarian family tree. Schleiermacher stands for an approach that situates the incarnation firmly in God's relating to what is not God in redemption; but he reads redemption from a supralapsarian perspective. Dorner represents a theology that situates the incarnation in God's relating to what is not God in creation. Barth exemplifies an approach that situates the incarnation in eschatological consummation. In turn, each of these approaches results in a different supralapsarian narrative.

In this chapter, I look again at each of these proposals, but this time I do not concentrate on their particularity, but approach them as representatives of one of the three branches of the supralapsarian family tree. The conclusions of this discussion will guide me in chapters 7 and 8, where I lay my own cards on the table and present an alternative supralapsarian proposal.

Felix Culpa

In the second chapter I discussed Schleiermacher's supralapsarian argument. I argued that the argument is directly based on Schleiermacher's doctrine of absolute dependence and divine causality. Because absolute dependence of humans on God implies a nonreciprocal relationship between God and creation, the incarnation cannot be conceived as a divine response to human sin. And since everything falls within the scope of divine causality, including sin, Schleiermacher cannot construe sin as opposite to the divine initiative, but needs to present sin as part of it. The solution Schleiermacher proposes is to see sin and subsequent redemption as the means by which God connects all humankind to Christ, through whom the divine impartation—the eschatological goal of creation—enters the world. For this solution to work, Schleiermacher appeals to the idea that it is sin that makes human beings receptive to the gifts of Christ: God ordained the consciousness of sin "in order to intensify that longing without which even the endowment possessed by Jesus would have met with no living faculty for the reception of what he communicates."[1] In other words: human beings will not be receptive to the divine gifts in Christ unless these gifts address an evil in their lives.

In my discussion of Schleiermacher's proposal, I charged him with a fatal inconsistency between his ontological framework and his theological proposal. At this point, however, I am interested in Schleiermacher's idea concerning the receptivity of human beings toward the gifts in Christ. For Schleierma-

1. Friedrich Schleiermacher, *The Christian Faith*, eds. H. R. Mackintosh and J. S. Stewart (Edinburgh: T and T Clark, 1999), § 89.1, 366.

cher's idea has a troubling implication: if there is no receptivity toward divine gifts unless these gifts address an evil, this means that the good is in need of the bad as much as the bad is in need of the good. The good needs the bad for the good to be needed, recognized, and received.

It is interesting that Schleiermacher introduces this idea without any defense. Evidently, he believed his idea to resonate with his readers, and he might have been right. Some reflection shows that similar ideas are deeply ingrained in the history of Christian theology. Schleiermacher's proposal can be read as a variation on the *felix culpa* tradition. The term *felix culpa* comes from a line in a hymn from the Latin liturgy sung on Holy Saturday:

> *O certa necessarium Adae peccatum, quod Christi morte deletum est!*
> *O felix culpa, quae talem ac tantum meruit habere redemptorem!*

"O truly necessary sin of Adam, which was blotted out by the death of Christ! O happy fault, that merited to possess such and so great a Redeemer!" Adam's sin should be praised, because it triggered greater gain than would otherwise be received. Without Adam's sin, the bad, the greater good of incarnation and consummation could neither have been given nor received. The thought expressed in the hymn can be found throughout the Western tradition.[2] For example, Gregory the Great says:

> What greater fault than that by which we all die? And what greater goodness than that by which we are freed from death? And certainly, unless Adam had sinned, it would not have behooved our redeemer to take on our flesh. Almighty God saw beforehand that from that evil because of which men were to die, he would bring about a good which would overcome that evil. How wonderfully the good surpasses the evil, what faithful believer can fail to see? Great, indeed, are the evils we deservedly suffer in consequence of the first sin; but who of the elect would not willingly endure still worse evils, rather than not have so great a redeemer?[3]

2. See for a history of the *felix culpa* tradition: Arthur O. Lovejoy, "Milton and the Paradox of the Fortunate Fall," *Journal of English Literary History* 4 (1937): 161–79.

3. *In Primum Regum Expositiones* 4,7 (J.P. Migne, Patrologia Latina 79, 222); quoted in Lovejoy, "Milton and the Paradox of the Fortunate Fall," 172–73.

About a millennium later, in John Milton's *Paradise Lost,* the Archangel Michael concludes his overview of the history of humanity with a prediction of the second coming and the final judgment, when Christ shall reward

> His faithful, and receive them into bliss,
> Whether in Heav'n or Earth, for then the Earth
> Shall all be Paradise, far happier place
> Then this of Eden, and far happier daies.
> So spake th' Archangel Michael, then paus'd,
> As at the Worlds great period; and our Sire
> Replete with joy and wonder thus repli'd.
> O goodness infinite, goodness immense!
> That all this good of evil shall produce,
> And evil turn to good; more wonderful
> Than that which by creation first brought forth
> Light out of darkness! full of doubt I stand,
> Whether I should repent me now of sin
> By mee done and occasiond, or rejoyce
> Much more, that much more good thereof shall spring,
> To God more glory, more good will to Men
> From God, and over wrauth grace shall abound.[4]

Gregory, Milton, and Schleiermacher approach the topic from a slightly different angle. Gregory and Milton write from the perspective of God, who is not able to show forth the fullness of the divine love unless triggered by human need: "unless Adam had sinned, it would not have behooved our redeemer to take on our flesh." Schleiermacher writes from the perspective of humanity, which is not receptive to the fullness of the divine love unless triggered by human need: "that longing without which even the endowment possessed by Jesus would have met with no living faculty for the reception of what he communicates." The underlying principle is nonetheless the same: the good is in need of the bad as much as the bad is in need of the good.

Even among the three theologians I discussed—Schleiermacher, Dorner, and Barth—Schleiermacher is not the only one who makes use of this notion; so does Barth. In the preceding chapter, I discussed Barth's ontology. I argued

4. John Milton, *Paradise Lost* XII.462–78.

that Barth's proposals are governed by two commitments: his supralapsarianism and his thesis of creational entropy. This thesis holds that when God calls into being what is not God, the latter, as long as it exists independently of God, will necessarily lapse into evil. Only incorporation into the divine being protects creational being from further downfall. I argued that this thesis explains the existence of *das Nichtige* as the sum of rejected *possibilia*, the ontological necessity of human sin, and Barth's construal of the eschaton.

However, if creational entropy is part of the ontological framework in which God's creative activity takes place, why did God not create human beings immediately incorporated into the divine being? Why choose the detour of sin and redemption? Because, says Barth:

> God's supreme and truest good for creation, and therefore the good determined for and promised to creation, is revealed in its full splendor only when its obedience and blessedness are not simply its nature, the self-evident fulfillment of its existence, its inevitable course, but when they are salvation from the edge of an abyss, when in its obedience and blessedness creation is constantly reminded of its creation out of nothing and its preservation from nothingness by the menacing proximity of the kingdom of darkness, when its obedience and blessedness are therefore grace and salvation. It is the very essence of our reconciliation as grace to depend on the existence of a divine *voluntas permittens*, and in virtue of this on the reality of disgrace, damnation and hell. If God is greater in the very fact that he is the God who forgives sins and saves from death, we have no right to complain but must praise him that his will also includes a permitting of sin and death.[5]

We find a comparable argument in Barth's redescription of the Calvinist "supralapsarian theory [concerning election] as detached and purified from the doubtful presuppositions of the older theology," a theory Barth says to support if "corrected and supplemented in a Christological direction," but "with no material alteration."[6] God wills, says Barth, "to impart and reveal himself—and

5. Karl Barth, *Church Dogmatics*, Vol. II.1 (Edinburgh: T and T Clark, 1956–75), 595. Hereafter, *Church Dogmatics* is cited as CD, followed by volume and part number, and page numbers.

6. CD II.2, 140, 143.

with himself his glory, he himself being the very essence of glory," and human beings as "the witness to his glory and the object of his love." It is not God's will that humans should fall into sin, but that they reject sin. However, for this purpose humans need to be confronted with evil, and—creational entropy!—"it is inevitable that this confrontation with what God repudiates, with evil, should mean for man, who is certainly not God and not almighty, that evil confronts him as a hostile power, a power which is, in fact, greater than his own power." In the sphere of creation, evil can therefore only be overcome in "a history: the history of an obstacle and its removing; the history of a death and a resurrection; the history of a judgment and a pardon; the history of a defeat and a victory." Thus, "God wills *homo labilis*, not in order that he may fall, but in order that when he has fallen he may testify to the fullness of God's glory."[7]

I did not discuss this part of Barth's thought in the previous chapter. Barth makes these comments almost in passing, in the small print of his argument, and it is not clear how deeply embedded they are in Barth's overall proposal.[8] However this may be, for present purposes it is important that Barth's argument in the passages quoted above turns on the same principle as Schleiermacher's idea: God "is greater in the very fact that he is the God who forgives sins and saves from death," and for God to show "the fullness of God's glory," it needs to be contrasted with a human history of defeat. The good is in need of the bad as much as the bad is in need of the good.

The notion of *felix culpa* plays an important role in the medieval debates concerning the incarnation, with infralapsarians looking to it for support, and supralapsarians arguing against it. There is no reason to embrace supra-

7. CD II.2, 140–42. In related passages, Barth situates his line of thought in the *felix culpa* tradition, and rightly so: CD II.1, 506–12; CD IV.1, 69.

8. In chapter 5, after expounding Barth's idea of *das Nichtige* as the threatening presence of *possibilia* who receive their existence in God's rejection, I posed three questions: Why is it that God's rejection causes its objects to exist? Why do these rejected objects have not only existence but also power? Why is this power evil? To the first question I answered that for Barth all *possibilia* are established by divine power, presumably, in the act of election and rejection. As an answer to the third question I suggested the thesis of creational entropy. Barth's adherence to the *felix culpa* motive may suggest an answer to the second, and unanswered question: God gives power to the rejected *possibilia* so that their evil may bring out "the fullness of God's glory." As far as I know, there is no textual evidence for this suggestion; its plausibility rests on its coherence. But if this suggestion is right, the passages identified above would have more importance than is suggested by the little prominence they have in Barth's text.

lapsarianism, Aquinas argues, "For God allows evil to happen in order to bring a greater good therefrom; ... hence, in the blessing of the Paschal candle, we say: 'O happy fault, that merited such a great Redeemer.' "[9] On the other hand, "*Valde improprie*," very improper, writes Aquinas' teacher Albert the Great concerning the *felix culpa* hymn, and rightly so, I believe.[10] It is *improprie* to the nature of the good to hold that the good needs the bad in order to be needed, recognized, or received. It is true that human beings find themselves psychologically often more receptive to the good in times of need. It is also true that Christians feel drawn to Christ especially in times of need and despair. This, however, should not lead us to the conclusion that the good is in principle in need of the bad in order to be needed, recognized, or received. That believers long for the soothing presence of Christ in times of need does not imply that Christ's presence is not also a good in time of fortune. If believers find themselves psychologically more receptive to the good in times of need, this should in itself rather be analyzed as a result of the sinful situation of humanity: if God needs to make use of the bad in order to make us see the good, this is because sin disturbed our abilities to recognize the good for what it is. The *felix culpa* argument, however, is based on the idea that the good needs the bad in principle. The sinful situation itself is introduced (Schleiermacher), needed (Gregory), or allowed (Milton, Barth), in order to create a need and receptivity for the good; but to do so devalues the excellence of the good and allots goodness to the bad. Supralapsarians, I believe, should explore the meaning of the incarnation, the presence of God among us, as an excellent good in and of itself, and not take refuge in a doctrine of sin to beef up incarnation's meaning. We do not need the bad to enjoy Christ.

My argument against the *felix culpa* motive is thus based on the excellence of the good. Most of the theologians discussed will be sensitive to this appeal to value, I expect. The exception is Schleiermacher. As I noted in my discussion of his Christology, the central religious experience on which his theology is built is one of absolute dependence, and the language of causality is the only acceptable framework to analyze God's actions. God is therefore conceived as supreme causality, but not as supreme value. Within this context,

9. Thomas Aquinas, *Summa Theologiae* III, q.1, a3 ad 3.

10. Quoted in Bruce Foss Westcott, *The Epistles of St. John: The Greek Text with Notes and Essays* (London: Macmillan, 1883), 297.

Schleiermacher can speak about human good and human sin, but this is only relative to the God-consciousness—that is, relative to the experience of human causal dependence.[11] Appealing to his theological method, Schleiermacher could thus consistently hold onto the *felix culpa* motive—but at the same time thereby also revealing its theological price: the inability to acknowledge any value to God's being.

Creation and Incarnation

One sample is a rather thin base to draw general conclusions about the strength and weaknesses of a supralapsarian Christology anchored in the doctrine of creation. Nonetheless, I believe a careful rehearsal of the arguments as analyzed in chapter 3, combined with a quick glance at some like-minded approaches, will allow us to separate the arguments particular to Dorner from the underlying general strategy, and to suggest some strengths and weaknesses of supralapsarian arguments based on God's relating to what is not God in creation.

Dorner's arguments are premised on the notion that God is a lover of love. In creating what is not God, God aims at aggrandizing the life of love: a twofold surrender of God to human beings, and of humans to God. This twofold surrender is embodied in religion. The divine contribution to religion is revelation; the consummation of revelation—and thereby of religion and, ultimately, of creation—is the incarnation. Dorner develops a threefold argument to support this last thesis. First, revelation attains perfection only in the incarnation, since God is only in the incarnate One completely communicated and perfectly received. Second, such complete revelation is necessary in order to make absolute religion possible. All existing religions are relative, because they are historical, finding their origin in the visionary leadership of an inspired personality. However, none of these religious founding fathers had received an absolute revelation, and therefore the religious communities founded by them can help their adherents to come only to a relative development of the life of love with God. By contrast, an absolute, all-embracing religion needs an absolute, all-embracing founder. Third, love is an ethical act.

11. Friedrich Schleiermacher, *The Christian Faith*, ed. H. R. Mackintosh and J. S. Stewart (Edinburgh: T and T Clark, 1999). See for the good: § 60, thesis, 244, and § 70.1–2, 282–84; and for the bad, § 66, 271–73.

The ethical is only had by a free, self-involved choice vis-à-vis the ethical. But to make such a choice, it is not enough to know the ethical; one needs an encounter with the ethical in an offer of interpersonal relationship with God, who is the ethical, and this offer comes to humans in the incarnation.

For Dorner, the incarnation is thus a necessary implication of the initial motivation for the divine act of creation, to aggrandize love. But this act and its motivation are themselves given with the ethical nature of God. The incarnation is thus not only necessarily implied by God's creating, but creation and incarnation are themselves necessary as well. As I argued above, this necessary nature of creation is at odds with the ethical relationship aimed at in the incarnation. For the divine love whereof Dorner speaks to be meaningful, it has to be a love for the particular. However, God's love for the particular needs to be understood as contingent, and so are the objects of God's love. In order to save his supralapsarian argument, Dorner will have to give up on the necessity of creation and incarnation.

Nevertheless, we would move too fast if we used the failure of Dorner's necessitarian approach to draw negative conclusions in general concerning supralapsarian arguments based on God's relating to what is not God in creation. By their very nature, such arguments do indeed hold a strict implication between creation and incarnation; but they do not need to hold the necessity of creation itself. I illustrate this by comparing Dorner's approach with two other supralapsarian proposals, one developed by a contemporary of Dorner, the Anglican New Testament scholar and bishop Brooke Foss Westcott (1825–1901), the other recorded by the medieval theologian and bishop Robert Grosseteste (c. 1168–1253).

In his *Christus Consummator*, Westcott presents a supralapsarian argument based on the idea that God created human beings in God's image—"the primal endowment and final goal of humanity."[12] Since we were created to carry the image of God, Westcott suggests, "the fitness and the necessity of the incarnation exists . . . from the moment when man was made."[13] The incarnation, Westcott argues, "corresponds with the perfection of man as he was constituted at first. . . . *Homo particeps Dei*—man made partaker of God—is the

12. Brooke Foss Westcott, *Christus Consummator: Some Aspects of the Work and Person of Christ in Relation to Modern Thought* (London: Macmillan, 1906), 104.

13. Ibid.

satisfaction, the only possible satisfaction, of *Homo capax Dei*—man capable of receiving God."[14] This is, suggests Westcott, the "Gospel of Creation."[15]

Two comments need to be made to unpack Westcott's argument. First, Westcott's argument equates *capax dei* with assumability: to be assumed by God is the fulfillment of humanity's capacity to receive God. However, traditionally these are very distinct notions. *Capax dei* is that which sets human beings apart from other creatures: the ability to know God and live in an interpersonal relationship with God. By contrast, assumability, the obediential potency (*potentia oboedientialis*), is something human beings share with all of creation. Every created entity can be brought into hypostatic union with a divine person; God can become incarnate in every part of creation.[16]

Second, the success of Westcott's argument depends on two additional premises. The first premise would need to say something to the effect that God, in the act of creation, commits God to fulfill all good potencies of creation. Only on such a premise does it make sense to say that from the presence of a mere potency we can predict its fulfillment. A second premise would explain why it nonetheless is not the case that all individual human beings are subject to divine assumption. After all, the argument implies that all human beings share in the same potency to be hypostatically united with the divine; however, in the Christian narrative, this potency is only fulfilled in one. What premises Westcott's argument is the notion of the unity of all humankind, whereby the fulfillment of a potency of one counts as the fulfillment of the potency of all. Westcott does not give a metaphysical underpinning of this premise; instead, he draws on biological and sociological arguments, such as the idea of evolution and the unity of humanity presupposed by the labor movement.[17] Based

14. Ibid., 105.

15. Ibid. Cf. Westcott's comments in an essay on supralapsarian Christology titled "The Gospel of Creation": "It will perhaps be said that the view which has been indicated makes the action of God dependent on creation. So far as there is force in this argument it extends not only to the perfection of creation but to creation itself. The very act of creation is a self-limitation of omnipotence. And as far as we dare speculate on such subjects it is easier for us to suppose that the crowning act of love, the consummation of all finite things, was included in the one creative act, than that it was contingent on man's conduct." *The Epistles of St. John*, 325.

16. Cf. the section "Assumability" in my "The Logic of Assumption," in *Exploring Kenotic Christology*, ed. C. Stephen Evans (New York: Oxford University Press, 2006), 277–81 [265–90].

17. Cf. Westcott, *Christus Consummator*, 106–14, 136–47; Westcott, *The Epistles of St. John*, 318–28; Brooke Foss Westcott, *The Gospel of Life: Thoughts Introductory to the Study of Christian Doctrine*, 2nd ed. (London: Macmillan, 1895), passim.

on this premise, Westcott rejects the particularity of the incarnate One's nature and holds its generality: that what was assumed by Christ was not a particular human nature, but a general humanity in which we all share.[18]

Before I make a comparison between Westcott's and Dorner's approaches, I want to give a second example of a supralapsarian argument from creation, as presented by the medieval theologian Robert Grosseteste. Being able to compare these three arguments will then allow us to draw some more general conclusions concerning this branch of the supralapsarian family tree. Grosseteste's argument hinges on the desirability of unity in creation. For any entity to be unified, it requires a unifying principle. Humanity, as made up out of body and soul, suggests itself as such. On the one hand, the human soul is linked with other creatures like angels by their common spiritual nature, while in itself it recapitulates the life activities of all vital entities. On the other hand, the human body is linked to all elements of the physical universe. However, a unifying principle must be greater than the parts that compose that unity, which undermines humanity's claim, since human beings cannot claim greater dignity than the angels. But angels themselves cannot function as the unifying principle, since they do not take the central position human beings have; while all other creatures also cannot function as the unifying principle, since they rank behind human beings in dignity. Creation itself is thus unable to function as its own unifier. Moreover, no creature has unity with its creator, which is necessary for creation's unity to be complete. However, if the creator were to assume human nature in hypostatic union, the desired unity is reached. The creator would be united with creation, and all of creation would be united with the God-man. Since it is a greater good for creation to be a unity than to be deprived of unity, and since it is possible for God to give unity and for creation to receive it, we can say "that in its perfection lies its necessity. As John of Damascus says: 'providence is that will of God by which all existing things receive suitable guidance through their end. But, if providence is God's will, then, according to right reason, everything that has come about through

18. Among many other places: "The Lord's humanity was universal and not individual, as including all that belongs to the essence of man, without regard to sex or race or time." Brooke Foss Westcott, *The Gospel According to St. John: The Authorised Version with Introduction and Notes*, reissued with a new introduction by A. Fox (London: James Clarke, 1958 [1882]), 11.

providence has quite necessarily come about in the best manner and that most befitting God, so that it could not have happened in a better way.' "[19]

I do not read these last comments as implying an absolute necessity concerning God's actions. God is free to create or not to create. But if God decides to create, the creative act and its result are governed by a series of conditions implied by the nature of God and what is befitting God mostly. In this, Westcott's and Grosseteste's strategies are structurally the same. This strategy turns on two arguments: first, an argument to the effect that the incarnation is the richest gift God can give creation, and second, an argument that God's commitment to creation is so strong that God will give it the richest gift God can give. Westcott holds, first, that the incarnation fulfills the primal endowment of human beings, namely, to be *capax dei*; and second, that God fulfills all good potencies of creation. For Grosseteste, incarnation gives creation desirable unity, and God, guided by right reason, always brings about what is more desirable than not. If we compare these two strategies with Dorner's necessitarian proposal, the latter can be read as a further variation on this approach. First, the incarnation is the consummation of religion as built on divine love, and thus the richest gift God can give creation. Second, God's commitment to creation is so strong that God will give it the richest gift God can give, since divine love is necessarily implied by God's ethical character. Further, in Dorner's proposal, not only is the incarnation necessarily implied by creation, but also creation is necessarily implied by God's being—but this position is the result of the particular arguments Dorner has chosen, not of the argumentative strategy Dorner shares with Westcott and Grosseteste.

I do not take any of these particular sets of arguments to be sound. I do not think that the incarnation is the fulfillment of humanity's *capax dei*, nor do I buy Westcott's argument that the fulfillment of all good creational potencies can be seen as a good. I think there is greater good in the fulfillment of particular sets of potencies by every creature—a fulfillment analyzed in Christian theology in terms of gifts, calling, and identity. I also do not share the Platonic metaphysics and esthetics on which Grosseteste's understanding of creational unity is built. Finally, in chapter 3 I have argued that Dorner's notion of divine necessary love is inconsistent with the contingent status of the objects of God's love.

19. Robert Grosseteste, *De Cessatione Legalium*, ed. Richard C. Dales and Edward B. King (London: Oxford University Press, 1986), 132; with reference to Ioannes Damascenus, *De fide orthodoxa*, II.29.

However, I am inclined to think that with different arguments the argumentative strategy itself will work. Most Christian theologians agree that the act of creation comes with a form of divine commitment to God's creatures. Further, many theologians will also agree that friendship with God counts as the richest gift God gives creatures. In the next chapter, I argue for the incarnation as the consummation of this friendship. If we can give an account of divine commitment to creation strong enough to necessarily imply God giving the richest gift to creation, the argument succeeds. Careful consideration should be given to the latest move. It is pertinent not to describe such divine gift giving as a moral obligation. Large strands of the biblical material, in particular wisdom literature, describe the divine delight in the goodness of creation, even in all its ambiguity, while being remarkably silent regarding both redemption and eschaton. Opponents of my argument could thus argue that in the biblical narrative, "nothing about the stories of God's creating entails that God must necessarily also draw what is created to eschatological consummation."[20] A more promising line of argument is, I think, to argue from the character of God. God is a God of extravagance, and the most extravagant gift is the gift of interpersonal communion with Godself. Nothing obliges God to give Godself; it is an unexacted gift. Given God's character, it is nonetheless a gift that can be expected. This line of argument could very well accommodate the thought that large strands of the biblical narrative on creation are silent on an eschatological consummation—since creation itself does not necessitate consummation. It refuses nonetheless to draw final conclusions concerning God's intentions from this material.

In appealing to the divine character, the argument comes close to a form of perfect being theology. This form of theology starts from the notion of God as the best possible being, who has all characteristics it is better to have than not to have. A central element in this approach is an ontological argument for God's existence: from the notion of the excellence of God's being it can be proven that God exists, and exists necessarily. A supralapsarian argument from creation could add to this that if such a God decides to create, this extravagantly giving God will also give Godself to this creation. In some simple steps, the perfect being theologian could thus attain three central elements of the

20. David H. Kelsey, *Eccentric Existence: A Theocentric Anthropology*, chapter III.A, 3 (forthcoming from Westminster/John Knox Press). See for a discussion of the biblical material especially the chapters IV.A and IV.B.

Christian faith: God's existence, goodness, and incarnation. In the simplicity of the argument lies beauty, and in its beauty lies its appeal.

Nonetheless, in the following I do not attempt to develop such an argument. Even if from the divine character a sound argument could be made that divine commitment to creation is strong enough to necessarily imply God giving the richest gift to creation, a second argument is needed—that the incarnation is in fact that richest gift God has in store. And this argument seems to be epistemologically secondary to consummation. How do we know that the incarnation is the richest gift God has to give except after it is given—that is, after the dawn of the consummation? At least from the perspective of the history of religion, it seems a good case can be made that incarnation as the Christian faith knows it—no mere appearance of God in human disguise, but the real presence of God in human form—is a concept only developed in response to the experience of the Christian community with Jesus of Nazareth. Further, conceptually, we could argue that if love is always particular—that is, bound up with the particular person of the lover—it is not until we experienced the richness of the love in Christ that we could know that his is the richest gift love can offer. All this does not, of course, make the argument from creation invalid. But it does mean that the argument is epistemologically posterior to an experience of consummation.

Christology and Pneumatology

In chapter 3 I argued that Dorner's proposal embodies a number of diverging supralapsarian interpretations of the incarnation. I raised several questions concerning the incarnation, suggesting for each question two different answers. Each answer amounts to a different supralapsarian profile, in need of a distinct set of arguments. Dorner, I argued, never faces those questions, and wavers between several supralapsarian approaches.

One such question concerns the character of the divine–human relationship established in the incarnation. Some supralapsarians see this relationship primarily as interpersonal. Dorner's proposal contains this approach: by becoming incarnate, God aims to establish a kingdom of love. God becomes present among us as a suitor, pursuing a relationship of mutual love and commitment. Other supralapsarians see this relationship primarily as ontological. By assuming a human nature, God is able to change and complete the ontological structure of reality. Dorner's proposal contains this approach, too. In the incarnation, Dorner argues, God joins divinity to humanity in such a way that the latter's time-space limitations are overcome—first for Christ, and in the eschaton, also for the beatified.

The difference between these two answers lies, first, in the way these answers conceive of the receiver of the gift of incarnation; and second, in the ontological presuppositions embedded in them. The first answer conceives of the incarnation as a gift given to human persons: by assuming a human nature, God makes Godself available for interpersonal interaction, from one human being to the other. The second answer conceives of the incarnation as given to human nature: by assuming human nature, God is able to change the ontological status of humanity from the inside out. The former option assumes that in the incarnation God takes up a human nature like ours, a nature that allows God to be present to us in human form. The latter option presupposes that in the incarnation God assumes a human nature that is ours, a nature that God will now change for the better. The former option is premised on the similarity of individual human natures; the second option is premised on the unity of human nature.

In Westcott's supralapsarian argument, discussed earlier in this chapter, we have another example of the second option. Humanity has the potency to be assumed by God, and God will fulfill all good potencies of creation. In assuming Christ's human nature, God assumed all, since humanity is one. Christ's human nature was therefore "universal and not individual, as including all that belongs to the essence of man, without regard to sex or race or time."[21]

Finally, Barth's proposal is also determined by the second option. Human beings are elected "in" Christ, and the "in" has the status of an ontological connection. This ontological connection is parsed out in terms of assumption. "Assumption" is thus understood as transitive. When in Christ God assumes human nature, it is not just Christ's individual human nature that is assumed, elevated, and exalted, but all of humanity. Unlike Westcott, Barth does not deny the individuality of Christ's human nature. But since our human natures are assumed by Christ's human nature, for God to assume Christ's human nature is identical with assuming our human natures:

21. See note 17.

> As we have seen already, the human nature elected by him and assumed into unity with his existence is implicitly that of all men. In his being as man God has implicitly assumed the human being of all men. In him not only are we all as *homines*, but our *humanitas* as such—for it is both his and ours—exists in and with God himself.[22]

I believe this account of the incarnation leads to a twofold problem. One problem lies in the idea of the unity of human nature. What ontological account should we give of "humanity" if, as Dorner's and Westcott's proposals imply, it is not an individual quality similarly held by all, but a single substance in which all share, and assumed by Christ? In particular, is it possible to hold this idea without relegating the individuating properties of human beings to the second plane? Westcott's position that "the Lord's humanity was universal and not individual, as including all that belongs to the essence of man, without regard to sex or race or time" suggests otherwise.

My question is theologically motivated. When Christianity made its entry into the pagan world, it was confronted by a philosophical tradition that tended to favor the universal over the particular, and to treat the particular as a disturbance of the essential structure of reality. For example, according to Aristotle individuation is only to be found in matter. Human beings are identical to one another in their form, in what is essential to them; they differ only in their matter. For theological reasons, Christian thinking resisted such an approach. Central notions of the Christian faith—love, sin, conversion, faith, forgiveness—cannot be understood in an ontological framework that devaluates individuality.

Barth escapes these problems of a single humanity by analyzing humanity not in terms of substance but in terms of history. This allows him to hold both to the individual human nature of Christ and to the inclusion of all of humanity in Christ. Christ's own human nature is established in the history of God's decision to reach out to what is not God. However, this history as such is not just a history of God in Christ: it is inclusive, a history aimed at what is not God. All human beings are included in this history as the intentional objects of God's action. Therefore, in this one single history, every human's history—and therefore its nature—finds its beginning.

22. CD IV.2, 59.

However, Barth's solution leads to another problem. In Barth's solution, our histories are included in Christ's history. As such, they began before we existed; they will be preserved even when we are no longer. The technical term for this inclusion of our history in Christ's history is *assumption*. Christ assumes an individual human nature, and in his individual human nature he assumes all. Included in him, every human nature is assumed, elevated, and exalted. But what about the human agents who are the subjects of these human natures? They did not exist yet when their histories started. Presumably, they were not objects of assumption. And indeed, they are not preserved in the eschaton. Their histories are; they are not. In this proposal, human agents seem to fall outside the reach of salvation.

The root of this problem lies in the use of the notion of assumption. *Assumption* is a Christological category. In the incarnation, the divine Word assumes a human nature. This human nature is, as Chalcedon says, "like us in all respects, except for sin." It is a nature with a mind, a will, and a body. However, whereas our human natures are had by human persons, this human nature is not. It is assumed by a divine person, the divine Word. Therefore, between this human nature and God there is no personal "over-againstness." Everything this human nature has, does, and undergoes is had, done, and undergone by God the Word. In the human being Jesus of Nazareth we meet the person of God.

There is, however, a personal over-againstness between the divine Word and our human natures. Our natures are not personified by the divine Word, but by human persons. What our natures have, do, or undergo is not had, done, or undergone by the person of the divine Word, but by our own persons. There is an I-Thou difference between God and us, which is not present between God and the human being Jesus of Nazareth. Exactly for this reason, it is unhelpful to apply the category *assumption* to the relationship between Christ and humanity. It ignores the I-Thou difference between God and us.[23]

Terms that do respect the ontological over-againstness between the divine and the human are terms like *inspiration, renewal, re-creation, imitation.* Notably, these are pneumatological categories, not Christological categories. Of

23. Note that nothing in this argument is dependent on a particular interpretation of what it is to be a "nature." In classical Christology, a nature is a set of attributes, powers, and agency. In Barth's proposal, a nature is a history. But for either, the logic of assumption applies.

course, for each of these the person of Christ is looming in the shadows. The Spirit takes what is Christ's and declares it to us (John 16:15). We are to be conformed to the image of Christ (Rom. 8:29), to put on Christ (Gal. 3:27), to love like him (Eph. 5:1), to be like him (Phil. 2:5). Our eschatological bodies will "bear the image of the man of heaven" (1 Cor. 15:49; cf. Phil. 3:21). The Christological is always present—but at the same time, none of these sayings would make sense if there were no over-againstness between Christ and the rest of humanity. A human being that is assumed by Christ need not be conformed to the image of Christ—she is Christ. Only a being that is different can be made alike.

There are things the Son does better than the Spirit, and there are things the Spirit does better than the Son.[24] The Son, by assuming a human nature, makes God present over-against us: God visible, tangible, and audible in our midst. But as soon as the Son would try to make us participate in the divine grace by assuming all our human natures, God is no longer present to us, since we, as the ultimate subjects of these natures, would no longer exist—we would be replaced by the Son. It is therefore the Spirit who makes us participate in grace. On the other hand, the Spirit, by re-creating, renewing, and inspiring us, reforms our persons and natures in the image of the Son. But without the Son assuming a human nature, the Spirit has no form in which to mold us. It is therefore the Son who makes grace present to us. Christology and pneumatology are structurally different.[25] A successful supralapsarian argument needs to respect these differences.

Let me sum up the results of this chapter. To set up a supralapsarian argument according to which God introduced sin and redemption in the world in order to make us receptive for the incarnation is a form of *felix culpa* argument. *Felix culpa* arguments are theologically problematic. They imply that God needs the

24. Cf. the judgment of Eugene F. Rogers Jr., writing about modern pneumatology, that "the upshot of two centuries of trinitarian revivals seems to be this: Anything the Spirit can do, the Son can do better," in *After the Spirit: A Constructive Pneumatology from Resources outside the Modern West* (Grand Rapids: Eerdmans, 2005), 33; cf. 19–32. If Rogers is correct, the supralapsarian use of Christological categories for what should be explained pneumatologically is embedded in a general theological trend in the modern era.

25. Cf. the important essay by A. A. van Ruler, "Structuurverschillen tussen het christologische en het pneumatologische gezichtspunt," in *Theologisch Werk* I (Nijkerk: G.F. Callenbach, 1969), 175–90. Without mentioning it, Van Ruler's article is directed against the strong Barthian influence on European theology in the 1950s and 1960s. A. A. van Ruler, Nederlands Reformed theologian, had a formative influence on Jürgen Moltmann.

bad in order to introduce the good; but this devaluates the excellence of the good and allots goodness to the bad. Therefore, Schleiermacher's route has to be rejected.

More interesting is a supralapsarian approach that situates the incarnation in God's relating to what is not God in creation. Such an approach turns on two arguments: first, an argument to the effect that the incarnation is the richest gift God can give creation, and second, an argument that God's commitment to creation is so strong that God will give it the richest gift God can give. The most fruitful way to make the second argument is to premise it on the nature of God. However, the notion that the incarnation is the richest gift God can give creation is premised on the actual experience of the incarnation—on the experience of consummation. Therefore, epistemologically, the primary supralapsarian approach is to start from eschatological consummation.

The preeminent example of a supralapsarian approach rooted in an account of eschatological consummation is Karl Barth's theology. Barth's proposals are, however, shaped not only by supralapsarian intuitions but also by the thesis of creational entropy. The latter holds that unless creation is incorporated into the divine being it will necessarily fall into evil. This inspires Barth to hold that the incarnate One not only assumes an individual human nature but, in this nature, assumes all natures. Grace comes to humanity by taking it up and assuming it into community with the divine. However, while such a construal can give an account of how grace comes to human natures, it cannot give an account of how it comes to us as persons. For this, we need a proposal that respects the over-againstness between the incarnate One and other human beings. It is such a proposal that I develop in the next chapter.

7

Supralapsarian Christology: A Proposal

I. Resurrection Life

Resurrection Morning

On a small table in our living room stands a statue of two persons: a standing man and a kneeling person in front of him. Whether the kneeling person is a man or woman, one cannot tell. The man holds the other in an embrace. His hands rest tenderly and protectively on the shoulder and head of the other. The kneeling person, overwhelmed with emotion, kneels with the head against the man's chest, hands holding him tight. The man's face rests on the other one's head. The kneeling person's body speaks of joy, relief. The man's face is filled with love. The whole scene suggests peace, completion, a wait that is finally over. "And I go and prepare a place for you, I will come again and will take you to myself, so that where I am, there you may be also" (John 14:3). The title of the statue is *Resurrection Morning.*

The statue expresses two central features of the New Testament's presentation of Christ's resurrection: eschatology and embodiment. Christ's resurrection is an eschatological event. Because of the resurrection, we no longer live in the last days, but in the first of a new aeon. Our time is no longer a time of only awaiting; it is a time of welcoming. The resurrection is the introduction of creation's consummation. Paul speaks of the resurrected Christ as the first fruits, the inauguration of a triumphant order of divine rule: "Christ the first fruits, then at his coming those who belong to Christ, then comes the end" (1 Cor. 15:23), when all things are subject to Christ's reign. The Spirit of him "who raised Jesus from the dead" now works to incorporate persons into this new reality, to conform them "to the image of [the] Son, in order that [he] might be the firstborn within a large family," and dwells in a creation groaning in labor pains and eagerly waiting to be set free from its bondage and to see the full revelation of the children of God (Rom. 8:9–26).

This resurrection life comes to us as an embodied existence. Especially, Luke's gospel emphasizes the reality of Christ's resurrection body.[1] The risen Lord meets two men on the road to Emmaus, walks home with them, and breaks bread (Luke 24:13–31). He meets with his disciples and, when they take him to be a ghost, invites them: "Look at my hands and my feet; see that it is I myself. Touch me and see; for a ghost does not have flesh and bones as you see that I have" (Luke 24:39). When they still disbelieve, he asks for food and eats a piece of fish in front of their eyes (24:42). Luke knows of his Hellenistic readers' dichotomous image of human existence and wants to make sure they do not take the resurrected Lord for a ghost without a body. At the same time, Luke is careful not to write about Jesus's resurrection as a return of Jesus's spirit to his old physical nature, in a way he did write about Jairus's daughter (Luke 8:55), or he could have written about the widow's son in Nain (Luke 7:11ff.), Tabitha (Acts 9:36ff.), or Eutychus (Acts 20:7ff.).[2] Christ's resurrected body is different. It partakes of a new reality, which is physical but also somehow wider, larger, with more possibilities than the old physical world. This new reality allows Christ to be recognized at some times but not at others (Luke 24:16, 24:31); it allows him to participate in our space-time reality without being restricted by it (Luke 24:36); and in this new reality Christ takes his residence,finally physically withdrawing from his disciples (Luke 24:51).

1. See in particular Hans-Joachim Eckstein, "Bodily Resurrection in Luke," in *Resurrection: Theological and Scientific Assessments*, ed. Ted Peters, Robert John Russell, and Michael Welker (Grand Rapids: Eerdmans, 2002), 115–23.

2. See ibid., 118–20.

Other gospel writers and Paul concur with this theme of bodily continuity and discontinuity. John tells how Jesus shows Thomas the marks of the nails and spear visible in his body (John 20:27) but also how he suddenly, without visibly entering the room, appears in the midst of his disciples (20:19, 20:26). He writes of Jesus eating fish and bread with them on the shore of the Sea of Tiberias (John 21:9–13), but also how they initially do not recognize him (21:4, 21:12). Paul explains that while Christ is resurrected in his body, it is a body now clothed in glory and power. There are different kinds of physicality throughout creation, he writes. Celestial bodies and earthly bodies obey very different physical laws, he concurs with the convictions of his time, but they are all perceived to be material. Likewise, both the bodies of creation and the bodies of consummation are material but governed by very different energy and physical laws. The former are animated by the ordinary breath of life; the latter by the Spirit of the living God (1 Cor. 15:35–47).

Christ is the first to receive a body animated by the Spirit. In him the eschatological consummation breaks through, and his body is, as Paul repeatedly asserts, the original of which ours will bear the image. The Spirit of him who raised Christ from the dead already dwells in us, as a first installment (2 Cor. 1:22), giving us the first fruits until we receive the full "redemption of our bodies" (Rom. 8:23), so that Christ might be "the firstborn within a large family" (Rom. 8:29). We "have borne the image of the man of dust," Adam, but we will "bear the image of the man of heaven" (1 Cor. 15:49). Christ "will transform the body of our humiliation that it may be conformed to the body of his glory, by the power that also enables him to make all things subject to himself" (Phil. 3:21).

Eschatological human beings are thus embodied creatures—Christ as the firstborn, than, in the general resurrection, followed by all others. If this is true, it will not do to say, as Barth does, that the being of Jesus Christ was perfect and complete by the time of his death, and that resurrection and ascension are no more than the revelation of Christ as the man he had been.[3] Nor will it do, as Barth's recapitulation model does, to conceptualize eschatological consummation as the preservation of the lived life, instead of the continuation of

3. Karl Barth, *Church Dogmatics*, IV.2 (Edinburgh: T and T Clark, 1956–75), 132–33; see this thesis, 115.

the creature's temporal life.[4] Embodiment implies a continuation of time. Bodily actions are, essentially, temporal events. Breaking bread, eating a fish, embracing a friend—these are actions that cannot take place in a timeless existence. Further, a life that still unfolds in time cannot be called completed. Therefore, Christ's being, Christ's life and identity cannot be presented as completed by the time of his death, nor can the resurrection be analyzed as solely a revelation of a life lived. A completed life has no future, but Christ does. A life lived no longer participates in time, but Christ does. The recapitulation model needs to be rejected: it falters on the embodied nature of the resurrected One.[5] The eschaton is not the conservation of a life definitively ended by death. Instead, the eschaton is the harvesting of new life; life born out of the old as the crop is born out of the seed.

This reading of the resurrection as the inauguration of eschatological consummation is neither infralapsarian nor supralapsarian. Proponents of both approaches can agree on my rejection of the recapitulation model and my emphasis of the embodied nature of the eschatological life. However, the question I want to raise in this chapter is this: can the infralapsarian explain why the history of the incarnate One does not just amount to a reconciliation between God and humanity, to a restoration of the life of the proton, the life of original creation, but also further unfolds in the inauguration of this eschatological life? If God becomes human only to take care of the sin problem, why does the incarnation continue once atonement is made, and why does it give us so much more than what sin made us lose? Put in the form of a thesis, the argument I will develop is this: if the incarnation inaugurates the eschatological life, in all the glory of Easter morning, the gift of the incarnation cannot be fully explained as a divine emergency measure triggered by human sin.

4. Ibid., III.2, 614; see this thesis, 113.

5. Günter Thomas, "Resurrection to New Life: Pneumatological Implications of the Eschatological Transition, in *Resurrection: Theological and Scientific Assessments*, ed. Peters, Russell, and Welker, 263–65 [255–76], makes a similar case against the recapitulation model, but without connecting embodiment and time, as I have done. It is interesting that, whereas the generation immediately after Barth largely accepted the recapitulation model, a younger generation rejects it. For its acceptance, see for instance: Eberhard Jüngel, *Death: The Riddle and the Mystery* (Philadelphia: Westminster Press, 1974); and Wolfhart Pannenberg, *Systematic Theology*, Vol. III (Grand Rapids: Eerdmans, 1998), 580–608. For its rejection, see: Miroslav Volf, "Enter into Joy! Sin, Death, and the Life of the World to Come," in *The End of the World and the Ends of God: Science and Theology on Eschatology*, ed. John Polkinghorne and Michael Welker (Harrisburg: Trinity Press International, 2000), 256–78; Douglas Farrow, "Karl Barth on the Ascension: An Appreciation and Critique," *International Journal of Systematic Theology* 2 (2000): 127–50; Ernst M. Conradie, "Resurrection, Finitude, and Ecology," in *Resurrection: Theological and Scientific Assessments*, ed. Peters, Russell, and Welker, 277–96; and Thomas, "Resurrection to New Life."

More than this is given; more than this is at stake. If Easter morning's implications are fully acknowledged, we need to understand the gift given in Christ as supralapsarian.

Ascension Day

Before I embark on my actual argument, I want to pause a moment to complement my reading of the resurrection with a reading of Christ's ascension. The ascension is virtually neglected in Christian theology, and here is not the place to repair this neglect.[6] Introducing the ascension is nonetheless felicitous for my argument in that it both confirms my rejection of the recapitulation model of eschatology and underscores the eschatological and material aspects of Jesus's postresurrection life. First, the ascension confirms that Christ's resurrection is not the same as coming to participate in God's eternal life. A lived life, on its death taken up in the embrace of eternity, need not ascend anywhere. In a recapitulation model of eschatological consummation, resurrection and ascension conflate. In a model that speaks of consummation as a continuation of the creature's temporal life, resurrection and ascension are two different events, both establishing new aspects of the history of the resurrected One. Both events speak of eschatology and embodiment, but they speak of it in two distinct ways.

Second, the eschatological aspects of the ascension are best understood from Daniel 7 and Mark 13. Daniel 7 describes from above what the disciples in Acts 1 see from below:

> I saw one like a human being
> coming with the clouds of heaven.
> And he came to the Ancient One
> and he was presented before him.
> To him is given dominion
> and glory and kingship,
> that all peoples, nations, and languages
> should serve him.
> His dominion is an everlasting dominion
> that shall not pass away,

6. But see Douglas Farrow, *Ascension and Ecclesia: On the Significance of the Ascension for Ecclesiology and Christian Theology* (Grand Rapids: Eerdmans, 1999).

and his kingship is one
that shall never be destroyed. (Dan. 7:13–14)

For first-century Jews, this apocalyptic vision spoke of the eschatological judgment of God in which the great empires that opposed God would be defeated and collapse, and the people of God would be vindicated. The people of God are represented by the "Son of Man," who did not come down toward the earth riding on a cloud, but who went upward from earth to heaven, inaugurated and exalted as the true king of an everlasting kingdom. Christ quotes from these verses in Mark:

You will see the Son of Man
seated at the right hand of the Power
and coming with the clouds of heaven. (Mark 14:62)

N. T. Wright is convincing when he writes that, in applying Daniel's vision to himself, Christ did not want to speak of a future return from heaven but spoke of his going to heaven, making the startling move of foretelling his own enthronement, by his sharing of the divine throne with the Ancient of Days.[7] Therefore, what Daniel envisioned from above, Luke is now able to chronicle from below. Resurrection speaks of the eschatological re-creation by the Spirit; ascension of the eschatological inauguration of the Son. In both cases, the object is embodied existence. In the resurrection, it is re-created. In the ascension, it is inaugurated in the heavenly realm from where it "will come in the same way as you saw him go into heaven" (Acts 1:11).

With this conceptualization of resurrection and ascension in hand, we can now develop three arguments for the need of supralapsarianism.

Supralapsarian Arguments

An Argument from Eschatological Superabundance

My first supralapsarian argument is premised on the relationship between the eschaton and the proton. The eschaton is not the restoration of the proton. In

7. N. T. Wright, *Jesus and the Victory of God* (Minneapolis: Fortress, 1996), 339–69. Cf. Richard B. Hays, "'Why Do You Stand Looking Up Toward Heaven?': New Testament Eschatology at the Turn of the Millennium," *Modern Theology* 16 (2000): 123–24 [115–35]; and Farrow, *Ascension and Ecclesia*, 15ff.

the eschaton there is an abundance, a richness in intimacy with God and in human transformation that the proton did not know. In Christ we gain more than we lost in Adam. However, the argument goes, such gain cannot be contingent upon sin. Sin, by its very nature, never brings us closer to God; it only alienates us from God. If we gained the richness of the eschaton because of sin, this would amount to *felix culpa*, and such an understanding has to be rejected, as I argued in the previous chapter. Therefore, the richness of the eschaton has to be understood in supralapsarian terms: it is not contingent upon sin. And since Christ is the embodiment of the abundance of the eschatological life, neither is the incarnation contingent upon sin.

Let me unpack the argument. That the eschaton is more than a restoration of the proton is a conviction held by proponents of infralapsarianism as well as supralapsarianism. The gain of the eschaton is usually understood to be twofold. First, it is a gain by way of human transformation, a human change for the better. The infralapsarian Augustine provided the authoritative formulation of this transformation. In the proton, human beings had "an ability not to sin, combined with the possibility of sinning." But the eschaton "will bring the impossibility of sinning." Human nature is then "set free by a more abundant gift of grace so that it may be brought to that condition of liberty in which it is incapable of sin."[8] This idea has become standard in all Western traditions.[9] The second eschatological gain is one of divine intimacy. In the eschaton, human beings come to see God as they never had before: face to face. Augustine is again a good spokesperson:

> Now let us see, as far as the Lord deigns to help us to see, what the saints will do in their immortal and spiritual bodies. . . . There will be that "peace of God which," as the Apostle says, "is beyond all understanding" (Phil. 4:7). . . . We must remember what a great man it was who said: "Our knowledge is partial, and our prophesying is partial, until perfection comes," and "we now see a dim reflection in a mirror; but then we shall see face to face" (1 Cor. 13:9ff.).

8. Augustine, *De Civitate Dei* XXII.30; quoted from *Concerning the City of God Against the Pagans*, new translation by Henry Bettenson with an introduction by John O'Meara (London: Penguin Books, 1984).

9. See, for instance, Heinrich Denzinger, *Enchiridion symbolorum definitionum et declarationum de rebus et declarationum de rebus fidei et morum*, 37. Auflage (Freiburg: Herder, 1991), nn. 403, 1000, 1001; H. Schmid, *Doctrinal Theology of the Evangelical Lutheran Church*, 3rd rev. ed. (Minneapolis: Augsburg, 1961), 225; Heinrich Heppe, *Reformed Dogmatics*, rev. and ed. Ernst Bizer (San Francisco: Harper Collins, 1956), 249–50.

> This is how the holy angels see already. . . . We also shall see as they see already. . . . This vision is reserved for us as the reward of faith; and the apostle John speaks of the vision in these words: "When he is fully revealed, we shall be like him, because we shall see him as he is" (1 John 3:2).[10]

Augustine refers here to a number of Scripture passages that underlie the notion of the beatific vision. With the last quotation he also brings the two eschatological gains together: "We shall be like him, because we shall see him as he is." Human transformation and beatific vision are intimately related. In the eschaton we change for the better, not because God remakes the blueprint of human nature, but because we are brought into such heightened intimacy with God. Having come so close to God, we lose all desire to go our own ways.

What is at stake for the supralapsarian is the centrality of Christ to eschatological consummation. The gifts of the eschaton are intimately bound up with his person: they are modeled after, brought about by, and directed at him. The person of Christ is the model for humanity's transformation (Rom. 8:28, Phil. 3:10, 2 Cor. 3:18). The intimacy by which this is brought about is an intimacy with him (Col. 3:4, John 14:12, 15:1–11). As the apocalyptic fragment in Philippians has it, it is his consummating power which "will transform the body of our humiliation that it may be conformed to the body of his glory," the same power which "also enables him to make all things subject to himself" (Phil. 3:21). Finally, the eschaton will be a revelation of the glory of Christ (John 17:3, 17:24), and satisfy the desire of those who long to see Christ (Heb. 12:14, 1 Pet. 1:8). In other words: the eschatological superabundance is a gain in Christ. The theological question pressed by the supralapsarian therefore is this: if the superabundance of the eschaton is thus so intimately bound up with the person of Christ, can Christ be contingent upon sin? Would this not make the eschaton itself contingent upon sin?

The infralapsarian can respond in two ways. First, she can embrace the last point, and say that, indeed, eschatological consummation is just as much contingent upon sin as the incarnation. This response takes the form of a *felix culpa* argument:

10. Augustine, *De Civitate Dei* XXII.29 (Concerning the City of God, 1081–82). Cf. Denzinger, *Enchiridion symbolorum*, nn. 1000, 1001; Schmid, *Doctrinal Theology of the Evangelical Lutheran Church*, 661–62; Heppe, *Reformed Dogmatics*, 706–8.

> O goodness infinite, goodness immense!
> That all this good of evil shall produce,
> And evil turn to good; more wonderful
> Than that which by creation first brought forth
> Light out of darkness!

as John Milton wrote. In the previous chapter, I expounded an important problem with this view: it suggests that God needs evil in order to bring out good, which is repugnant to the excellence of the good. Moreover, this infralapsarian take on the eschaton is at odds with a strong tendency in Western theology to think of the two gains of the eschaton—human transformation and beatific vision—as the telos of human history. Different traditions within Western thought use different conceptual frameworks to express this idea. For example, medieval theologians speak about it in terms of happiness: ultimate happiness lies only in the beatific vision of God.[11] Such ultimate happiness was not given to Adam yet, but was to be given at a later stage.[12] As another example, Reformed theology conceives of it in terms of covenant. God made a covenant of works with Adam, asking of Adam obedience to the divine commandments and promising eternal life as reward for their observation.[13] While different from one another, both conceptual frameworks are premised on the notion that the eschaton is not contingent upon sin, but part of God's dealing with humanity from the beginning.

Another strategy is to hold to an infralapsarian Christology while combining it with a supralapsarian eschatology. One might then hold that the same superabundant gifts of the eschaton, while now modeled on and given through Christ, could also have been received in a different way. An example of such a strategy is Reformed infralapsarian covenantal theology. Adam received creation, and not consummation, but by virtue of the covenant of works that God entered into with him, Adam was able to gain eschatological abundance. When Adam fell, God introduced a covenant of grace, holding that humanity could now receive through Christ what it had otherwise received through Adam:

11. Thomas Aquinas, *Summa Theologiae* Ia.II.ae., q.3, a.1, responsio; q.3, a.3, responsio.

12. Ibid., Ia, q. 94, a.1.

13. Heinrich Heppe, *Reformed Dogmatics,* 283; H. Bavinck, *Gereformeerde Dogmatiek* II, seventh, unaltered edition (Kok: Kampen, 1998), 524–38, translated in Herman Bavinck, *In the Beginning: Foundations of Creation Theology*, ed. John Bolt, trans. John Vriend (Grand Rapids: Baker Books, 1999), 197–212.

> Hence Christ does not [merely] restore his own to the state of Adam before the fall. He acquired and bestows much more, namely, that which Adam would have received had he not fallen. He positions us not at the beginning but at the end of the journey that Adam had to complete. He accomplished not only the passive but also the active obedience required; he not only delivers us from guilt and punishment, but out of grace immediately grants us the right to eternal life.[14]

While this strategy is consistent in its understanding of the relation between Christ, creation, and consummation, it has a significant drawback: it demands a reading of the relationship between Christ and the eschaton as strictly extrinsic. While after the fall the eschaton is modeled after and inaugurated by Christ, it could, with the same results, have been modeled after and inaugurated by Adam. This can only be true, though, if Christ's life, as the pattern by which our lives will be transformed, and Christ's power, by which he inaugurates the consummation, and Christ's presence, which will enlighten the heavenly city, are not intrinsically bound up with Christ's identity. And that is wrong. It is given Christ's identity that Christ can be present in the way he is and act in the way he acts, and not the other way around—that is, it is because Christ is the one in whom God is present in our midst that he has the power to inaugurate creation's consummation, that he will enlighten the heavenly city, and that it should be after him, and no one else, that the transformation of our lives should be patterned. If it is true that what differentiates the eschaton from the proton is that in the consummation humanity is no longer able to sin, and that such is dependent on a heightened intimacy with God brought in Christ, then the nature of the eschaton is intrinsically bound up with the incarnation.[15]

The abundance of the eschatological consummation is intrinsically bound up with Christ, and since these eschatological gifts should not be conceived as infralapsarian, neither should Christ. This is the upshot of the supralapsarian argument. At this point, the supralapsarian can point to several New Testament documents that seem to draw the same conclusion. Spread out over the

14. Bavinck, *Gereformeerde Dogmatiek* II, 534 (*In the Beginning*, 208). Cf. Michael S. Horton, *Lord and Servant: A Covenant Christology* (Louisville: Westminster John Knox Press, 2005), xi–xii.

15. Cf. Barth's argument that only because Christ is not just an elect creature but primarily and supremely the electing creator that humanity can be elected "in him" (see above, 154).

traditional Pauline and Johannine corpus, as well as in Hebrews, several passages identify Christ as the agent not only of eschatological consummation but also of creation (1 Cor. 8:6; Col. 1:16–17; Heb. 1:2; and 1 John 1:1–3). What happens here is premised on Jewish apocalyptic logic, that God governs history and that therefore all things correspond to God's predetermined purposes. If this is true, what is central in the eschatological triumph must be central to the purpose of creation. If Christ is the "firstborn from the dead," his existence cannot be equivalent to a divine emergency measure, but he must also be the "firstborn of creation."[16] A similar argument is implied elsewhere, not with reference to the notion of creation but concerning divine election: "Blessed be the God and Father of our Lord Jesus Christ, who has blessed us in Christ with every spiritual blessing in the heavenly places, just as he chose us in Christ before the foundation of the world to be holy and blameless before him in love" (Eph. 1:3–4; cf. Rom. 8:29–30). The eschatological blessing is based on an election "in Christ" that is situated "before the foundation of the world" and is therefore as primordial as God's commitment to creation, independent of human sin and need for reconciliation. Infralapsarian Christology cannot account for the logic implied in such an idea; only supralapsarianism can.

An Argument from the Vision of God

A second supralapsarian argument zooms in on a detail of the argument from eschatological abundance. This argument explains the eschaton in terms of human transformation and the vision of God. These abundant gifts are intimately bound up with the person of Christ, so the argument goes, and since the former are supralapsarian, so is the latter. Christ ushers in the eschaton, and eschatological human transformation is modeled after him. The second argument concerns an aspect of the relationship between Christ and the eschaton that stayed underexposed in the first argument: Christ's role in the beatific vision. Christ is instrumental to eschatological human transformation; but is he similarly instrumental to the beatific vision?

The medieval theologian Robert Grosseteste argued that Christ is indeed instrumental. The beatific vision gives human beings complete joy. Human

16. See Larry H. Hurtado, *Lord Jesus Christ: Devotion to Jesus in Earliest Christianity* (Grand Rapids: Eerdmans, 2003), 123–25.

beings' internal sense, intellect, finds fulfillment in the contemplation of Christ's divinity, but their external sense finds fulfillment only in the contemplation of Christ's humanity, as Grosseteste quotes Pseudo-Augustine. Thus, if the beatific vision is supralapsarian, so is the incarnation, because only God incarnate gives human intellect and senses complete joy.[17]

I would not want to cast the argument purely in epistemological terms, as Grosseteste does, but for the rest, I believe this argument is correct. The eschaton brings humanity the enjoyment of full intimacy with God. For bodily, sensory beings this includes sensory contact. And eschatological humans will be bodily, sensory beings, as the Gospel depictions of Christ's resurrection attest. Therefore, if the eschatological goal of humanity is to enjoy God in the beatific vision, this vision should not be understood purely in terms of intellectual cognition, but should also imply sensory perception. However, this can only take place if God makes Godself present in bodily form.

To conceive of the beatific vision as being as much sensory as it is intellectual goes against the grain of traditional understanding of the eschatological enjoyment of God. Not that the tradition banned the sensory completely; but usually it takes second rank to the intellectual. A good example is, again, Augustine. In the same chapter of the *City of God* in which Augustine considers the impeccability of the eschatological world, he gives an extensive discussion of the bodies of the resurrected, including that of Jesus. At the end of the discussion he raises the question whether the resurrected will see God with their bodily eyes. It is true that "everyone will see the Christ of God"; he "has been seen in physical form, and he will be so seen when he comes to judge the living and the dead."[18] But Augustine continues that Paul's phrase "face to face," a key notion for the doctrine of the beatific vision, "does not compel us to believe that we shall see God by means of this [our] corporal face, with its corporal eyes. We shall see God by the spirit without any interruption."[19] Evidently, for Augustine the seeing of "the Christ of God" and the beatific vision are two different things, and it is the latter, not the former, which is the telos of human life.

17. Robert Grosseteste, *De Cessatione Legalium*, ed. Richard C. Dales and Edward B. King (London: Oxford University Press, 1986), 128.

18. Augustine, *De Civitate Dei* XXII.29 (*Concerning the City of God*, 1085).

19. Ibid.

In later writers we find the same distinctions. The beatific vision is to see the essence of God through the intellect, Aquinas holds.[20] In response to Grosseteste, Aquinas writes that while it might be true that both body and soul will be beatified in the eschaton, "since man is not through his body but through his soul, and the body is essential to man, in so far as it is perfected by the soul: it follows that man's beatitude does not consist chiefly otherwise than in an act of the soul, and passes from the soul on to the body by a kind of overflow." Nonetheless, Aquinas admits, "our bodies will have a certain beatitude from seeing God in sensible creatures: and especially in Christ's body."[21] Or, for another illustration, take the reformed scholastic theologian Antonius Waleaus. His beginning is promising: "We agree that God's glory will be most fully seen in Christ's human nature." But then he continues, "yet we grant that this actual vision, which is as it were the supreme basis of eternal life, will not be of bodily, but of the soul's eye."[22]

While my supralapsarian argument thus breaks with the standard explanation of the beatific vision in intellectual terms, I think it receives support from the biblical material on which the theological notion of the beatific vision is based. The idea goes back to a small number of texts that speak about the eschatological "seeing of God's face" or "meeting God face to face" (Matt. 5:8, 1 Cor. 13:12, Heb. 12:14, 1 John 3:2, Rev. 22:4). Both expressions have their roots in the Hebrew Bible: Jacob, Moses, and Gideon are all said to have met God face to face (Gen. 32:30, Exod. 33:11, Judg. 6:22) while the faithful go up to the temple to see God's face (Ps. 11:4–7, 42:2).[23] Important to the supralapsarian argument is that none of these uses in the Hebrew Bible suggests that seeing God's face implies an intellectual vision—quite the contrary; they are all used for a meeting with God through an embodied medium. The faithful in the Psalms do not go to the temple to enjoy God by their intellect, but to participate in a very sensual temple ritual. Jacob sees God face to face by wrestling with a

20. Aquinas, *Summa Theologiae* Ia, q.12, a.3, responsio.

21. Ibid., suppl., q. 92, a.2, ad 6.

22. Quoted in Heppe, *Reformed Dogmatics*, 707. See also Schmid, *Doctrinal Theology of the Evangelical Lutheran Church*, 661.

23. By then the term has become a *terminus technicus* for participation in the temple cult. See: F. Nötscher, *"Das Angesicht Gottes schauen" nach biblischer und babylonischer Auffassung* (Darmstadt: Wissenschaftliche Buchgesellschaft, 1969), 89. We find the same use in the rabbinical literature: Hermann L. Strack and Paul Billerbeck, *Kommentar zum Neuen Testament aus Talmud und Midrasch. Erster Band: Das Evangelium nach Matthäus* (München: C.H. Beck'sche Verlagsbuchhandlung, 1986), 206–7.

man. Gideon meets God face to face by engaging an angel sitting under the oak at Ophrah. Moses speaks with God face to face when the pillar of cloud comes to the tent of meeting. And, very tellingly, while Moses is thus said to have regular face-to-face meetings with God, at the same time he asks God to see God, just once, not through an intermediary but directly, as God is. God assents to Moses's request but does not allow him to see God's face, "for no one shall see me and live" (Exod. 33:20). Clearly, meeting God face to face does not mean seeing God immediately. If this is the background against which the New Testament writers speak of the eschatological vision of God, it seems wrong to interpret the New Testament references to the seeing of God as talking about a vision of solely, or even primarily, intellectual nature.[24] It would be better to read them as speaking of a seeing of God that is bound up with the person of Christ, as all other eschatological superabundance is. This would fit well with Pauline concepts of Christ as the image of God (1 Cor. 11:7, 2 Cor. 4:4, Col. 1:15) and John's notion that, while "no one has ever seen God, it is God the only Son, who is close to the Father's heart, who has made him known" (John 1:18; cf. 6:46, 14:9). And indeed, none of the New Testament passages that speak of the eschatological seeing of God suggests that they want to be understood differently from their Hebrew roots, intellectual rather than sensible.

Whether this means that, in fact, the eschatological seeing of God is purely a sensible seeing of the Son as the one in whom God has become visibly present, or whether it includes both an intellectual and a visible component, the supralapsarian does not have to decide.[25] All I need for my argument is that

24. Modern commentaries read the expression "face to face" as referring to personal intimacy with God, not to knowledge of primarily intellectual nature. See, for instance, on 1 Cor 13:12: C. K. Barrett, *The First Epistle to the Corinthians* (Peabody: Hendrickson, 1968), 306–7; Gordon D. Fee, *The First Epistle to the Corinthians* (Grand Rapids: Eerdmans, 1987), 647–49; Anthony C. Thiselton, *The First Epistle to the Corinthians: A Commentary on the Greek Text* (Grand Rapids: Eerdmans, 2000), 1069–71; on Matt. 5:8: John Nolland, *The Gospel of Matthew: A Commentary on the Greek Text* (Grand Rapids: Eerdmans, 2005), 204–5; on Rev. 22:4: David E. Aune, *Revelation 17–22* (Nashville: Thomas Nelson, 1998), 1179–81.

25. In this context, an important exegetical and theological question is whether it is impossible to "see God and live" (cf. Gen. 32:30; Exod. 33:20; Judg. 6:22) as a result of human sin (thus infralapsarian) or of divine ontological otherness (thus supralapsarian). In the latter case, the beatific vision cannot be otherwise than only a seeing of Christ: eschatological consummation does not abolish the ontological difference between God and creation. Commentators differ on the object of the eschatological seeing of God in the classical beatific vision passages: see, for example, on Heb. 12:14: William L. Lane, *Hebrews 9–13* (Dallas: Word Books, 1991), 451 (the object is God; with literature references to others), and Paul Ellingworth, *The Epistle to theHebrews: A Commentary on the Greek Text* (Grand Rapids: Eerdmans, 1993), 662–63 (the object might be Christ, or God and Christ); on 1 John 3:2: Raymond E. Brown, S.S., *The Epistles of John* (Garden City: Doubleday, 1982), 394–95 (the object is God, with literature references to others), and Stephen S. Smalley, *1,2,3 John* (Dallas: Word Books, 1984),

the sensible presence is decisively part of the biblical understanding of the beatific vision, a presence consummated in the incarnate One. If this is true, and if the beatific vision is the supralapsarian goal of the relationship between God and humanity, then so is the incarnation.

An Argument from Divine Friendship

"Show me your glory, I pray," said Moses to God (Exod. 33:18). Show me yourself, come to me not through a medium, but directly, show yourself to me as you are. Moses asks for a reason; because the Lord is his friend.

In the narrative, Moses is on his way with the people of Israel to Canaan. He just had a difficult conversation with God. The Lord had come to Moses in a pillar of cloud, as God used to do, and had talked with Moses "face to face, as one speaks with a friend" (Exod. 33:11). The Lord had told Moses to tell the people to break up their camp and leave for Canaan, and the Lord would send an angel before him. Moses had argued with the Lord: an angel won't do; you yourself will have to escort us. Three times he cajoles God, and finally the Lord caves in: "My presence will go with you, and I will give you rest" (33:14). The conversation thus seems to go to an end; but for Moses it is not enough. The public need is met; but not Moses's need. Moses, the religious-political leader of Israel, is satisfied; but not Moses, the friend, the lover of God. "Show me your glory" (33:18). And God goes along with it. Moses hides in the rock, and God strolls past in something like a body, and Moses gets a glimpse of God's exquisite beauty, a private showing of the Lord.[26]

"Show me your glory." For Moses, it is not enough that God will lead his way, that God will clear a path through the desert, or even that God communicates with him from a pillar of cloud. Moses desires God's own presence; for Moses is God's friend. And for friends, presence is what counts. Not just

145–47 (the object is Christ, with literature references to others); on Rev. 22:4: Aune, *Revelation 17–22* (the object is God, but Aune's reading suggests that God's inaccessibility is ontological, and God is therefore seen only indirectly), and G. K. Beale, *The Book of Revelation: A Commentary on the Greek Text* (Grand Rapids: Eerdmans, 1999), 1113–14 (the objects are God and Christ, who together occupy the throne).

26. Cf. for a reading of Moses's request as motivated by his personal love for God: Ellen F. Davis, *Getting Involved with God: Rediscovering the Old Testament* (Cambridge: Cowley, 2001), 153–59; and Jacqueline E. Lapsley, "Friendship with God? Moses and the Possibility of Covenantal Friendship," *Interpretation* 58 (2004): 117–29; see also Brevard S. Childs, *Exodus: A Commentary* (London: SCM Press, 1974), 596. For a different interpretation: Cornelis Houtman, *Exodus*, Vol. 3 (Leuven: Peeters, 2000), 700.

appropriate advice, not just a letter from afar, but the personal presence of the beloved. God understands; because Moses is God's friend.

There is a small but discernible line in the biblical narrative that conceives of the relationship between God and God's people as a form of friendship. Not only Moses, but also Abraham is called a friend of God (Isa. 41:8; see 2 Chron. 20:7, James 2:23). The rabbinical sources feel free to think of Israel as the friend of God and read Psalm 122:8 as God speaking to God's people: "For the sake of my relatives and friends I will say: 'Peace be within you.'"[27] Finally, Christ picks up on the friendship language and says to his disciples: "I do not call you servants any longer . . . but I have called you friends" (John 15:15).[28]

The theologically important point about conceiving of God's relating to humanity as a form of friendship is friendship's motivational structure. Friendship is motivated by a delight in and a love for the other. It enjoys the other's goodness and the goodness the relationship with the other embodies. Of course, friendship can be disrupted, disregarded, betrayed. All of these can motivate friends to seek forgiveness, reconciliation, healing of their relationship. The friendship itself is not based on the episodes of disruption and reconciliation, but on a deeper sense of love and delight. Therefore, when God calls Abraham, Moses, and the people of Israel God's friends, and when Jesus addresses his disciples as friends, not slaves, this defines these relationships as motivated not only by human sin and need for reconciliation, but by a deeper, preordinate sense of love. Of course, none of these relationships can be characterized as just delight and love. All of them are tainted by human failure and betrayal. The narratives of Abraham, Moses, and Israel are full of stories of distrust, disobedience, and unbelief. Jesus calls his disciples friends in the context of a conversation about his imminent death: "No one has greater love than this,

27. Hermann L. Strack and Paul Billerbeck, *Kommentar zum Neuen Testament aus Talmud und Midrasch. Zweiter Band: Das Evangelium nach Markus, Lukas und Johannes und die Apostelgeschichte* (München: C.H. Beck'sche Verlagsbuchhandlung, 1983), 564–65.

28. Lately, a lot of attention has been paid to the Hellenistic background of Jesus's use of the notion of friendship in John: see G. R. O'Day, "Jesus as Friend in the Gospel of John," *Interpretation* 58 (2004): 144–57; J. M. Ford, *Redeemer-Friend and Mother: Salvation in Antiquity and in the Gospel of John* (Minneapolis: Fortress, 1997); and Sharon H. Ringe, *Wisdom's Friends: Community and Christology in the Fourth Gospel* (Louisville: Westminster John Knox Press, 1999); but see Gustav Stählin in *Theological Dictionary of the New Testament* IX, ed. Gerhard Kittel and Gerhard Friedrich (Grand Rapids: Eerdmans, 1974), 151–54. However, I believe a case can be made to read the Johannine use of concepts of friendship against the background of the sparse but present use of such concepts in the Hebrew Bible and literature of the Second Temple period (see Ringe, *Wisdom's Friends*, 69–75).

to lay down one's life for one's friends" (John 15:13). But while the death is motivated by the friendship, the friendship is not motivated by death. Jesus becomes his disciples' savior because he is their friend; not the other way around.

If this is true, it would be an impoverishment to read all Jesus's actions, all his words, and finally, his very presence, as motivated by human sin and the need for reconciliation. To do so would be to lose sight of other feelings and emotions, of a deeper layer of motivations that might be at play in the relationship between God and human beings. One of these motivations, I suggest, is laid bare in the story of Moses: Moses, the friend of God, longs for the visible, tangible presence of the Lord, and the Lord understands the longing of God's friend, and makes Godself available to him. Could we not read the incarnation as God's final and permanent answer to humanity's longing, the ultimate availability of the Lord, no longer in a pillar of cloud, no longer in a momentary appearance of dazzling glory, but in a human form, with a human face, visible, tangible, audible?

It is, I believe, no wonder that it is especially in the Johaninne literature, presented as the work of the disciple whom Jesus loved, that the visibility, the tangibility, the embodiment of Jesus is emphasized. In him the Word became flesh and tabernacled among us (John 1:14); he is the one who made known the God no one had ever seen (1:18), who makes the Father visible (14:9), who can be touched when resurrected (20:17, 20:27), and of whom the first letter of John says: "We declare to you what was from the beginning, what we have heard, what we have seen with our eyes, what we have looked at and touched with our hands, concerning the word of life" (1 John 1:1). It is a proclamation of one who laid down his life for his friends, for certain, but also more than that, the proclamation of God having become present to God's friends in human form.

It is also by this reading of the incarnation that its permanence can be explained. If the incarnation only happened as a function of God's reconciling action, there would be no need for a continued bodily existence of Christ after crucifixion and death. The sacrifice had been made; life had been laid down, atonement given—in whatever form conceived—and the relationship between God and humanity restored. There would have been no need for a bodily resurrection; resurrection morning and ascension day could collapse into one event. That this did not happen, that Christ did return in bodily form to his friends the disciples and went up in embodied form on a victory parade into heaven, suggests that more is at stake.

Here is, therefore, a third supralapsarian argument: there is a discernible line in both the Hebrew Bible and the New Testament which suggests that God's ultimate goal is to be a friend of his creatures. The more deeply friends are involved, the more available they make themselves to each other. The incarnation can be interpreted as God making Godself ultimately available, by offering the friendship in a mode previously not present—visible, tangible, audible in human form, and with a human face. This friendship is not based on the divine desire to reconcile estranged humanity; it is the other way around—the divine desire to reconcile strayed humanity is based on, and therefore logically follows, divine friendship. Therefore, if the incarnation is the fullest expression of this divine friendship, the incarnation also logically does not follow human estrangement and divine reconciliation, but precedes it—in other words, is supralapsarian.

8

Epilogue: Consummation, Creation, and Redemption

In the preceding chapter, I presented three arguments for supralapsarianism. The first started from the superabundance of the eschaton over the proton, and I argued that since, on the one hand, the eschaton is essentially bound up with Christ, and, on the other hand, it would be problematic to say that the eschatological superabundance can somehow be contingent upon sin, we have to say that Christ himself is not contingent upon sin. Second, I looked at one aspect of the superabundance of the eschaton, the vision of God, which is said to be that for which we were created, and I argued that since such a vision is to allow us to fully enjoy God, and for embodied human beings full enjoyment of God implies enjoyment not only with our minds but also our senses, our eyes and ears and touch, full enjoyment of God implies that we will be able to see God, hear God, embrace God—but this can happen only if God is incarnate, in the flesh. Finally, I argued that in scripture there is a small but discernible line that speaks of God's desire to be friends with God's creatures, and that in this friendship God comes as close to his friends as God can, that is, by becoming humanly present himself.

These three arguments together amount to an eschatological vision: a vision of lively, intimate, abundant enjoyment of the incarnate Lord as the goal of creation. In this epilogue I want to compare this vision to some of the other supralapsarian approaches, and tease out its implications for our spiritual life and eschatological imagination.

Speculation

The first thing to point out is how my approach differs from most traditional arguments for supralapsarian Christology. Traditionally, the matter at stake in supralapsarian Christology is formulated as a positive answer to this question: "Would God have become human if human beings had not sinned?" This is how the medievals formulated the matter and how it has been discussed for centuries. Note the nature of this question: it is a counterfactual. It talks about a situation that did not obtain—human beings never sinned—and asks what God would have done under those hypothetical circumstances. Because of this counterfactual way of raising the issue, supralapsarianism's opponents accused the supralapsarians of engaging in nothing more than speculation, and that, the infralapsarians believed, was a bad thing. As John Calvin, one of these opponents, says: in speculating about what would have happened if humans had not sinned, you are trying to get away from the fact that you actually did sin and you only show that you are not "content with this very Christ who was given to us as the price of our redemption."[1] That is serious criticism. Is it indeed the case that supralapsarians have trouble accepting that they are sinners and are in need of redemption, and that therefore they would rather speculate about a hypothetical situation in which neither sin nor redemption obtained? Maybe such criticism applies to those who discuss this issue in the traditional hypothetical form, although I doubt it. But note that my arguments do not concern such a hypothetical situation. I do not ask what would have happened if we had not sinned; I ask about the incarnation as it happened, about the Christ as we have him; and my point is that the incarnation as it happened gives us so much, is so rich in gifts of divine friendship and intimacy, that it cannot be explained as only a divine countermeasure against sin. There is no speculation here about a hypothetical situation; there is no discontent with the Christ as he is; rather, I am

1. John Calvin, *Institutiones* II.xii.5, quoted from *Institutes of the Christian Religion*, Vol. 1, ed. John T. McNeill, trans. Ford Lewis Battles (Philadelphia, Westminster Press, 1960), 469.

so impressed with the Christ as he is that I argue that the category of redemption is not rich enough to explain the wonder of his presence.

Supralapsarian Spirituality

Rather than an exercise in speculation, I hold that a supralapsarian understanding actually leads to a deepened spiritual relationship with Christ. In an understanding governed by the infralapsarian logic of creation, redemption, and consummation, our relationship to Christ is triggered by a problem. The relationship is in its origin therapeutic: Christ is the troubleshooter. The relationship is therefore by nature functional. The believer needs Christ for something. But what happens when the problem is solved? What basis is there for a continuing relationship? There seems to be none. The believer may grow in her understanding of herself and her relationship with God. She may come to see herself as a forgiven creature, destined for an eschatological future in which the stain of sin is permanently removed, sin's guilt and shame permanently cast behind God's back (Isa. 38:17). But in relationship to Christ, there never is such a future. Since, by infralapsarian logic, the believer's relationship to him is purely functional, it is a relationship permanently defined in terms of sinner and Savior, problem and solution, sickness and medicine; and, once the problem of sin is removed, the basis for the relationship is removed as well. For a faith so centered on the person of Christ as Christianity is, this is a serious theological, spiritual, and psychological problem. But in my supralapsarian understanding of Christ we do not need sin in order to benefit from the incarnation; we do not need sin in order to relate to Christ. If the intimate presence of God in Christ is the goal of all things, all aspects of our lives are related to him. It is here, I believe, that supralapsarianism has an important contribution to make.

In this respect, my approach differs from Schleiermacher's. In my supralapsarian narrative, consummation precedes redemption, and not the other way around. I reject the notion of *felix culpa*, which underlies Schleiermacher's approach. However, I believe this point is important not only theologically but also spiritually. One of the consequences of the logic of both infralapsarianism and Schleiermacher is that by such logic, in preaching Christ we first need to introduce people to "sin" before we can introduce them to Christ. We first need to tell them that they have a problem before we can tell them what the solution is. The problems with this are manifold, especially in a time such as ours in which the sense of sin is minimal. Moreover, it leaves us open to the misunderstanding that the first and most important thing the Christian faith has to say about human beings is that they are sinners. And of course, that is not the case—the first and most important thing the Christian faith has to say about human beings is that they are offered the love of God. My proposal allows us exactly to say that. In my proposal, we do not have to preach sin before we can preach Christ; we can preach Christ as the offer of love and friendship with God; and it is thereafter, in the light of that offer of friendship and love, that human beings discover themselves as sinners.

The Recipient of the Gift of Incarnation

In preceding chapters, I introduced a distinction between incarnation as a gift to human nature and as a gift to human persons that is not often acknowledged by supralapsarian writers. On the one hand, that human nature is the recipient of the gift of the incarnation is implied by those writers who hold that by assuming human nature, God is able to change the ontological status of humanity from the inside out. Such a view presupposes that in the incarnation God assumes a human nature that is ours, a nature that God will now change for the better, a presupposition which in turn is premised on the unity of human nature. On the other hand, that human persons are the recipients of the gift of incarnation is implied by those writers who hold that by assuming a human nature, God makes Godself available for interpersonal interaction, from one human being to the other. Such a view presupposes that in the incarnation God takes up a human nature like ours, a nature that allows God to be present to us in human form. This presupposition is in turn premised on the similarity of individual human natures.

As I argued before, the first view is problematic, first of all for its ontological account of the unity of all humanity, and second, for the fact that it does not respect the "over-againstness" between the Word made flesh and our human natures. It has the relationship between the incarnate One and other human beings governed by the logic of assumption, but assumption is a category which implies that there is no over-againstness between the assumer and the assumed. If the Word were to try to make us participate in God's grace by assuming our human natures, he would no longer be God-with-us, since the us, the ultimate subjects of our natures, would no longer exist—what is assumed by the Word has no person of its own but is personified by the Word himself. Therefore, we should hold that the incarnation is a gift to human persons—the Word, by assuming a human nature, makes God present over-against us: God visible, tangible, and audible in our midst. It is exactly this understanding of the incarnation that is expressed in my supralapsarian arguments.

Supralapsarian Eschatology

Finally, in my arguments I speak about the eschatological seeing of God with our eyes, touching God with our hands, hearing God with our ears—and this because I read both Christ's and our eschatological resurrection as events that concern real bodies. My arguments thus both presuppose and lend support to ideas of eschatological continuation of agency and eschatological embodiment. With both positions I disagree strongly with some of my conversation partners. Concerning the eschatological continuation of agency, I resist the popular twentieth-century understanding of the eschaton as the conservation of the lived life—as, for example, exemplified by Barth. Concerning eschatological embodiment, I disagree with all those who see space and time as imperfections of our current reality—as, for example, Dorner holds. I argue that consummated creation is embodied creation. Where there is embodiment, there is space; and where there is spatial action, there is time. I do not look at space and time suspiciously, as if they were part of an unredeemable reality that will be left behind once the new aeon breaks through. They themselves are ushered into this new reality, allowing it to be what it is: the consummation, not of lived lives, not of times completed, but of living, acting, embodied human beings. Certainly, space and time are expressions of a limitation. Spacial entities are not omnipresent but limited to one location. Temporal beings are not eternal, but know of a past that is gone and a future to look forward to. But these limitations are not particular to our current existence; they are essential to being created. We are in time because we once were not; we are localized because our being is not without end.

Nonetheless, eschatological consummation does not leave space and time untouched. Interestingly, whereas most theologians' eschatological speculations have to do with the transformation of time, the resurrection stories seem to suggest more about the transformation of space. The resurrected Christ is able to appear suddenly in the midst of his disciples (note that the texts nowhere suggest that he comes through the walls or door, as popular understanding has it). Likewise, he suddenly vanishes from the sight of the men at Emmaus. Sometimes he is recognized; but sometimes his face does not betray who he is. He walks with his disciples out to Bethany, and a cloud comes and withdraws him from their sight. And if my reading of the resurrection and ascension stories is correct, the embodied Christ is, right now, somewhere—he has a space. Resurrection space is thus more than the three-dimensional space we are currently acquainted with. Three-dimensionality is not enough to contain the resurrected One. What this suggests, I believe, is that we should not imagine eschatological consummation as the end of space but as its expansion. A good illustration of the eschatological imagination I propose is found in Luco J. van den Brom's *Divine Presence in the World.*[2] In the context of a discussion of divine omnipresence, Van den Brom develops a mathematical account of how we could understand the space to which Christ ascended. Van den Brom makes use of the notion of "more dimensionality." Mathematically, it is possible that reality contains more than the three dimensions we are visibly acquainted with. There might be a fourth, a fifth, or even a much higher number of dimensions. In this more-dimensional reality, our three-dimensional reality can be described as a subsystem of a larger system. We could now think of the resurrected and ascended Christ as participating in a greater reality than our three-dimensional reality. But since our reality is a subsystem of Christ's reality, our reality is still directly accessible to Christ. In fact, in such a model the puzzling aspects of Christ's appearances make perfect sense. To see this, we can think of our three-dimensional reality as itself encompassing one- and two- dimensional reality. Imagine a two-dimensional world with two-dimensional entities: for example, this sheet of paper and the letters printered thereupon. Also, imagine that these two-dimensional entities are gifted with consciousness. Such creatures are aware of before and after, and left and right, but not of above and below. Imagine now a three-dimensional creature entering such a two-dimensional reality from above: for example, your finger, moving toward the sheet of paper until it touches it. The two-dimensional

2. Luco J. van den Brom, *Divine Presence in the World: A Critical Analysis of the Notion of Divine Omnipresence* (Kampen: Kok Pharos, 1993), 266–316.

creatures would not be aware of your approaching finger. But as soon as it touches the sheet of paper, that is, enters their reality, your finger would be "suddenly in their midst." Your finger could move around on the paper: these creatures would be aware of this. But once you move your finger away from the paper, these creatures would not know where it was going. It would be "taken out of their sight." It would not imply, of course, that your finger had left space altogether. It had only left the space of which these creatures were aware. This also would not mean that their space was no longer accessible to them. This would not even mean that your finger was far away from their space. It could be very close by; it would just not be visibly present to them.

We can think about Christ's ascension along similar lines. No longer is he visibly present; but that does not mean he has left space altogether. Instead, as the firstborn of a new creation, he has entered a wider, more-dimensional reality, a reality where he has gone to prepare a place for us, and from where he will come again and take us to himself, so that where he is, there we may be also (John 14:3).

When that happens, time will be consummated as well. It will not be ended, but it will be healed and renewed. We will always be temporal beings, with a past that is gone and a future to look forward to. But our past will be reconciled—our sins judged and forgiven, the wrongs acknowledged and the wronged vindicated, and friends and enemies will have entered the world of love in mutual embrace.[3] And our future will be unending—the unending exploration of the inexhaustible riches of God, the joy of the heavenly banquet, and the unending delight in the presence of Christ, who is

> The image of the invisible God,
> the firstborn of all creation;
> for in him all things were created,
> in heaven and on earth,
> things visible and invisible,
> whether thrones or dominions or rules or powers—
> all things have been created through him and for him.
> He himself is before all things,

3. Cf. Miroslav Volf, "The Final Reconciliation: Reflections on a Social Dimension of the Eschatological Transition," *Modern Theology* 16 (2000): 91–113. See also for the notion of time in the eschaton, John Polkinghorne, *The God of Hope and the End of the World* (New Haven: Yale University Press, 2002), 117–22, 143–44.

and in him all things hold together.
He is the head of the body, the church;
he is the beginning,
the firstborn from the dead,
so that he might come to have first place in everything.
For in him all the fullness was pleased to dwell,
and through him to reconcile all things to him,
whether things on earth or in heaven,
by making peace through the blood of his cross. (Col. 1:15–20)

Bibliographical Appendix: The Genealogy of Supralapsarianism

While this is a constructive and not a historical study, I would like to provide future students of supralapsarianism with some bibliographical help on the genealogy of supralapsarian Christology. There is a deplorable lack of research on this topic, with only a series of partial studies like book chapters and essays sketching some of supralapsarian Christology's history, even while this history stretches in a continuous tradition from the eleventh to the twenty-first centuries.[1]

The first author we know who explicitly discussed the issues of supralapsarian Christology is Rupert of Deutz (c. 1075–1129/30). Rupert is also responsible for the counterfactual formulation under which most subsequent premodern authors would discuss the issue: "whether the Son of God . . . would have become human or not even

1. See Brooke Foss Westcott, "The Gospel of Creation," in: *The Epistles of St. John: The Greek Text with Notes and Essays* (London: Macmillan, 1883), 286–328; Fr. Chrysostome, O.F.M., "La Rédemption est-elle le motif de l'incarnation?" *La France franciscain* 14 (1931): 113–67; J. M. Bissen, "La tradition sur la predestination absolue de Jésus-Christ du VIIe au XIVe siècles," *La France franciscain* 22 (1939): 9–34; J.-F. Bonnefoy, "La Question hypothétique *Utrum si Adam non peccesset . . .* au XIIIe siècle," *Revista Esponola de Teologi* 14 (1954): 327–68; M. Mückshoff, "Die mariologische Prädestination im Denken der franziskanischen Theologie," *Franziskanische Studien* 39 (1957): 290–361; and the historical essays in Nico den Bok and Guus Labooy, eds., *Wat God bewoog mens te worden: Gedachten over de incarnatie* (Zoetermeer: Boekencentrum, 2003).

if sin . . . had not intervened."[2] We do not know whether or by whom the issue was discussed after Rupert. However, Robert Grosseteste (c. 1168–1253), chancellor of Oxford University, wrote extensively on the issue and reports a handful of arguments for supralapsarianism, seemingly not of his own making but collected from other literature.[3] This suggests that the issue received widespread attention in the twelfth century. After Grosseteste, most medieval theologians took up the issue, with people like Bonaventure[4] and Aquinas[5] defending the infralapsarian cause, and Alexander of Hales,[6] Albert the Great,[7] and Duns Scotus[8] defending supralapsarianism. Scotus's approach is decisively different from those of his fellow medieval theologians in that he[9] does

2. Quoted in Westcott, *The Epistles of St. John*, 290. Cf. John H. van Ingen, *Rupert of Deutz* (Berkeley: University of California Press, 1983), 252–60.

3. For the text, see Robert Grosseteste, *De Cessatione Legalium*, ed. Richard C. Dales and Edward B. King (London: Oxford University Press, 1986), 119–32. For a discussion, see James McEvoy, "The Absolute Predestination of Christ in the Theology of Robert Grosseteste," in *Sapientiae Doctrina: Mélanges de théologie et de literature médiévales offerts à Dom Hildebrand Bascour O.S.B.* (Leuven, Abbaye du Mont César, 1980), 212–30; James McEvoy, *Robert Grosseteste* (Oxford: Oxford University Press, 2000), 127–30; James R. Ginther, *Master of the Sacred Page: A Study of the Theology of Robert Grosseteste, ca. 1229/30–1235* (Aldershot: Ashgate, 2004), 121–28.

4. *Sententiae* III, d.20, a.1, qq. 2, 5, 6. Bonaventure is an interesting case in the infralapsarian–supralapsarian debate. His theological emphasis on the primacy of Christ tends strongly toward supralapsarianism, and in his discussion of supralapsarian arguments he concedes as much. However, in the end he decides for infralapsarianism since he believes it inflames the faithful more than supralapsarianism. Cf. A. Gerken, "Bonaventuras Konvenienzgründe für die Inkarnation des Sohnes," *Wissenschaft und Weisheit* 23 (1960): 131–46; A. Gerken, *Theologie des Wortes: Das Verhältnis von Schöpfung und Inkarnation bei Bonaventura* (Düsseldorf: Patmos, 1963), 131–46; Marilyn McCord Adams, *What Sort of Human Nature? Medieval Philosophy and the Systematics of Christology* (Milwaukee: Marquette University Press, 1999), 24–28.

5. Thomas Aquinas, *Summa Theologiae* IIIa, q.1, a.3.

6. Alexander of Hales, *Summa Theologiae* III, q.3, a.13.

7. Albert the Great, *Sententiae* III, d.20, a.4.

8. Duns Scotus, *Ordinatio* III, d.7, q.3, and suppl. D. 19. Both texts are published and translated in Damian McElrath, *Franciscan Christology: Selected Texts, Translations, and Introductory Essays* (St. Bonaventure: Franciscan Institute, 1980), 146–52.

9. There is a host of literature on Scotus's supralapsarian Christology: Karl M. Balić, "Duns Skotus' Lehre über Christi Prädestination im Lichte der neuesten Forschungen," in *Wissenschaft und Weisheit* 3 (1936): 19–35; Werner Dettloff, "Die Geistigkeit des hl. Franziskus in der Christologie des Johannes Duns Scotus," *Wissenschaft und Weisheit* 22 (1959): 17–28; Agathon Kandler, "Die Heilsdynamik im Christusbild des Johannes Duns Scotus," *Wissenschaft und Weisheit* 27 (1964): 175–96, 28 (1965): 1–14; Johannes Schlageter, "Das Menschsein Jesu Christi in seiner zentralen Bedeutung für Schöpfung und Geschichte bei Johannes Duns Scotus und heute," *Wissenschaft und Weisheit* 47 (1984): 23–36; Werner Dettloff, "Die Christozentrische Konzeption des Johannes Duns Scotus als Ansatz für eine Theologie der Welt," *Wissenschaft und Weisheit* 48 (1985): 182–96; Giovanni Iammarrone, "Wert und Grenzen der Christologie des Johannes Duns Scotus in heutigen Zeit," *Wissenschaft und Weisheit* 52 (1989): 1–20; M. Burger, *Personalität im Horizont absoluter Prädestination. Untersuchungen zur Christologie des Johannes Duns Scotus und ihrer Rezeption in modernen theologischen Ansätzen* (Münster: Aschendorff, 1994); Nico den Bok, "Liefde op zoek naar een geliefde: Over persoon-zijn in

not present supralapsarianism as an argument concerning a counterfactual situation, but rather argues that Christ's election has priority over ours. Since election is supralapsarian (as Scotus argues), so is the incarnation. Later generations had difficulty distinguishing Scotus's approach from the counterfactual approach and reverted to the latter. After the thirteenth century the issue became a point of controversy between Thomists and Scotists.[10] The writings of the reformers and the Protestant confessional documents are all infralapsarian in nature. In part, this was a consequence of the strong emphasis on topics of sin and reconciliation in their theology. In all likelihood, another factor was that in their time the supralapsarian cause was taken up by some writers who were theologically rather suspect, like Andreas Osiander, Michael Servetus, and Faustus Socinus.[11] The reformer John Calvin, however, left his followers a complicated heritage. He rejected the notion that the incarnation is not contingent upon sin, but he did believe that Christ's mediatorship is not contingent upon sin.[12] This led both to an almost unanimous rejection among the Reformed of the supralapsarian position on the incarnation[13] and to

---

Augustijns-franciscaanse zin, belicht vanuit christologie en verkiezingsleer," *Kerk en Theologie* 49 (1998): 184–98; Nico den Bok, "Geven om de ander: Scotus' visie op God's liefde, verkiezing en menswording als moment in de geschiedenis van het volheidsbeginsel," *Bijdragen* 60 (1999): 25–53; Henri Veldhuis, "De hermeneutische betekenis van de supralapsarische christologie van Johannes Duns Scotus," *Bijdragen* 61 (2000): 152–74; Herbert Schneider, ed., *Menschwerdung Gottes—Hoffnung des Menschen* (Kevelaer: Butzon and Bercker, 2000); Nico den Bok, "De twee klassieke motiveringen van de menswording: Anselmus en Scotus," in *Wat God bewoog mens te worden*, eds. den Bok and Labooy, 38–58.

10. P. Kreling, "Het motief der menschwording," *Studia Catholica* 15 (1939): 89–101.

11. Cf., as noted earlier, Calvin, who rejected supralapsarian Christology in discussion with Andreas Osiander: *Institutiones* ii.XII.5; John Calvin, *Institutes of the Christian Religion*, ed. John T. McNeil (Philadelphia: Westminster Press, 1960), 469. Calvin writes against Osiander's supralapsarian tract *An filius Dei fuerit incarnandus, si peccatum non introivisset in mundum, item: De imagine Dei, quid sit* (1950), critical edition in Andreas Osiander, *Gesamtausgabe Band 9: Schriften und Briefe 1549 bis August 1551*, ed. Gerhard Müller and Gottfried Seebaß (Gütersloh: Gütersloher Verlagshaus, 1994), 450–91. For Servetus and Socinus as supralapsarians, see Westcott, *The Epistles of St. John*, 315–16.

12. Calvin, *Institutiones* II.xii.1 (*Institutes*, 465). Cf. for the most recent study on this issue: Stephen Edmondson, *Calvin's Christology* (Cambridge: Cambridge University Press, 2004), esp. 143–51. Unfortunately, Edmondson does not further explore Calvin's relationship to Bonaventure, although their systematic positions seem rather similar.

13. See, for instance, Heinrich Heppe, *Reformed Dogmatics*, rev. and ed. Ernst Bizer (San Francisco: Harper Collins, 1956), 448, and Francis Turretin, *Institutio theologiae elencticae* II.xiii.iii (*Institutes of Elenctic Theology*, Vol. 2, trans. George Musgrave Giger, ed. James T. Dennison Jr. [Philipsburg: P&R Publishing, 1994], 299). The only exception I am aware of is the Dutch theologian Alexander Comrie (1706–74), who gives a supralapsarian argument in the context of his discussion of predestination, very similar to Duns Scotus (see: A. Vos, "Supralapsarisme en de gereformeerde theologie," in *Wat God bewoog mens te worden*, ed. den Bok and Labooy, 192–96 [175–97]).

an extensive discussion about Christ's mediatorship. If Calvin was right, then what is the nature of Christ's supralapsarian, but nonincarnate, mediatorship?[14] On the Roman Catholic side, the infralapsarian approach had taken the upper hand with the Thomistic orientation of post-Trentian theology, although supralapsarianism stayed alive among the Jesuits.[15] The seventeenth and eighteenth centuries were thus the low tide of supralapsarian thinking. Interestingly, the nineteenth century brought a recovery in popularity for supralapsarian Christology. A supralapsarian incarnation was central to both Hegel's and Schleiermacher's theology.[16] The next generation of theologians counted a number of supralapsarians, in Germany,[17] England,[18] and the Netherlands,[19] as well as Scandinavia.[20] For a genealogical study, this would raise a series of interesting questions: what caused the popularity of supralapsarianism in this time period? Was it inspired by Hegel, or Schleiermacher, or both? How do Hegel's and Schleiermacher's Christologies relate; and what influenced their turn to supralapsarianism? In the twentieth century, supralapsarianism's popularity continued, both on the Protestant and on the Roman

14. See A. Kuyper, *De Vleeschwording des Woords* (Amsterdam: J.A. Wormser, 1887), 23–26.

15. Cf. the discussions in Rudolph Haubst, *Vom Sinn der Menschwerdung* (München: Max Hueber Verlag, 1969). For Jesuit supralapsarianism, see Francisco Suárez, *Theologiae Summa*, II.v.ii–vi.

16. For Hegel, cf. Eugene TeSelle, *Christ in Context: Divine Purpose and Human Possibility* (Philadelphia: Fortress Press, 1975), 86–105; for Schleiermacher, see chapter 2, this volume.

17. For a discussion, see I. A. Dorner, *History of the Development of the Doctrine of the Person of Christ*, Vol. III (Edinburgh: T and T Clark, 1878), 236–48. Dorner mentions, among others, Karl Immanuel Nitzsch, Richard Rothe, and Theodor A. Liebner. For Dorner himself, see chapter 3, this volume. The turn to supralapsarianism was not only a Protestant affair; see M. J. Scheeben, *Gesammelte Schriften*, Vol. VI.2: *Handbuch der katholischen Dogmatik*, Vol. V.2, 2nd ed., ed. C. Feckes (Freiburg: Herder, 1954), 221–26.

18. For example, Brooke Foss Westcott, bishop of Durham, whose supralapsarian arguments are discussed in chapter 6, this volume; and F. D. Maurice. See F. D. Maurice, *Theological Essays* (London: Macmillan, 1871), 192f; F. D. Maurice, *The Doctrine of Sacrifice* (London: Macmillan, 1893), 192. Based on the dissertation by Lewis B. Smedes, *The Incarnation: Trends in Modern Anglican Thought* (Kampen: Kok, 1953), Charles Gore is also regularly mentioned as a proponent of supralapsarian Christology (e.g., by B. Wentsel, *God en mens verzoend: Incarnatie, verzoening, koninkrijk van God*, dogmatiek deel 3b [Kampen: Kok, 1991], 176), but Gore nowhere explicitly endorses supralapsarianism. Cf. James Carpenter, *Gore: A Study in Liberal Catholic Thought* (London: Faith Press, 1959), 173–76.

19. Daniel Chantepie de la Saussaye, *Verzameld Werk*, deel II (Zoetermeer: Boekencentrum, 2000), 83–84, 177–81, 216, 220–21, 270–74; J. J. van Oosterzee, *Christelijke Dogmatiek* II (Utrecht: Kemink, 1870), 107; J. J. van Oosterzee, *Christologie* III (Rotterdam: Van der Meer en Verbruggen, 1861), 85; J. H. Gunning, *Blikken in de Openbaring*, derde deel (Amsterdam: H. Höveker, 1868), 132.

20. H. Martensen, *Christian Dogmatics: A Compendium of the Doctrines of Christianity* (Edinburgh: T and T Clark, 1898), 260–63.

Catholic side of the theological spectrum. Karl Barth put supralapsarianism at the center of Reformed theology,[21] followed by the Lutherans Wolfgang Pannenberg[22] and Robert W. Jenson,[23] and the Reformed theologian Jürgen Moltmann.[24] On the Roman Catholic side, supralapsarianism had proponents in Karl Rahner,[25] Michael Schmauss,[26] and Hans Küng.[27]

21. On Barth, see chapters 4 and 5, this volume.

22. Wolfgang Pannenberg, *Systematic Theology*, Vol. 2 (Grand Rapids: Eerdmans, 1991), 24–25, 63–66.

23. Robert W. Jenson, *Systematic Theology, Volume 1: The Triune God* (New York: Oxford University Press, 1997), 72–74.

24. Jürgen Moltmann, *The Trinity and the Kingdom: The Doctrine of God* (Minneapolis: Fortress Press, 1993), 114–18.

25. Among many places: Karl Rahner, "Current Problems in Christology," in *Theological Investigations* I (Baltimore: Helicon Press, 1961), 164–65 [149–200]; Karl Rahner, "On the Theology of the Incarnation," *Theological Investigations* IV (Baltimore: Helicon Press, 1966), 116–17 [105–20].

26. Michael Schmauss, *Dogma 1: God in Revelation* (New York: Sheed and Ward, 1968), 47–52.

27. Hans Küng, *Justification: The Doctrine of Karl Barth and a Catholic Reflection* (Louisville: Westminster John Knox Press, 2004 [1964]).

Bibliography

Adams, Marilyn McCord. "The Metaphysical Size Gap." *Sewanee Theological Review* 47 (2004): 129–44.

Adams, Marilyn McCord. "The Primacy of Christ." *Sewanee Theological Review* 47 (2004): 164–80.

Adams, Marilyn McCord. *What Sort of Human Nature? Medieval Philosophy and the Systematics of Christology*. Milwaukee: Marquette University Press, 1999.

Adams, Robert Merrihew. "Faith and Religious Knowledge." In *The Cambridge Companion to Friedrich Schleiermacher*, edited by Jacqueline Mariña, 35–52. Cambridge: Cambridge University Press, 2005.

Adams, Robert Merrihew. *Finite and Infinite Goods: A Framework for Ethics*. New York: Oxford University Press, 1999.

Adams, Robert Merrihew. *Leibniz: Determinist, Theist, Idealist*. New York: Oxford University Press, 1994.

Adams, Robert Merrihew. "Schleiermacher on Evil." *Faith and Philosophy* 13 (1996): 563–83.

Augustine. *Concerning the City of God against the Pagans*. New translation by Henry Bettenson, with an introduction by John O'Meara. London: Penguin Books, 1984.

Augustine. *The Trinity*. Introduction, translation, and notes by Edmund Hill. Edited by John E. Rotelle. New York: New City Press, 1991.

Aune, David E. *Revelation 17–22*. Nashville: Thomas Nelson, 1998.

Axt-Piscalar, Christine. *Der Grund des Glaubens: Eine theologiegeschichtliche Untersuchung zum Verhältnis von Glaube und Trinität in der Theologie Isaak August Dorners*. Tübingen: J.C.B. Mohr (Paul Siebeck), 1990.

Backhaus, Knut. "'Licht von Licht'—Die Präexistenz Christi im Hebräerbrief." In *Gottes ewiger Sohn: Die Präexistenz Christi*, edited by Ruldolf Laufen, 95–114. Paderborn: Ferdinand Schöningh, 1997.

Baillie, John. *The Idea of Revelation in Recent Thought*. New York: Columbia University Press, 1956.

Balić, Karl M. "Duns Skotus' Lehre über Christi Prädestination im Lichte der neuesten Forschungen." *Wissenschaft und Weisheit* 3 (1936): 19–35.

Barrett, C. K. *The First Epistle to the Corinthians*. Peabody: Hendrickson, 1968.

Barth, Karl. *Church Dogmatics*, Vols. I–IV. Edinburgh: T and T Clark, 1956–70.

Barth, Karl. *The Göttingen Dogmatics: Instruction in the Christian Religion*, Vol. I. Edited by Hannelotte Reiffen. Translated by Geoffrey W. Bromiley. Grand Rapids, MI: Eerdmans, 1991.

Barth, Karl. *The Humanity of God*. Translated by John Newton Thomas. Atlanta: John Knox Press, 1976.

Barth, Karl. *Kirchliche Dogmatik*, Vols. I–IV. Zurich: EVZ–Verlag, 1932–67.

Barth, Karl. *Protestant Theology in the Nineteenth Century: Its Background and History*. Translated by Brian Cozens and John Bowden. Grand Rapids, MI: Eerdmans, 2002.

Bavinck, H. *Gereformeerde Dogmatiek*. Seventh unaltered edition. Kampen: Kok, 1998.

Bavinck, Herman. *In the Beginning: Foundations of Creation Theology*. Edited by John Bolt. Translated by John Vriend. Grand Rapids, MI: Baker Books, 1999.

Beale, G. K. *The Book of Revelation: A Commentary on the Greek Text*. Grand Rapids, MI: Eerdmans, 1999.

Beisser, Friedrich. *Schleiermachers Lehre von Gott; dargestellt nach seiner Reden und seiner Glaubenslehre*. Göttingen: Vandenhoeck und Ruprecht, 1970.

Berkouwer, G. C. *The Triumph of Grace in the Theology of Karl Barth*. Translated by Harry R. Boer. Grand Rapids, MI: Eerdmans, 1956.

Bissen, J. M. "La tradition sur la predestination absolue de Jésus-Christ du VIIe au XIVe siècles." *La France franciscain* 22 (1939): 9–34.

Bok, Nico den. "De twee klassieke motiveringen van de menswording; *Anselmus en Scotus*." In *Wat God bewoog mens te worden: Gedachten over de Incarnatie*, edited by Nico den Bok and Guus Labooy, 38–58. Zoetermeer: Boekencentrum, 2003.

Bok, Nico den. "Geven om de ander: Scotus' visie op God's liefde, verkiezing en menswording als moment in de geschiedenis van het volheidsbeginsel." *Bijdragen* 60 (1999): 25–53.

Bok, Nico den. "Liefde op zoek naar een geliefde: Over persoon-zijn in Augustijns-Franciscaanse zin, belicht vanuit christologie en verkiezingsleer." *Kerk en Theologie* 49 (1998): 184–98.

Bok, Nico den, and Guus Labooy, eds. *Wat God bewoog mens te worden: Gedachten over de Incarnatie*. Zoetermeer: Boekencentrum, 2003.

Bonnefoy, J.-F. "La Question hypothétique *Utrum si Adam non peccesset*... au XIIIe siècle." *Revista Esponola de Teologi* 14 (1954): 327–68.

Boyer, Bruce L. "Schleiermacher on the Divine Causality." *Religious Studies* 22 (1986): 113–23.

Brink, Gijsbert van den. "Descartes, Modalities, and God." *International Journal for Philosophy of Religion* 33 (1993): 1–15.

Brom, Luco J. van den. *Divine Presence in the World: A Critical Analysis of the Notion of Divine Omnipresence.* Kampen: Kok Pharos, 1993.

Brom, Luco J. van den. "Eschatology and Time: Reversal of the Time Direction?" In *The Future as God's Gift: Explorations in Christian Eschatology,* edited by David Fergusson and Marcel Sarot, 159–67. Edinburgh: T and T Clark, 2000.

Brown, Raymond E. *The Epistles of John.* Garden City, NJ: Doubleday, 1982.

Brown, Robert. "On God's Ontic and Noetic Absoluteness: A Critique of Barth." *Scottish Journal of Theology* 33 (1980): 533–49.

Brunner, Emil. *The Christian Doctrine of God. Dogmatics*: Vol. I. Translated by Olive Wyon. Philadelphia: Westminster Press, 1949.

Burgess, Andrew. *The Ascension in Karl Barth.* Aldershot: Ashgate, 2004.

Busch, Eberhard. *The Great Passion: An Introduction to Karl Barth's Theology.* Translated by Geoffrey W. Bromiley. Edited and annotated by Darrell L. Guder and Judith J. Guder. Grand Rapids, MI: Eerdmans, 2004.

Calvin, John. *Institutes of the Christian Religion.* Edited by John T. McNeil. Philadelphia: Westminster Press, 1960.

Carpenter, James. *Gore: A Study in Liberal Catholic Thought.* London: Faith Press, 1959.

Chantepie de la Saussaye, D. *Verzameld Werk,* volume 2. Zoetermeer: Boekencentrum, 2000.

Childs, Brevard S. *Exodus: A Commentary.* London: SCM Press, 1974.

Chrysostome, Fr. OFM. "La Rédemption est-elle le motif de l'incarnation?" *La France franciscain* 14 (1931): 113–67.

Colwell, John. *Actuality and Provisionality: Eternity and Election in the Theology of Karl Barth.* Edinburgh: Rutherford House, 1989.

Conradie, Ernst M. "Resurrection, Finitude, and Ecology." In *Resurrection: Theological and Scientific Assessments,* edited by Ted Peters, Robert John Russell, and Michael Welker, 277–96. Grand Rapids, MI: Eerdmans, 2002.

Cunningham, Mary Kathleen. *What Is Theological Exegesis? Interpretation and Use of Scripture in Karl Barth's Doctrine of Election.* Valley Forge, PA: Trinity Press International, 1995.

Daley, Brian E. "A Richer Union: Leontius of Byzantium and the Relationship of Human and Divine in Christ." *Studia Patristica* 24 (1993): 239–65.

Dalferth, Ingolf U. "Karl Barth's Eschatological Realism." In *Karl Barth: Centenary Essays,* edited by S. W. Sykes, 14–45. Cambridge: Cambridge University Press, 1989.

Davidson, Ivor. "Theologizing the Human Jesus: An Ancient (and Modern) Approach to Christology Reassessed." *International Journal of Systematic Theology* 3 (2001): 129–53.

Davies, Oliver. *The Creativity of God: World, Eucharist, Reason.* Cambridge: Cambridge University Press, 2004.

Davis, Ellen F. *Getting Involved with God: Rediscovering the Old Testament.* Cambridge: Cowley, 2001.

Denzinger, Heinrich. *Enchiridion symbolorum definitionum et declarationum de rebus et declarationum de rebus fidei et morum.* Improved, expanded, and translated into German, and with assistance of Helmut Hoping edited by Peter Hünermann. 37th edition. Freiburg: Herder, 1991.

DeVries, Dawn, and B. A. Gerrish. "Providence and Grace: Schleiermacher on Justification and Election." In *The Cambridge Companion to Friedrich Schleiermacher,* edited by Jacqueline Mariña, 189–208. Cambridge: Cambridge University Press, 2005.

Dorner, Isaak August. *Divine Immutability: A Critical Reconstruction.* Translated by Robert R. Williams and Claude Welch, with an introduction by Robert R. Williams. Minneapolis: Fortress Press, 1994.

Dorner, Isaak August. *History of the Development of the Doctrine of the Person of Christ,* Vol. III. Edinburgh: T and T Clark, 1878.

Dorner, Isaak August. *A System of Christian Doctrine,* Vols. I–IV. Translated by Alfred Cave and J. S. Banks. Edinburgh: T and T Clark, 1882–91.

Driel, Edwin Chr. van. "Karl Barth on the Eternal Existence of Jesus Christ." *Scottish Journal of Theology* 60 (2007): 45–61.

Driel, Edwin Chr. van. "The Logic of Assumption." In *Exploring Kenotic Christology,* edited by C. Stephen Evans, 265–90. New York: Oxford University Press, 2006.

Driel, Edwin Chr. van. "Schleiermacher's supralapsarian Christology." *Scottish Journal of Theology* 60 (2007): 251–70.

Ebeling, Gerhard. "Interpretatorische Bemerkungen zu Schleiermachers Christologie." In, *Schleiermacher und die wissenschaftliche Kultur des Christentums,* edited by Günter Meckenstock, 125–46. Berlin: Walter de Gruyter, 1991.

Eckstein, Hans-Joachim. "Bodily Resurrection in Luke." In *Resurrection: Theological and Scientific Assessments,* edited by Ted Peters, Robert John Russell, and Michael Welker, 115–23. Grand Rapids, MI: Eerdmans, 2002.

Edmondson, Stephen. *Calvin's Christology.* Cambridge: Cambridge University Press, 2004.

Ellingworth, Paul. *The Epistle to the Hebrews: A Commentary on the Greek Text.* Grand Rapids, MI: Eerdmans, 1993.

Farrow, Douglas. *Ascension and Ecclesia: On the Significance of the Doctrine of the Ascension for Ecclesiology and Christian Cosmology.* Grand Rapids, MI: Eerdmans, 1999.

Farrow, Douglas. "Karl Barth on the Ascension: An Appreciation and Critique." *International Journal of Systematic Theology* 2 (2000): 127–50.

Fee, Gordon D. *The First Epistle to the Corinthians.* Grand Rapids, MI: Eerdmans, 1987.

Ferrara, D. M. " 'Hypostatized in the Logos': Leontius of Byzantium, Leontius of Jerusalem and the Unfinished Business of the Council of Chalcedon." *Louvain Studies* 22 (1997): 311–27.

Ford, David. *Barth and God's Story: Biblical Narrative and the Theological Method of Karl Barth in the "Church Dogmatics."* Frankfurt am Main: Verlag Peter Lang, 1981.

Ford, J. M. *Redeemer-Friend and Mother: Salvation in Antiquity and in the Gospel of John.* Minneapolis: Fortress Press, 1997.

Gerdes, Hayo. *Der geschichtliche biblische Jesus oder der Christus der Philosophen: Erwägungen zur Christologie Kierkegaards, Hegels und Schleiermachers.* Berlin: Verlag Die Spur, 1974.

Gerken, A. "Bonaventuras Konvenienzgründe für die Inkarnation des Sohnes." *Wissenschaft und Weisheit* 23 (1960): 131–46.

Gerken, A. *Theologie des Wortes: Das Verhältnis von Schöpfung und Inkarnation bei Bonaventura.* Düsseldorf: Patmos, 1963.

Ginther, James R. *Master of the Sacred Page: A Study of the Theology of Robert Grosseteste, ca. 1229/30–1235.* Aldershot: Ashgate, 2004.

Gloege, Gerhard. "Zur Prädestinationslehre Karl Barths: Fragmentarische Erwägungen über den Ansatz ihrer Neufassung." *Kerygma und Dogma* 2 (1956): 193–217, 233–55.

Gockel, Matthias. *Barth and Schleiermacher on the Doctrine of Election: A Systematic-Theological Comparison.* Oxford: Oxford University Press, 2006.

Gockel, Matthias. "New Perspectives on an Old Debate: Friedrich Schleiermacher's Essay on Election." *International Journal of Systematic Theology* 6 (2004): 301–18.

Graß, Hans. "Die durch Jesum von Nazareth vollbrachte Erlösung: Ein Beitrag zur Erlösungslehre Schleiermachers." In *Denkender Glaube: Festschrift Carl Heinz Ratschow,* edited by Otto Kaiser, 152–69. Berlin: Walter de Gruyter, 1976.

Greer, Rowan A. *Christian Hope and Christian Life: Raids on the Inarticulate.* New York: Crossroad, 2001.

Grossesteste, Robert. *De Cessatione Legalium.* Edited by Richard C. Dales and Edward B. King. London: Oxford University Press, 1986.

Gunning, J. H. *Blikken in de Openbaring.* Third volume. Amsterdam: H. Höveker, 1868.

Gunton, Colin E. *Becoming and Being: The Doctrine of God in Charles Hartshorne and Karl Barth.* 2nd ed. London: SCM Press, 2001.

Gunton, Colin E. "Karl Barth's doctrine of election as part of his doctrine of God." *Journal of Theological Studies* new series 25 (1974): 381–92.

Härle, Wilfried. *Sein und Gnade: Die Ontologie in Karl Barths Kirchlicher Dogmatik.* Berlin: Walter de Gruyter, 1975.

Hart, David Bentley. *The Beauty of the Infinite: The Aesthetics of Christian Truth.* Grand Rapids, MI: Eerdmans, 2003.

Haubst, Rudolph. *Vom Sinn der Menschwerdung.* Munich: Max Hueber Verlag, 1969.

Hays, Richard B. " 'Why Do You Stand Looking Up Toward Heaven?': New Testament Eschatology at the Turn of the Millennium." *Modern Theology* 16 (2000): 115–35.

Hector, Kevin W. "God's Triunity and Self-Determination: A Conversation with Karl Barth, Bruce McCormack and Paul Molnar." *International Journal of Systematic Theology* 7 (2005): 246–61.

Hendry, George S. "The Freedom of God in the Theology of Karl Barth." *Scottish Journal of Theology* 31 (1978): 229–44.

Heppe, Heinrich. *Reformed Dogmatics*. Revised and edited by Ernst Bizer. Translated by G. T. Thompson. San Francisco: Harper Collins, 1956.

Herms, Eilert. "Schleiermachers Eschatologie nach der zweiten Auflage der 'Glaubenslehre.'" *Theologische Zeitschrift* 46 (1990): 97–123.

Hick, John. *Evil and the God of Love*. Rev. ed. San Francisco: Harper and Row, 1977.

Houtman, Cornelis. *Exodus*, Vol. 3. Leuven: Peeters, 2000.

Hunsinger, George. "The Daybreak of the New Creation: Christ's Resurrection in Recent Theology." *Scottish Journal of Theology* 57 (2004): 163–81.

Hunsinger, George. *Disruptive Grace: Studies in the Theology of Karl Barth*. Grand Rapids, MI: Eerdmans, 2000.

Hunsinger, George. *How to Read Karl Barth: The Shape of His Theology*. New York: Oxford University Press, 1991.

Hurtado, Larry W. *Lord Jesus Christ: Devotion to Jesus in Earliest Christianity*. Grand Rapids, MI: Eerdmans, 2003.

Hüttenhoff, Michael. *Erkenntnistheorie und Dogmatik: Das erkenntnistheoretische Problem der Theologie bei I.A. Dorner, Fr. H.R. Frank und R.A. Lipsius*. Bielefeld: Luther Verlag, 1991.

Ingen, John H. van. *Rupert of Deutz*. Berkeley: University of California Press, 1983.

Jager, O. "Is the Incarnatie meer dan een noodmaatregel?" *Rondom het Woord* 10 (1968): 71–102.

Jenson, Robert W. *Alpha and Omega: A Study in the Theology of Karl Barth*. New York: Thomas Nelson, 1963.

Jenson, Robert W. *God after God: The God of the Past and the God of the Future, Seen in the Work of Karl Barth*. Indianapolis: Bobbs-Merrill, 1969.

Jenson, Robert W. "The Great Transformation." In *The Last Things: Biblical and Theological Perspectives on Eschatology*, edited by Carl E. Braaten and Robert W. Jenson, 33–42. Grand Rapids, MI: Eerdmans, 2002.

Jenson, Robert W. *Systematic Theology I: The Triune God*. New York: Oxford University Press, 1997.

Jenson, Robert W. *Systematic Theology II: The Works of God*. New York: Oxford University Press, 1999.

John of Damascus. *The Orthodox Faith*. In *Saint John of Damascus: Writings*, translated by Frederic H. Chase Jr., 165–406. New York: Fathers of the Church, 1958.

Johnson, William Stacy. *The Mystery of God: Karl Barth and the Postmodern Foundations of Theology*. Louisville: Westminster John Knox Press, 1997.

Jones, Paul Dafydd. "Karl Barth on Gethsemane." *International Journal of Systematic Theology* 9 (2007): 148–171.

Jüngel, Eberhard. *Death: The Riddle and the Mystery*. Philadelphia: Westminster Press, 1974.

Jüngel, Eberhard. *God's Being Is in Becoming: The Trinitarian Being of God in the Theology of Karl Barth*. Translated and with a new introduction by John Webster. Grand Rapids, MI: Eerdmans, 2001.

Kelsey, Catherine L. *Thinking About Christ with Schleiermacher*. Louisville: Westminster John Knox Press, 2003.

Kelsey, David H. "Aquinas and Barth on the Human Body." *The Thomist* 50 (1986): 643–89.

Kelsey, David H. *Eccentric Existence: A Theocentric Anthropology*. Forthcoming from Westminster John Knox Press, Louisville.

Kittel, Gerhard, and Gerhard Friedrich. *Theological Dictionary of the New Testament*, Vols. I–X. Grand Rapids, MI: Eerdmans, 1964–78.

Knijff, Hans de. "Karl Barth over de menselijke natuur." In *Bijna goddelijk gemaakt: Gedachten over de menselijke gerichtheid op God*, edited by Nico den Bok and Arjan Plaisier, 200–23. Zoetermeer: Boekencentrum, 2005.

Köjiro, Masami. "God's Eternal Election in the Theology of Karl Barth." PhD dissertation, University of Aberdeen, 1996.

Kooi, C. van der. *As in a Mirror: John Calvin and Karl Barth on Knowing God*. Leiden: Brill, 2005.

Koppehl, Thomas. *Der Wissenschaftliche Standpunkt der Theologie Isaak August Dorners*. Berlin: Walter de Gruyter, 1997.

Krause, Burghard. *Leiden Gottes—Leiden des Menschen: Eine Untersuchung zur Kirchlichen Dogmatik Karl Barths*. Stuttgart: Calwer Verlag, 1980.

Kreck, Walter. *Grundentscheidungen in Karl Barths Dogmatik: Zur Diskussion seines Verständnisses von Offenbarung und Erwählung*. Neukirchen-Vluyn: Neukirchener Verlag, 1978.

Kreling, P. "Het motief der menschwording." *Studia Catholica* 15 (1939): 89–101.

Kretzmann, Norman. "A General Problem of Creation: Why Would God Create Anything at All?" In *Being and Goodness: The Concept of the Good in Metaphysics and Philosophical Theology*, edited by Scott MacDonald, 208–28. Ithaca, NY: Cornell University Press, 1991.

Kretzmann, Norman. "A Particular Problem of Creation: Why Would God Create This World?" In *Being and Goodness: The Concept of the Good in Metaphysics and Philosophical Theology*, edited by Scott MacDonald, 229–49. Ithaca, NY: Cornell University Press, 1991.

Krötke, Wolf. *Sünde und Nichtiges bei Karl Barth*. 2nd ed., revised and expanded edition. Neukirchen-Vluyn: Neukirchener Verlag, 1983.

Küng, Hans. *Justification: The Doctrine of Karl Barth and a Catholic Reflection*. Louisville: Westminster John Knox Press, 2004 [1964].

Kuyper, A. *De Vleeschwording des Woords*. Amsterdam: J.A. Wormser, 1887.

Lamm, Julia A. *The Living God: Schleiermacher's Theological Appropriation of Spinoza*. University Park: Pennsylvania State University Press, 1997.

Lane, William L. *Hebrews 9–13*. Dallas: Word Books, 1991.

Lang, U. M. "Anhypostatos-Enhypostatos: Church Fathers, Protestant Orthodoxy, and Karl Barth." *Journal of Theological Studies* 49 (1998): 630–57.

Lange, Dietz. *Historischer Jesus oder mythischer Christus: Untersuchungen zu dem Gegensatz zwischen Friedrich Schleiermacher und David Friedrich Strauß*. Gütersloh: Gütersloher Verlagshaus, 1975.

Lapsley, Jacqueline E. "Friendship with God? Moses and the Possibility of Covenantal Friendship." *Interpretation* 58 (2004): 117–29.

Laufen, Rudolf. "Der anfanglose Sohn. Eine christologische Problemanzeige." In *Gottes ewiger Sohn: Die Präexistenz Christi,* edited by Ruldolf Laufen, 9–30. Paderborn: Ferdinand Schöningh, 1997.

Leftow, Brian. "God and Abstract Properties." *Faith and Philosophy* 2 (1990): 193–217.

Loon, J. C. van. "Karl Barth und Chalkedon." *Zeitschrift für Dialektische Theologie* 19 (2003): 162–82.

Lovejoy, Arthur O. *The Great Chain of Being: A Study of the History of an Idea.* Cambridge: Harvard University Press, 1964 [1936].

Lovejoy, Arthur O. "Milton and the Paradox of the Fortunate Fall." *A Journal of English Literary History* 4 (1937): 161–79. Reprinted in: Arthur O. Lovejoy, *Essays in the History of Ideas* (Baltimore: 1948), 277–95.

Mariña, Jacqueline, ed. *The Cambridge Companion to Friedrich Schleiermacher.* Cambridge: Cambridge University Press, 2005.

Mariña, Jacqueline. "Christology and Anthropology in Friedrich Schleiermacher." In *The Cambridge Companion to Friedrich Schleiermacher,* edited by Jacqueline Mariña, 151–70. Cambridge: Cambridge University Press, 2005.

Mariña, Jacqueline. "Schleiermacher's Christology Revisited: A Reply to His Critics." *Scottish Journal of Theology* 49 (1996): 177–200.

Martensen, H. *Christian Dogmatics: A Compendium of the Doctrines of Christianity.* Edinburgh: T and T Clark, 1898.

Maurice, F. D. *The Doctrine of Sacrifice.* London: Macmillan, 1893.

Maurice, F. D. *Theological Essays.* London: Macmillan, 1871.

McCormack, Bruce L. "Barth's grundsätzliche Chalkedonismus?" *Zeitschrift für Dialektische Theologie* 18 (2002): 138–73.

McCormack, Bruce L. "Beyond Nonfoundational and Postmodern Readings of Barth: Critically Realistic Dialectical Theology." *Zeitschrift für Dialektische Theologie* 13 (1997): 67–95, 170–94.

McCormack, Bruce L. "Grace and Being: The Role of God's Gracious Election in Karl Barth's Theological Ontology." In *The Cambridge Companion to Karl Barth,* edited by John Webster, 92–110. Cambridge: Cambridge University Press, 2000.

McCormack, Bruce L. *Karl Barth's Critically Realistic Dialectical Theology: Its Genesis and Development 1909–1936.* Oxford: Clarendon Press, 1995.

McCormack, Bruce L. "The Ontological Presuppositions of Barth's Doctrine of the Atonement." In *The Glory of the Atonement: Biblical, Historical, and Practical Perspectives,* edited by Charles E. Hill and Frank A. James III, 346–66. Downers Grove, IL: InterVarsity Press, 2004.

McCormack, Bruce L. "Participation in God, Yes, Deification, No: Two Modern Protestant Responses to an Ancient Question." In *Denkwürdiges Geheimnis: Beiträge zur Gotteslehre. Festschrift für Eberhard Jüngel zum siebtigsten Geburtstag,* edited by Ingolf U. Dalferth, Johannes Fischer, and Hans-Peter Großhans, 347–74. Tübingen: Mohr Siebeck, 2004.

McCormack, Bruce L. "§27 'The Limits of the Knowledge of God': Theses on the Theological Epistemology of Karl Barth." *Zeitschrift für Dialektische Theologie* 15 (1999): 75–86.

McCormack, Bruce L. "Seek God Where He May Be Found: A Response to Edwin Chr. van Driel." *Scottish Journal of Theology* 60 (2007): 62–79.

McCormack, Bruce L. "What's at Stake in Current Debates over Justification? The Crisis of Protestantism in the West." In *Justification: What's at Stake in the Current Debates?* edited by Mark Husbands and Daniel J. Treier, 81–117. Downers Grove, IL: InterVarsity Press, 2004.

McDowell, John C. *Hope in Barth's Eschatology: Interrogations and Transformations beyond Tragedy*. Aldershot: Ashgate, 2000.

McDowell, John C. " 'Mend Your Speech a Little': Reading Karl Barth's *das Nichtige* through Donald MacKinnon's Tragic Vision." In *Conversing with Barth*, edited by John C. McDowell and Mike Higton, 142–72. Aldershot: Ashgate, 2004.

McDowell, John C. "Much Ado about Nothing: Karl Barth's Being Unable to Do Nothing about Nothingness." *International Journal of Systematic Theology* 4 (2002): 319–35.

McElrath, Damian. *Franciscan Christology: Selected Texts, Translations, and Introductory Essays*. St. Bonaventure: Franciscan Institute, 1980.

McEvoy, James. "The Absolute Predestination of Christ in the Theology of Robert Grosseteste." In *Sapientiae Doctrina: Mélanges de théologie et de literature médiévales offerts à Dom Hildebrand Bascour O.S.B.*, 212–30. Leuven: Abbaye du Mont César, 1980.

McEvoy, James. *Robert Grosseteste*. Oxford: Oxford University Press, 2000.

McGrath, Alister. "Karl Barth als Aufklärer? Der Zusammenhang seiner Lehre vom Werke Christi mit der Erwählungslehre." *Kerygma und Dogma* 30 (1984): 273–83.

Molnar, Paul D. *Divine Freedom and the Doctrine of the Immanent Trinity: In Dialogue with Karl Barth and Contemporary Theology*. Edinburgh: T and T Clark, 2002.

Molnar, Paul D. "The Trinity, Election, and God's Ontological Freedom: A Response to Kevin W. Hector." *International Journal of Systematic Theology* 8 (2006): 294–306.

Moltmann, Jürgen. *The Trinity and the Kingdom: The Doctrine of God*. Minneapolis: Fortress Press, 1993.

Moore, Walter L. "Schleiermacher as a Calvinist: A Comparison of Calvin and Schleiermacher on Providence and Predestination." *Scottish Journal of Theology* 24 (1971): 167–83.

Morris, Thomas V., and Christopher Menzel. "Absolute Creation." *American Philosophical Quarterly* 23 (1986): 353–62. Reprinted in Thomas V. Morris, *Anselmian Explorations* (Notre Dame: University of Notre Dame Press, 1987), 161–78.

Mückshoff, M. "Die mariologische Prädestination im Denken der franziskanischen Theologie." *Franziskanische Studien* 39 (1957): 290–361.

Mueller, David L. *Foundation of Karl Barth's Doctrine of Reconciliation: Jesus Christ Crucified and Risen*. Lewinston, NY: Edwin Mellen Press, 1990.

Neder, Adam. " 'A Differentiated Fellowship of Action': Participation in Christ in Karl Barth's *Church Dogmatics*." Dissertation, Princeton Theological Seminary, Princeton, NJ, 2005.

Nellas, Panayiotis. *Deification in Christ: Orthodox Perspectives on the Nature of the Human Person.* Translated from the Greek by Norman Russell; with a foreword by Bishop Kallistos Ware of Diokleia. Crestwood: St. Vladimir's Seminary Press, 1997.

Niebuhr, Richard R. "Christ, Nature, and Consciousness: Reflections on Schleiermacher in the Light of Barth's Early Criticism." In *Barth and Schleiermacher: Beyond the Impasse?* edited by James O. Duke and Robert F. Streetman, 23–42. Philadelphia: Fortress Press, 1988.

Niebuhr, Richard R. "Schleiermacher and the Names of God." In *Schleiermacher as Contemporary*, edited by Robert W. Funk, 176–215. New York: Herder and Herder, 1970.

Niebuhr, Richard R. *Schleiermacher on Christ and Religion: A New Introduction.* New York: Charles Scribner's Sons, 1964.

Nimmo, Paul T. "The Mediation of Redemption in Schleiermacher's *Glaubenslehre.*" *International Journal of Systematic Theology* 5 (2003): 187–99.

Nolland, John. *The Gospel of Matthew: A Commentary on the Greek Text.* Grand Rapids, MI: Eerdmans, 2005.

Oberdorfer, Bernd. "Schleiermacher on Eschatology and Resurrection." In *Resurrection: Theological and Scientific Assessments*, edited by Ted Peters, Robert John Russell, and Michael Welker, 165–82. Grand Rapids, MI: Eerdmans, 2002.

Oblau, Gotthard. *Gotteszeit und Menschenzeit: Eschatologie in der Kirchlichen Dogmatik von Karl Barth.* Neukirchen-Vluyn: Neukirchener Verlag, 1988.

O'Brien, Peter T. *Colossians, Philemon.* Word Biblical Commentary. Waco: Word Books, 1982.

O'Day, G. R. "Jesus as Friend in the Gospel of John." *Interpretation* 58 (2004): 144–57.

Ogletree, Thomas W. *Christian Faith and History: A Critical Comparison of Ernst Troeltsch and Karl Barth.* Nashville: Abingdon Press, 1965.

Oosterzee, J. J. van. *Christelijke Dogmatiek*, Vol. II. Utrecht: Kemink, 1870.

Oosterzee, J. J. van. *Christologie*, Vol. III. Rotterdam: Van der Meer en Verbruggen, 1861.

Osiander, Andreas. *Gesamtausgabe Band 9: Schriften und Briefe 1549 bis August 1551.* Edited by Gerhard Müller and Gottfried Seebaß. Gütersloh: Gütersloher Verlagshaus, 1994.

Pannenberg, Wolfgang. *Systematic Theology*, Vols. I–III. Grand Rapids, MI: Eerdmans, 1991–98.

Plantinga, Alvin. *Does God Have a Nature?* Milwaukee: Marquette University Press, 1980.

Pleisier, Arjan. "Motieven voor incarnatie bij Barth." In *Wat God bewoog mens te worden*, edited by Nico den Bok and Guus Labooy, 198–216. Zoetermeer: Boekencentrum, 2003.

Polkinghorne, John. *The God of Hope and the End of the World.* New Haven: Yale University Press, 2002.

Rahner, Karl. "Current Problems in Christology." *Theological Investigations*, Vol. I, 149–200. Baltimore: Helicon Press, 1961.

Rahner, Karl. "Grace." In *Sacramentum Mundi*, Vol. II, edited by Karl Rahner, 415–24. New York: Herder and Herder, 1968.
Rahner, Karl. "On the Theology of the Incarnation." *Theological Investigations*, Vol. IV, 105–20. Baltimore: Helicon Press, 1966.
Richards, Jay Wesley. *The Untamed God: A Philosophical Exploration of Divine Perfection, Simplicity and Immutability*. Downers Grove, IL: InterVarsity Press, 2003.
Ringe, Sharon H. *Wisdom's Friends: Community and Christology in the Fourth Gospel*. Louisville: Westminster John Knox Press, 1999.
Roberts, Richard H. "Karl Barth's Doctrine of Time: Its Nature and Implications." In *Karl Barth: Studies of his Theological Method*, edited by S. W. Sykes, 88–146. Oxford: Oxford University Press, 1979.
Rodin, R. Scott. *Evil and Theodicy in the Theology of Karl Barth*. New York: Peter Lang, 1997.
Rogers, Eugene F. Jr. *After the Spirit: A Constructive Pneumatology from Resources outside the Modern West*. Grand Rapids, MI: Eerdmans, 2005.
Root, Michael. "Schleiermacher as Innovator and Inheritor: God, Dependence, and Election." *Scottish Journal of Theology* 43 (1990): 87–110.
Rothermundt, Jörg. *Personale Synthese: Isaak August Dorners dogmatische Methode*. Göttingen: Vandenhoeck und Ruprecht, 1968.
Rowland, Christopher. "Interpreting the Resurrection." In *The Resurrection of Jesus Christ*, edited by Paul Avis, 68–84. London: Darton, Longman, and Todd, 1993.
Ruler, A. A. van. "Structuurverschillen tussen het christologische en het pneumatologische gezichtspunt." In *Theologisch Werk*, Vol. I, 175–90. Nijkerk: G.F. Callenbach, 1969.
Russell, Robert John. "Bodily Resurrection, Eschatology, and Scientific Cosmology." In *Resurrection: Theological and Scientific Assessments*, edited by Ted Peters, Robert John Russell, and Michael Welker, 3–30. Grand Rapids, MI: Eerdmans, 2002.
Scheeben, M. J. *Gesammelte Schriften*, Vol. VI.2: *Handbuch der katholischen Dogmatik*, Vol. V.2. 2nd ed., edited by C. Feckes. Freiburg: Verlag Herder, 1954.
Scheel, Hans. *Die Theorie von Christus als dem zweiten Adam bei Schleiermacher*. Leibzig: A. Deichert'sche Verlagsbuchhandlung, 1913.
Schleiermacher, Friedrich. *The Christian Faith*. Edited by H. R. Mackintosh and J. S. Stewart. Edinburgh: T and T Clark, 1999.
Schleiermacher, Friedrich. *Der christliche Glaube nach den Grundsätzen der Evangelischen Kirche im Zusammenhange dargestellt (1830/31)*. Edited by Martin Redeker. Berlin: Walter de Gruyter, 1999.
Schleiermacher, Friedrich D. E. *On the Glaubenslehre: Two Letters to Dr. Lütcke*. Translated by James Duke and Francis Fiorenza. Chico: Scholars Press, 1981.
Schleiermacher, Friedrich D. E. *Ueber die Lehre von der Erwählung, besonders in Beziehung auf Hernn Dr. Bretschneiders Aphorismen*. In *Kritische Gesamtausgabe* I/10, edited by H.-F. Traulsen and M. Ohst, 147–222. Berlin: De Gruyter, 1990.
Schleiermacher, Friedrich. *Servant of the Word: Selected Sermons*. Translated with an introduction by Dawn De Vries. Philadelphia: Fortress Press, 1987.

Schmauss, Michael. *Dogma 1: God in Revelation*. New York: Sheed and Ward, 1968.

Schmid, H. *Doctrinal Theology of the Evangelical Lutheran Church*. 3rd rev. ed. Minneapolis: Augsburg, 1961.

Schüssler Fiorenza, Elisabeth. *Priester für Gott: Studien zum Herrschafts- und Priestermotiv in der Apokalypse*. Münster: Verlag Aschendorff, 1972.

Scott, Charles E. "Schleiermacher and the Problem of Divine Immediacy." *Religious Studies* 3 (1968): 499–512.

Sharp, Douglas R. *The Hermeneutics of Election: The Significance of the Doctrine in Barth's Church Dogmatics*. Lanham, MD: University of America Press, 1990.

Sherman, Robert James. *The Shift to Modernity: Christ and the Doctrine of Creation in the Theologies of Schleiermacher and Barth*. New York: T and T Clark, 2005.

Shults, F. LeRon. "A Dubious Christological Formula: From Leontius of Byzantium to Karl Barth." *Theological Studies* 57 (1996): 431–46.

Slot, Edward van 't. "Karl Barth over 'das Nichtige.'" *Nederlands Theologisch Tijdschrift* 58 (2004): 226–38.

Smalley, Stephen S. *1,2,3 John*. Dallas: Word Books, 1984.

Smedes, Lewis B. *The Incarnation: Trends in Modern Anglican Thought*. Kampen: Kok, 1953.

Söding, Thomas. "Gottes Sohn von Anfang an. Präexistenzchristologie bei Paulus und den Deuteropaulinen." In *Gottes ewiger Sohn: Die Präexistenz Christi*, edited by Ruldolf Laufen, 57–94. Paderborn: Ferdinand Schöningh, 1997.

Sparn, Walter. "'Extra Internum': Die Christologische Revision der Prädestinationslehre in Karl Barths Erwählungslehre." In *Die Realisierung der Freiheit: Beiträge zur Kritik der Theologie Barths*, edited by T. Rendtorff, 44–75. Gütersloh: Gütersloher Verlagshaus Gerd Mohn, 1975.

Stickelberger, Hans. *Ipsa assumptione creatur: Karl Barth's Rückgriff auf die klassische Christologie und die Frage nach der Sebständigkeit des Menschen*. Bern: Peter Lang, 1979.

Strack, Hermann L., and Paul Billerbeck, *Kommentar zum Neuen Testament aus Talmud und Midrasch*. Munich: C.H. Beck'sche Verlagsbuchhandlung, 1986.

Tanner, Kathryn. "Jesus Christ." In *The Cambridge Companion to Christian Doctrine*, edited by Colin E. Gunton, 245–72. Cambridge: Cambridge University Press, 1997.

Tanner, Kathryn. *Jesus, Humanity, and the Trinity: A Brief Systematic Theology*. Minneapolis: Fortress Press, 2001.

TeSelle, Eugene. *Christ in Context: Divine Purpose and Human Possibility*. Philadelphia: Fortress Press, 1975.

Thiselton, Anthony C. *The First Epistle to the Corinthians: A Commentary on the Greek Text*. Grand Rapids, MI: Eerdmans, 2000.

Thomas, Günter. "'Er ist nicht hier . . .': Die Rede vom leeren Grab als Zeichen der neuen Schöpfung." In *Die Wirklichkeit der Auferstehung*, edited by Hans-Joachim Eckstein and Michael Welker, 183–220. Neukirchen-Vluyn: Neukirchener Verlag, 2002.

Thomas, Günter. "Resurrection to New Life: Pneumatological Implications of the Eschatological Transition." In *Resurrection: Theological and Scientific Assessments*, edited by Ted Peters, Robert John Russell, and Michael Welker, 255–76. Grand Rapids, MI: Eerdmans, 2002.

Torrance, Alan J. *Persons in Communion: An Essay on Trinitarian Description and Human Participation*. Edinburgh: T and T Clark, 1996.

Torrance, Thomas F. *Space, Time, and Incarnation*. New York: Oxford University Press, 1969.

Torrance, Thomas F. *Space, Time, and Resurrection*. Grand Rapids, MI: Eerdmans, 1976.

Turretin, Francis. *Institutes of Elenctic Theology*. Translated by George Musgrave Giger. Edited by James T. Dennison Jr. Phillipsburg, NJ: P&R Publishing, 1992.

Veldhuis, Henri. "De hermeneutische betekenis van de supralapsarische christologie van Johannes Duns Scotus." *Bijdragen* 61 (2000): 152–74.

Veldhuis, Henri. *Kijk op geloof: Christelijk geloof uitgelegd*. Zoetermeer: Boekencentrum, 2005.

Veldhuis, Henri. "Moderniteit en motieven voor de menswording. Een eigentijds pleidooi voor verdieping van de incarnatieleer." In *Wat God bewoog mens te worden: Gedachten over de Incarnatie*, edited by Nico den Bok and Guus Labooy, 12–32. Zoetermeer: Boekencentrum, 2003.

Volf, Miroslav. "Enter into Joy! Sin, Death, and the Life of the World to Come." In *The End of the World and the Ends of God: Science and Theology on Eschatology*, edited by John Polkinghorne and Michael Welker, 256–78. Harrisburg, PA: Trinity Press International, 2000.

Volf, Miroslav. *Exclusion and Embrace: A Theological Exploration of Identity, Otherness, and Reconciliation*. Nashville: Abingdon Press, 1996.

Volf, Miroslav. "The Final Reconciliation: Reflections on a Social Dimension of the Eschatological Transition." *Modern Theology* 16 (2000): 91–108.

Volf, Miroslav. *The End of Memory: Remembering Rightly in a Violent Word*. Grand Rapids, MI: Eerdmans, 2006.

Vos, A. "Supralapsarisme en de gereformeerde theologie." In *Wat God bewoog mens te worden: Gedachten over de Incarnatie*, edited by Nico den Bok and Guus Labooy, 175–96. Zoetermeer: Boekencentrum, 2003.

Vos, Antonie. *Het is de Heer: De opstanding voorstelbaar*. Kampen: Kok, 1990.

Vos, Antonie. *Kennis en Noodzakelijkheid: Een kritische analyse van het absolute eidentialisme in wijsbegeerte en theologie*. Kampen: Kok, 1981.

Vos, A. Jaczn., H. Veldhuis, A. H. Looman-Graaskamp, E. Dekker, and N. W. den Bok. *John Duns Scotus: Freedom and Contingency. Lectura I.39*. Dordrecht: Kluwer, 1992.

Webster, John. *Barth*. London: Continuum, 2000.

Webster, John. "Barth, Modernity and Postmodernity." In *Karl Barth: A Future for Postmodern Theology?* edited by Geoff Thompson and Christiaan Mostert, 1–69. Hindmarsh: Australian Theological Forum, 2000.

Webster, John. *Barth's Ethics of Reconciliation*. Cambridge: Cambridge University Press, 1995.

Webster, John. *Barth's Moral Theology: Human Action in Barth's Thought*. Grand Rapids, MI: Eerdmans, 1998.

Webster, John, ed. *The Cambridge Companion to Karl Barth*. Cambridge: Cambridge University Press, 2000.

Welker, Michael. "Theological Realism and Eschatological Symbol Systems." In *Resurrection: Theological and Scientific Assessments*, edited by Ted Peters, Robert John Russell, and Michael Welker, 31–42. Grand Rapids, MI: Eerdmans, 2002.

Wentsel, B. *God en mens verzoend: Incarnatie, verzoening, koninkrijk van God*. Dogmatics volume 3b. Kampen: Kok, 1991.

Westcott, Brooke Foss. *Christus Consummator: Some Aspects of the Work and Person of Christ in Relation to Modern Thought*. London: Macmillan, 1906.

Westcott, Brooke Foss. *The Epistles of St. John: The Greek Text with Notes and Essays*. London: Macmillan, 1883.

Westcott, Brooke Foss. *The Gospel According to St. John: The Authorised Version with Introduction and Notes*. Reissued with a new introduction by A. Fox. London: James Clarke, 1958 (1882).

Westcott, Brooke Foss. *The Gospel of Life: Thoughts Introductory to the Study of Christian Doctrine*. 2nd ed. London: Macmillan, 1895.

Wolter, Allan. "John Duns Scotus on the primacy and personality of Christ." In *Franciscan Christology: Selected Texts, Translations, and Introductory Essays*, edited by Damian McElrath, 139–82. New York: St. Bonaventure, 1980, 1994.

Wolterstorff, Nicholas. "Barth on Evil." *Faith and Philosophy* 13 (1996): 584–608.

Wolterstorff, Nicholas. *Divine Discourse: Philosophical Reflections on the Claim That God Speaks*. Cambridge: Cambridge University Press, 1995.

Wright, N. T. *The Climax of the Covenant: Christ and the Law in Pauline Theology*. Edinburgh: T and T Clark, 1991.

Wright, N. T. *Jesus and the Victory of God. Christian Origins and the Question of God*, Vol. 2. Minneapolis: Fortress Press, 1996.

Wright, N. T. *The Resurrection of the Son of God. Christian Origins and the Question of God*, Vol. 3. Minneapolis: Fortress Press, 2003.

Wyman, Walter E. Jr. "Rethinking the Christian Doctrine of Sin: Friedrich Schleiermacher and Hick's 'Irenaean Type.'" *Journal of Religion* 74 (1994): 199–217.

Wyman, Walter E. Jr. "Sin and Redemption." In *The Cambridge Companion to Friedrich Schleiermacher*, edited by Jacqueline Mariña, 129–50. Cambridge: Cambridge University Press, 2005.

Zagzebski, Linda Trinkaus. *Divine Motivation Theory*. Cambridge: Cambridge University Press, 2004.

Index